RALPH KINER

Ralph Kiner
A Baseball Biography

Robert P. Broadwater

McFarland & Company, Inc., Publishers
Jefferson, North Carolina

ALSO BY ROBERT P. BROADWATER AND FROM MCFARLAND
Lefty Grove and the 1931 Philadelphia Athletics (2014); *The Battle of Fair Oaks* (2011); *Gettysburg as the Generals Remembered It* (2010); *General George H. Thomas* (2009); *Did Lincoln and the Republican Party Create the Civil War?* (2008); *Civil War Medal of Honor Recipients* (2007; paperback, 2012); *American Generals of the Revolutionary War* (2007; paperback, 2012); *The Battle of Perryville, 1862* (2005; paperback, 2011); *The Battle of Olustee, 1864* (2006); *Chickamauga, Andersonville, Fort Sumter and Guard Duty at Home* (edited, 2006)

All photographs are from the National Baseball Hall of Fame Library, Cooperstown, New York.

LIBRARY OF CONGRESS CATALOGUING-IN-PUBLICATION DATA

Names: Broadwater, Robert P., 1958–
Title: Ralph Kiner : a baseball biography / Robert P. Broadwater.
Description: Jefferson, North Carolina : McFarland & Company, Inc., Publishers, 2016 | Includes bibliographical references and index.
Identifiers: LCCN 2016009945 | ISBN 9780786498178 (softcover : acid free paper) ♾
Subjects: LCSH: Kiner, Ralph. | Baseball players—United States—Biography. | Sportscasters—United States—Biography.
Classification: LCC GV865.K53 B76 2016 | DDC 796.357092—dc23
LC record available at http://lccn.loc.gov/2016009945

BRITISH LIBRARY CATALOGUING DATA ARE AVAILABLE

ISBN (print) 978-0-7864-9817-8
ISBN (ebook) 978-1-4766-2273-6

© 2016 Robert P. Broadwater. All rights reserved

No part of this book may be reproduced or transmitted in any form or by any means, electronic or mechanical, including photocopying or recording, or by any information storage and retrieval system, without permission in writing from the publisher.

Front cover image of Ralph Kiner in 1947 (National Baseball Hall of Fame Library, Cooperstown, New York)

Printed in the United States of America

*McFarland & Company, Inc., Publishers
Box 611, Jefferson, North Carolina 28640
www.mcfarlandpub.com*

Table of Contents

Introduction — 1

1: Learning to Love the Game — 5
2: Off to the Minors — 19
3: A World at War — 31
4: Breaking into the Bigs — 38
5: Making a Splash in Pittsburgh — 48
6: A Mentor for Ralph — 59
7: The Assault on Ruth's Record — 69
8: Earning a Tie with the Babe — 85
9: Best Player on Bad Teams — 94
10: Traded to the Cubs — 107
11: Last Stand with the Indians — 120
12: Out of the Game — 129
13: Kiner's Korner Moves to New York — 140
14: A World Series and a Trip to the Hall — 151
15: Mr. Met — 162

Epilogue — 173
Appendix One: Career Stats and Comparison to Other Hall of Fame Members — 177

Table of Contents

Appendix Two: Major League Players' Career Home Run Totals — 181

Appendix Three: Pittsburgh Pirates Hall of Famers — 183

Chapter Notes — 185

Bibliography — 189

Index — 191

Introduction

Ralph McPherran Kiner was one of the most feared power hitters in the Major Leagues in the years immediately following World War II. "King Kiner," as he was sometimes called, led the National League in home runs for seven consecutive years from his debut in 1946 through 1952. During this streak, he broke Babe Ruth's record of consecutive home run championships and became the first National League star to hit 50 or more home runs twice. In seven full seasons with the Pittsburgh Pirates he averaged 42 home runs, 103 runs scored, and 110 runs driven in. In addition, he was one of the most frequently walked players in the game, averaging 110 bases on balls per year in his seven full seasons with the Pirates. Pittsburgh was a storied franchise with a great baseball tradition and boasted a long list of star players and legends. Honus Wagner, Pie Traynor, Arky Vaughan, Max Carey, Fred Clarke, Lloyd Waner, and Paul Waner had all been stars of powerful Pirates teams. Other well-known legends like Heinie Manush, Waite Hoyt, Rabbit Maranville, Dazzy Vance, Freddie Lindstrom, and Rube Waddell made career stopovers in Pittsburgh to wear a Pirates uniform for short stints.

Pirates sluggers had won 14 batting titles in the National League by the time Kiner donned a Pittsburgh uniform. The great Honus Wagner had won the title eight times from 1900 to 1911. Paul Waner captured four titles, and Ginger Beaumont, Arky Vaughan, and Debs Garms each earned one crown. As accustomed as Pittsburgh fans were to having stars on their team, Ralph Kiner emerged as a sensation, a power threat who could regularly launch pitchers' mistakes over the left field fence in what would eventually become known as Kiner's Korner at old Forbes Field. Home run power was something that Pirates fans had never been exposed to. The only time in franchise history that a Pirate had won a

Introduction

home run title was in 1902, when Tommy Leach led the National League with a grand total of six round-trippers. The great Honus Wagner had stroked only 101 of them in a career that spanned two decades, 82 while wearing a Pirates uniform. Paul Waner boasted the most round-trippers of any Pirate who spent appreciable time in a Pittsburgh uniform, but his two decades in the majors accounted for only 113 homers, less than a home run a year more than Wagner's total, and four of those were hit when he was no longer a Pirate. Then came Kiner. His explosive bat thrilled Pittsburgh fans as he became the Pirates' all-time home run leader in his first three years in the league, stroking 114 round-trippers. Adding an exclamation point to his stats in his fourth campaign, Kiner belted another 54 homers to lead the National League for the fourth of his seven consecutive seasons.

These lofty statistics are all the more incredible when one considers the teams Kiner played on during his career. Though the Pirates had won six National League pennants and two World Series in their history, the team had recently declined and dropped out of contention. In the years after World War II, the Pittsburgh Pirates fell on hard times, as a lack of talent condemned them to be perennial cellar dwellers in the league. From 1946 through 1953, the team averaged 92 losses per season, with 1948 the only season the Pirates posted a winning record with a mark of 83–71, good enough to finish fourth in the league. During the other seven years that Kiner spent in Pittsburgh, the team finished no higher than sixth, was seventh three seasons, and finished dead last three times.

Kiner was the lone superstar on a team that provided him little or no protection in the lineup. His great number of walks each season bears testament to the fact that opposing hurlers were able to pitch around him when the game was on the line and take their chances with one of the lesser bats in the Pirates' lineup. One can only imagine what his home run totals could have been with more depth in the Pittsburgh batting order. As it was, Kiner became the sole attraction for Pirates fans during these years of fading fortunes, and what an attraction he was. Pirates faithful came to Forbes Field in droves, hoping to see Kiner go long with a majestic fly ball to deep left or center.

So great was Kiner's drawing power that the team saw more than 1,200,000 fans come through the turnstiles in 1947, the first time the

Introduction

franchise had ever topped one million fans in a season. In 1948, attendance soared to more than 1.5 million, tops in the National League, despite the fact that the team finished fourth. In far too many games, the hometown faithful had little hope of ending up on the winning side of the ledger. But they had come to see Kiner, and their devotion was rewarded by dramatics often enough to keep them chanting his name. It became a regular occurrence in Pittsburgh for fans to depart the stadium before the game had ended. One thing could keep them in their seats in the later innings when the team was trailing. Kiner was coming to bat. In these instances, the fans would stay to see their slugger take his final swings before a mass exodus for the parking lot took place.

In a ten-year career, delayed in its beginning by two and a half years serving as a Navy pilot in World War II, and cut short by back problems that forced his retirement in 1955, Kiner was able to amass 369 home runs, 1,015 runs batted in, and 971 runs scored. These are not great stats when one considers the totals of other legends of the game, but when examined in the context of a shortened career that spanned only a decade, they compare favorably with the greats of the game enshrined in the Baseball Hall of Fame in Cooperstown. The fact is that for the period of time Ralph Kiner was able to play in the Major Leagues, he was one of the most feared and respected sluggers in the game, and he accomplished these feats on an inferior team he often carried alone on his shoulders.

In 1975, Kiner's final year of eligibility on the ballot, sports writers elected him to the Baseball Hall of Fame. Though he had ranked 6th for home runs hit at the time of his early retirement, he narrowly squeaked through with 75 percent of the vote, the minimum required for enshrinement in Cooperstown. He was one of the most feared power hitters of his generation, but the short nature of his career, also the minimum to be considered for Hall of Fame voting, caused many writers to leave him off their ballots.

But the story of Ralph Kiner is much more than merely a slugging superstar for an underachieving team. Kiner was the sort of player and man that made him easy to root for. A gentleman at all times, his kind interaction with all those with whom he came in contact made him a beloved ambassador of the game he championed. When Bing Crosby became a minority owner of the Pirates in the latter portion of the 1946

Introduction

season, he took an immediate liking to Kiner, taking the young player under his wing and introducing him to the Hollywood set. Kiner was frequently in the gossip columns for his off-field dates with Hollywood starlets, including Elizabeth Taylor. In 1951, Kiner married tennis star Nancy Chaffee, and the pair became national sweethearts overnight, gracing the covers of several magazines. The majority owner of the team, John Galbreath, pointed Kiner toward real estate investments in his home state of California. Kiner built a home in Palm Springs, where he counted among his friends and neighbors celebrities like Frank Sinatra, Lucille Ball, and Phil Harris. His winning personality and affable nature made Kiner a favorite with the Hollywood crowd, as celebrities like Chuck Connors and George Carlin joined his ever-increasing list of friends.

With the end of his playing career, the 33-year-old Kiner was left looking for a job. Two old friends from his playing days, Al Lopez and Hank Greenberg, offered him a manager's position with a minor league team in the Cleveland Indians organization. Money was so tight in the minor leagues that Kiner cut expenditures by doing the play-by-play broadcast for the team himself. In 1961, he was offered the position of play-by-play announcer for the Chicago White Sox, and when the expansion New York Mets began their inaugural season of play in 1962, Kiner was part of a broadcast team that included Lindsey Nelson and Bob Murphy. For more than 50 years, Kiner would be the voice of the Mets, and his post-game interviews with players in the new version of Kiner's Korner became a favorite of fans not just in New York, but across the nation. Prone to verbal gaffes similar to those made famous by Yogi Berra, his "Kinerisms" like "solo home runs usually take place with no one on base" became a treasured part of his broadcasting legacy. In later years, Kiner continued to broadcast for the Mets, but in a reduced capacity. At the age of 91, he was still gracing New York fans with his own special style of wit and wisdom, right up until his death on February 6, 2014. With his passing, the game of baseball lost one of its best goodwill ambassadors. Tim McCarver, the All-Star catcher and veteran broadcaster, worked with Kiner for 16 years in the booth covering Mets games. McCarver paid tribute to his old colleague's charm when he said that "What Ralph learned was how to treat people, and he evidently learned that at an early age because he was across the board nice to everybody."[1]

CHAPTER 1

Learning to Love the Game

Ralph McPherran Kiner was born in Santa Rita, New Mexico, on October 27, 1922. His father, Ralph Macklin Kiner, had been born and raised in Pennsylvania, as was his grandfather, Andrew Kiner. His father was born in 1883 and was a baker by profession. The elder Ralph got a late start on settling down and starting a family when he married Beatrice Grayson in 1921, at the age of 38. Beatrice was getting a late start on married life herself, as she was only months younger than Ralph. Born and raised in Oregon, Beatrice had met Ralph in Santa Rita, where he was working as a steam-shovel operator at the local copper mine that employed the majority of the town's workers. Unlike most women of the time period, Beatrice had a profession of her own. She was a trained nurse who had served with the United States military during World War I.[1]

Kiner's father was a great baseball fan and loved to play the game. He was not good enough to play on Santa Rita's talented hometown team, however. A few of the Chicago White Sox players who had thrown the 1919 World Series had taken jobs at Santa Rita, and while they had received a lifetime ban from the Major Leagues, they continued to play for other leagues. The Santa Rita team was part of the Cop-per League, made up of teams from copper mining towns. Though Kiner was not good enough to play on the team, he was considered to be a reliable and honest member of the community, and was often selected to hold the money that was bet on the games.[2]

Young Ralph was only four years old when his father died in 1926. Beatrice was faced with the prospect of being the sole provider for herself and her son. Luckily, she had a profession to fall back on, so she sought a job in the nursing field. Beatrice was a small woman, standing only

4'11" tall, but she had a take-charge nature and sense of purpose that would add stability to Kiner's early life and made her far more imposing than her diminutive stature. Through a friend, she found a job in Alhambra, California, working as an office nurse for an insurance and trust company. Her pay was $125 per month, a handsome sum for the time, especially for a woman. Alhambra was still a young city when Kiner and his mother moved there. Located in the western San Gabriel Valley region of Los Angeles County, it was a suburb of the city of Los Angeles, its close neighbor to the east. Beatrice spent all her time working at her job or at her home, and Ralph remembered that she had "an aura of gentility and culture" about her, evidenced by the manner in which she kept house. Ralph recalled that their surroundings always included nice furniture and elegant china and silverware." Indeed, Beatrice gained such an enviable reputation as a homemaker and decorator among her neighbors that "many friends asked her to teach them how to keep their houses as prim and proper as ours was."[3]

Though Kiner's father never had a chance to play baseball with his son, the love of the game must have been in the blood, for Ralph became enamored of baseball at an early age. There were many vacant lots in the young town of Alhambra which provided perfect sites for games of catch and more. However, Ralph's mother had little appreciation for sports. To Beatrice, time well spent was time immersed in hard work and learning. To her, sports were a waste of time that could be better utilized in preparing oneself for a professional career as a doctor or lawyer. Young Ralph found little support or encouragement for his developing passion for baseball from his mother, even when it became apparent that he had a special talent for playing the sport. To Beatrice, the prospect of playing baseball for a living held little promise, and she did not consider it a reputable vocation for her son to aspire to.[4]

Luckily for Kiner, there was a nearby oasis in which he could indulge his love of baseball and find kindred spirits for his passion for the game. Bob and Rose Bodkin lived directly across the street from the Kiner residence, along with their son, Robert. Bob Bodkin had been a semi-pro pitcher in his younger days, and as such had a deep and abiding love for the game. He was doing his best to instill that love in his son, who was several years older than Kiner. "The Bodkins became my surrogate family," Kiner later wrote. "I was always hanging around, always nearby in case an impromptu batting-practice session was called." Bob often threw to Robert in order to improve his swing, and Kiner got into the act when the elder Bodkin tossed him a glove one day and asked if he would shag the batted balls. Kiner readily agreed, and for quite some time he performed the duties of designated fielder for the simulated games. At length, however, Kiner grew tired of just running down batted balls and asked to bat, as "it occurred to me that it might be more fun to hit a ball than chase it down." His request was initially denied, but when he proclaimed, "I'm going to quit unless you let me hit," he was finally granted a chance to trade in his glove. Kiner had already played a great deal of softball, but this was the first time he would use a regulation bat against a regulation baseball thrown overhand. It took him a while to adjust to the timing, but once he did, he began whacking the ball regularly, to the astonishment of his tutors. Now it was Bodkin in the field and Kiner at the bat, "a circumstance that I enjoyed more than he."[5]

With Beatrice working, Ralph spent a great deal of time home alone. Usually he was to be found at the Bodkin home, where he said he was "practically adopted." Kiner reflected that it was amazing that Robert Bodkin wasn't annoyed by his continual presence or his horning in on father-son time playing ball. Instead, Robert welcomed Kiner much like a younger brother, and their shared love of the game meant that they spent a great deal of time playing ball together.

The years during which Kiner and Robert Bodkin spent their boyhood were the golden age of baseball. Players like Babe Ruth, Lou Gehrig, Rogers Hornsby, Jimmie Foxx, and Lefty Grove were some of the leading stars in an era that produced nearly 100 members of the Hall of Fame. It was indeed a great time to be a baseball fan, but though the game had already become the national pastime, the Major Leagues were far from being national in their scope. The St. Louis Cardinals were located the furthest west of any big league team in a sport that was concentrated in the Northeast, Mid-Atlantic, and Midwest regions. In the South and far West, professional baseball meant minor league teams, usually of the Class A or AA variety.

In California, the minor league play was of an elevated variety owing to the success of the Pacific Coast League, which included teams like the Hollywood Stars, San Francisco Seals, and San Diego Padres. With no Major League baseball west of St. Louis, the Pacific Coast League evolved into a quality organization that rivaled the National and American Leagues in the level of play. Revenues for the owners were such that player salaries were nearly on par with the big leagues as well. Indeed, the Pacific Coast League produced a wealth of stars who went on to become legends in the sport, like Joe DiMaggio, Ted Williams, Tony Lazzeri, Paul Waner, Earl Averill, Bobby Doerr, Joe Gordon, and Ernie Lombardi.[6] Also, there were a few Major League teams that held

When Kiner was a boy, stars of the game included players like Ty Cobb, Lou Gehrig and Walter "the Train" Johnson. Babe Ruth, shown here, with his prodigious home run power, brought a new aspect to the game and attracted a new crop of baseball fans who thrilled in his ability to win games with a single swing of the bat. Kiner would grow up to add his name to an ever-increasing list of sluggers, following in the footsteps of Ruth, who became home run kings.

1: Learning to Love the Game

their spring training in California, which helped to fill the void for residents of the West Coast. It would be more than two decades from the time of Kiner's youth until Major League baseball would reach California.

Following Major League baseball in California meant listening to the games on the radio. All of the games were played during the day until 1935, when the Cincinnati Reds hosted the Philadelphia Phillies at Crosley Field under the lights. Afternoon games were fine during the summer, when school was out and Kiner's mother was at work, but they were almost impossible to follow during the school year. In 1934, Kiner adopted the Detroit Tigers as his favorite team. The Tigers fielded an awesome lineup of stars including Mickey Cochrane, Hank Greenberg, Charlie Gehringer, and Goose Goslin, with Schoolboy Rowe serving as their ace on the mound. Kiner's favorite player was Greenberg, and though he didn't know it yet, his boyhood hero was destined to have a great impact on his life. The Tigers captured the American League pennant that season and were poised to take on the St. Louis Cardinals in the World Series. The Cardinals were a great team in their own right. With stars like Frankie Frisch, Pepper Martin, and Joe Medwick, and a pitching staff that included the likes of Dizzy Dean, Dazzy Vance, and Jesse Haines, the Redbirds presented a formidable challenge for the Tigers.

Kiner was intent on following the World Series, but there were no radios in the school on which to listen to the play-by-play action. Mrs. Bodkin came to the rescue. The Bodkin home was 150 to 200 yards from the school, but their front porch could be seen by looking out the schoolhouse window. She would listen to the games on the radio, and when something of importance took place she would come out onto the porch and whistle loudly. Kiner would look out the window to see her give signs they had previously made up to inform him of what was going on in the game.[7] It was a hard-fought Series through the first six games, coming down to a winner-take-all contest in Game Seven. Dizzy Dean slammed the door on the Tigers by pitching a complete game shutout, and the Cardinals walked away as world champions.

Radio broadcasts of the games was still very much in their infancy at the time Mrs. Bodkin was relaying signals during the 1934 World

Series. Though the first game had been broadcast back in 1921 when KDKA Radio aired a game between the Pittsburgh Pirates and the Philadelphia Phillies, the concept had taken some time to catch on with the owners. Most team executives felt that broadcasting the games would keep people from coming to the ballpark and buying tickets, and they were reluctant to embrace this new technology. Most owners who did agree to allow their games to be broadcast only permitted the team's away games to go on the air. It wasn't until the 1930s that owners fully realized the impact that regularly broadcast games could have in promoting their teams' popularity. To be sure, the broadcasting of games served to increase interest among the fans, and instead of keeping them away from the turnstiles, brought more paying customers into the ballparks.

Kiner's mother was not yet fully aware of how deeply his love of baseball went, or how much time he was devoting to it. Beatrice would undoubtedly have been unhappy with Rose Bodkin if she had known how she was fueling the fire of Ralph's baseball passions during the World Series. Beatrice had only recently finished disciplining the boy for wayward actions that had been caused by excessive playing of baseball. Beatrice made good money for the time, especially when one considers that Ralph's boyhood took place largely during the Great Depression. Being the practical woman she was, Beatrice wanted Ralph to learn the lessons of hard work and responsibility, as well as the value of a dollar. Therefore, she arranged for him to get a job selling the *Saturday Evening Post* door to door. The magazine cost five cents, and Ralph was given 20 of them each week to peddle in his neighborhood. The magazines cost Ralph four cents per copy, meaning that he would make a profit of 20 cents if he sold them all. This money was turned over to Beatrice to help with family expenses. In reality, it is doubtful that Beatrice needed the money to make ends meet. She was making more than $30 a week at the time, and it may easily be assumed that she was merely attempting to teach Ralph work ethics and the meaning of contributing to the greater good.

Ralph found that it was a difficult chore to get rid of all of the magazines each week. It took a great deal of time to find enough people willing to part with a nickel to meet his quota. After a few weeks of toiling

1: Learning to Love the Game

to sell all the magazines, the boy's keen mind settled on a plan that he thought would satisfy his mother without eating in to so much of his baseball time. His neighborhood was made up of single family homes, all of them on small, 50 by 100-foot lots. The going rate for lawn mowing services in Alhambra was 25 cents per yard, and Ralph determined that he could easily mow a lot in half an hour. That meant that in two hours he could earn a dollar, enough money to pay the 80 cents to the magazine company and give his mother the 20 cents profit he would have made if he had sold all the copies. As the two hours of mowing time was a fraction of the time it took him to sell the magazines, Ralph thought he had come up with a solution that would satisfy everyone concerned. The only problem was what to do with all the unsold magazines. The family had an incinerator on their property, but burn day did not coincide with the day the magazines arrived. Ralph concluded that his best method of disposal was to bury the unsold magazines under a tree with low-hanging branches in the back yard. His scheme worked to perfection for some time. Beatrice thought that her son was a sales genius, as he was always able to get rid of his quota in very little time. Obviously, he was learning the traits she wanted to instill in him and was well on his way to becoming a productive member of society.

Then it happened. The burial ground became overladen with magazines. One fall day, while burning rubbish in the incinerator, Beatrice noticed something amiss under the tree in the back yard. Upon examination, she discovered that the *Saturday Evening Post* seemed to be sprouting from the roots of the tree, and the jig was up. As Ralph later put it, "I was tried, convicted, and sentenced in one afternoon." Beatrice was so incensed over Ralph's actions that she determined to send him to a place where he could more fully be taught the discipline he lacked. Accordingly, she enrolled him in the Long Beach Military School, where he would get continual supervision. Ralph hated the school, probably more for the fact that he could not play baseball than for the regulations and restraint. Luckily, for him, Beatrice felt that he had learned his lesson after six months and allowed him to return home and attend public school again.[8]

This wasn't the only time playing baseball got Kiner into trouble. Another incident resulted in his being arrested. During the summer of

1933, Ralph played in a supervised league that had its home games on a field at Fremont Grammar School. The sixth-grade building fronted the baseball diamond in left field, at what was assumed to be a safe distance from batted balls. Ralph proved that assumption to be wrong. During the course of the summer, he hit eight long home runs to left that shattered windows in the building, much to the dismay of the sixth-grade teacher, a Miss Bloomingdale. As he was the first boy to hit a ball that far, the incidents brought about an unusual question of who was at fault for the shattered windows. The day after the summer league ended, Ralph was at home when the door bell rang. Peering out from between the slats of the venetian blinds, Ralph saw police officers in front of the house. Miss Bloomingdale had filed a complaint with the authorities over Ralph's destruction of public property, and the police were there to arrest him. The officers took the boy to the city jail, and though it was only a ten-minute drive, it was the longest ten minutes in young Kiner's life. He remembered that he felt as if his life were over, and contemplated that "Even military school seemed a joyride by comparison to what lay ahead. The thought of my mother's reaction frightened me even more than the men in uniform," a sentiment well-known to anyone raised in a strict home.

When they reached the police station, the case was turned over to the truant officer. Once apprised of all the facts, this man reached into his desk and picked up a book. Paging to his desired spot, he began to read aloud the baseball poem "Casey at the Bat." The officers had checked out Miss Bloomingdale's complaint and had concluded that the problem was the positioning of the baseball diamond in relation to the school. Ralph was found to be innocent of any wrong-doing. The diamond was subsequently moved so that it did not face the sixth-grade building, and his record was expunged. The incident had a profound effect on the young boy. "Casey at the Bat" would hold special meaning for him the rest of his life. The truant officer who had read him the poem was Lieutenant John Casey, and to commemorate the event, he would later name his first daughter Katherine Chaffee, though he always "called her K.C."[9]

During this time, Ralph was actually a switch-hitter, and according to him "could hit the ball just as far" from the left side as he could from the right. Ralph also played a lot of softball and had adopted a left-handed stance when playing those games so as not to mess up his swing when playing hardball. But in those days, it wasn't considered an advantage to be a switch-hitter, so he continued to bat only right-handed in baseball games.[10]

Kiner's troubles may have seemed monumental to him at the time, but in actuality he was living a dream existence when compared with so many boys and girls across the country. The Great Depression had caused hundreds of thousands of Americans to become homeless. Unemployment in the nation reached 25 percent at its highest point in 1933.[11] With many Americans living in shanty towns, and many more worried over where their next meal would come from, Kiner's troubles were small indeed. His experience at military school merely served to show that his mother had the extra income, during these hard times, to send her son away to a boarding school with an appreciable tuition rate. To be sure, the Kiners were not wealthy, but they lived a comfortable lifestyle at a time when many of their fellow Americans were experiencing destitution and misery.

Though the Kiners and their neighbors in Alhambra seem to have escaped the severe financial worries that plagued many Americans during that time, they were never extravagant or wasteful. Things were meant to last, and not to be purchased over and over again. Bob Bodkin taught Kiner lessons of frugality by showing him how to nail and tape a broken bat properly and how to stitch up baseballs that had come apart. In Kiner's case, the latter had become very important, for he was already blossoming into a power hitter. The Bodkins continued to be an important part of his life and provided him with tutelage in many other facets of life. Rose Bodkin taught him how to drive a car, and he learned how to dance by tagging along with Robert Bodkin and his friends to the Pasadena Civic Auditorium.[12]

Another close friend of Kiner's during his boyhood was Lefty Johnston. Naturally, the foundation of the boy's friendship was their mutual love of baseball. Johnston's father, like Bob Bodkin, was also a great enthusiast of the game. The Johnstons took Kiner to an occasional Pacific Coast League game to see aspiring Major Leaguers in action, but they made a far greater contribution to Kiner's future career by enhancing his opportunities to play the game. Lefty's father, Harry, drove his son outside of Alhambra to allow him to play at other sites in other leagues. Kiner was regularly included on these trips, allowing him to play competitively against some better players than he saw in his home town. It also allowed him to play on several better fields. Through the Johnstons, Kiner had the chance to play at Gilmore Field and Wrigley Field, the home of the Pacific Coast League's Hollywood Stars and Los Angeles Angels, respectively. Harry Johnston obviously recognized the talent that Kiner had for the game. The elder Johnston had an eye for talent gained through experience. He had been a minor league pitcher himself, and he managed a semi-pro team in the Los Angeles area. Kiner and Johnston both pursued their dreams of playing professional ball when they got older, and Johnston was signed to a minor league contract. He never made it to the majors, however, and eventually quit baseball to make his living as a banker.[13]

Bob Bodkin also helped to hone the boy's skill by introducing him to league play of a higher caliber than he would have gotten playing on local sandlot teams. There was an adult pickup game in Alhambra every Sunday in which the men of the neighborhood would play. When Ralph was only 13 or 14, he began attending these games and playing regularly against the men. His position was usually right field, and though he described himself as "the worst player on the team" he was still good enough to compete "and help them with their winning games."[14]

By the time Kiner began his freshman year at Alhambra High School, he was already as good, or better, than most of the players on the team. The team had a rule that freshmen couldn't play, however, so he was forced to sit out his first year. In his sophomore year, Kiner took the field as a starter and remained so throughout his high school career. The Alhambra High Moors already had produced a star baseball player who would pave the way for Kiner into the majors. Max West was a hard-hitting outfielder on the Alhambra team who had been signed to play in the minor leagues. In 1938, while Kiner was still making a name for himself in the Alhambra lineup, West broke into the Major Leagues with the Boston Braves. He had a seven-year career in the majors, playing for the Braves and the Cincinnati Reds from 1938 through 1946. After being out of baseball in 1947, West tried to make a comeback and was ironically signed by the Pittsburgh Pirates in 1948, becoming a teammate of Kiner's and placing both of Alhambra's favorite sons on the same roster. West hit a respectable .254 for his career, but his claim to fame in the game came in 1940 during his only selection to the All-Star Game. In his first at-bat, he homered, becoming the first player to do so in All-Star play.[15]

Kiner didn't let the fact that he couldn't play on the high school team in his freshman year slow him down or limit his time on the diamond. He continued to play in sandlot pickup games, as well as in the Sunday adult games and on Saturdays as well. In addition, he started playing American Legion ball and was recruited by Dan Crowley, a player in the Pacific Coast League, to play for the Junior Yankees, a team sponsored by the New York Yankees. Crowley served as the manager of the team, with Bill Essick, the Yankees' influential West Coast scout, overseeing the team's operation. It was Essick who had recommended that the Yankees purchase Joe DiMaggio's contract from the Pacific Coast League.[16] At that time, the Yankees were the class of the Major Leagues. With players like Babe Ruth, Lou Gehrig, and Bill Dickey, they had dominated the game since the early 1920s. By the time Kiner graduated from high school, the Yankees had been crowned world champions eight times, the most of any team in the game. In keeping with an era where nothing was allowed to go to waste, the players on the Junior Yankees received their uniforms in an unusual way. "We used to get the hand-down uniforms of the Yankee players that played in the majors," Kiner remembered. "It was quite a thrill to wear an old Yankee uniform. I never got Ruth's uniform, or Gehrig's, but I did get Selkirk's uniform, which I treasured like any kid would, when he had it."[17] George Selkirk took over in right field for the Yankees when Babe Ruth was released in 1935. At the time Kiner was playing for the Junior Yankees, Selkirk was establishing himself as a legitimate star with the Major League squad, hitting over .300 for five of his first six seasons while belting 83 home runs. While playing for the Junior Yankees, Kiner was converted into an infielder and pitcher. He had a short stint in baseball as a pitcher, and later, when he reached the majors, he would help to shorten the pitching careers of hurlers he faced.

Kiner may not have gotten to wear one of Ruth's cast-off uniforms when he played for the Junior Yankees, but he would have the opportunity to meet the famed slugger in person when the Babe made a visit close to his home. Ruth was playing himself in the movie being made about Lou Gehrig, *Pride of the Yankees*, in 1942, and was on set in Hollywood. Babe Herman, a former Major Leaguer, was a scout for the Pittsburgh Pirates and offered to introduce Kiner to the Babe. Though Hank Greenberg was his favorite baseball player, Kiner must have been thrilled to meet the all-time home run king of the game, and he took the opportunity to obtain any pointers that could improve his own swing. Kiner watched as Ruth swung a bat on the set and remembered that "Ruth was an old man when I saw him swing, but I saw that he got plenty of wrist and forearm into his swing, more than anybody I ever saw." That observation led to Kiner to adopting special exercises to build up the strength of his wrists.[18]

At that time, there was an unwritten agreement that players with Major League-sponsored junior teams would be signed by the parent organizations when they became old enough. As such, Kiner seemed to be on the fast track to becoming a member of the Yankees, if only on a minor league squad, but he was already attracting the attention of scouts outside the Yankees organization, as other teams vied to acquire his talents. Beatrice was still hoping that her son would outgrow his boyhood passion for baseball and settle on a profession she deemed more reliable and stable, but it was becoming more and more difficult for her to dismiss the fact that her son had a great talent for the game. Dutch Ruether, a scout for the Chicago Cubs, informed his team management that he had found two bright prospects he thought they should sign. Kiner was the first, and Ruether recommended the team offer a $3,000 signing bonus to the slugger. The other prospect Ruether was hot on was Ewell Blackwell, a pitcher, who only wanted $750 to sign. The Cubs' brass declined to make an offer to either player, stating that the signing amounts were too high. Kiner, of course, would go on to post a Hall of Fame career in his ten years in the majors. Blackwell became a six-time All-Star while pitching for the Cincinnati Reds, and finished 2nd in the MVP voting in 1947 after compiling a record of 22–8 with an ERA of 2.47.

But the Cubs' scout was not the only one who had taken notice of Kiner's potential. Several others had tabbed him as a hot prospect and were urging their teams to sign him. The Hollywood Stars didn't offer a signing bonus, but if he played for them he would be able to remain at home while in the minors. The main inducement the Stars offered was that when a Major League team eventually purchased his contract, he would receive 50 percent of the amount paid. The Yankees weren't offering a signing bonus either, at least not in cash. Beatrice still wasn't convinced that baseball was the proper career for her son and preferred that he attend college instead. The Yankees offered to pay for him to attend the University of Southern California during the off-season so he could get his degree. To be sure, he would be signed into the Yankees' organization, but he was told that he would be starting his career in their Class D affiliate, the lowest classification in the minor leagues.

Hollis Thurston, a scout for the Pittsburgh Pirates, made Kiner another offer. Thurston said the Pirates would give him a $3,000 signing bonus and another $5,000 when he made it to the majors. In addition, he was promised that he would start his Pirates career at the Class A level, several positions higher than the Yankees were offering. As Kiner put it, "The decision was made by a committee of three: my mother, me, and Harry Johnston, the father of my high school teammate Lefty Johnston and the man who was my unofficial baseball guidance counselor in those days. Of the three, I had the least to say about my future course."

Johnston convinced both Beatrice and Ralph that the Pirates' offer was by far the best one. In 1940, $3,000 was a huge sum of money, and all by itself that signing bonus would have been enough to sway the decision toward the Pirates. Johnston pointed out that whatever prestige being in the Yankees' organization might have would be muted by the fact that the Bronx Bombers were stacked with talent at every level, and he might languish in the minors for years. With the Pirates, on the other hand, he would already be starting in Class A ball for a team that was relatively thin on talent. His road to the big leagues would therefore be much shorter with the Pirates, which would also result in his receiving the additional $5,000 bonus Thurston had promised.[19]

The day Kiner signed his contract he took his mother, Mr. and Mrs. Johnston, and his friend Lefty out to dinner on La Cienega Boulevard, a popular spot with the Los Angeles elite. Kiner said, "For the first time in my life dinner was on me." Dinner was the only extravagance spent out of the signing bonus. The bulk of the money was put toward a much more practical use: paying off the mortgage on the family home. Beatrice referred to herself as "Cinderella" from that day forward, and adopted a new acceptance of her son's career choice.[20]

All of Kiner's passion and practice had finally come to fruition. He was going to play professional baseball with a better than average chance of making it to the big show. His father must have been looking down on him with pride. The boy he had never gotten to play catch with had inherited his love of the game and had put himself in a position to make his dreams come true.

Chapter 2

Off to the Minors

Kiner did not report to the minors immediately following his graduation from Alhambra High School. Spring training had already begun by the time he received his diploma, and it was decided that his pro career would begin with the 1941 season. In the meantime, he would continue to play in the various leagues around his home town to keep himself sharp and his swing well timed.

When the 1941 season approached, Kiner received instructions from the Pirates to report to the Albany Senators, the Pirates' Class A club in the Eastern League. The Senators had been playing baseball in Albany, New York, since 1885, and had been affiliated with several leagues, including the New York State League, the International League, and the New York–Pennsylvania League. In 1938, the team became part of the Eastern League, an affiliation it would maintain until 1959. The Senators had been a minor league squad of the Cincinnati Reds for a couple years before Pittsburgh became the parent club in 1940. The Pirates would be the Major League affiliate of this Class A team for a decade, from 1940–1950, during which time the Senators made it to the Eastern League playoffs six times and won the title in 1945. The team played their games at Hawkins Stadium, one of the spacious fields that favored pitchers which seemed to define the Eastern League.

America embraced the advent of the 1941 season with enthusiasm. Newspapers and movie newsreels were filled with reports of the war that was raging in Europe and Asia, but most Americans were content to let the world take care of itself and advocated isolationism. After all, it had been little more than two decades since the nation had sent its sons to fight in the "war to end all wars," and the peace won in that conflict had lasted only a single generation. Most Americans found it abhorrent to dive into this latest European power struggle and wished to sit this one out. Everything would change before the year ended, however, as a rush to war resulted from the attack on Pearl Harbor.

In the meantime, the 1941 baseball season provided fans with all the excitement they could handle, despite occasional interruptions causing thoughts to turn to war. Hank Greenberg, the star slugger of the Detroit Tigers, had been runner-up for the American League Most Valuable Player Award in 1940, and was expected to have another big season in 1941. But Greenberg played for only three weeks before being drafted into the army. He had been one of the highest paid players in the game, with an annual salary of $55,000, which quickly diminished to a soldier's pay of $21 a month. Before the season was over, four more Major Leaguers would be drafted into the military.

Joe DiMaggio had replaced Babe Ruth and Lou Gehrig as the face of the New York Yankees, and he started the season with a glimpse of the greatness that would put him in the record book. After hitting safely in his last 19 games of spring training, he started off the regular season by reaching safely in the first eight games before falling into a slight slump. On May 15, DiMaggio singled against Chicago White Sox pitcher Edgar Smith in what would be the beginning of a record streak that stands to this day. For 56 straight games, the "Yankee Clipper" hit safely, until the hot streak finally came to an end on July 17 against the Cleveland Indians. Wee Willie Keeler's record of 44 straight games, set in 1897, had been decisively beaten. Amazingly, DiMaggio started another streak the following day, hitting in another 16 straight games, recording hits in 72 of 73 games.

While one unbelievable streak was being set, the holder of another record most baseball fans thought would never be broken lost his battle with ALS. Lou Gehrig died on June 2, three weeks before his 38th birthday. Gehrig, nicknamed the "Iron Horse" because of his never missing a game, had put together a string of 2,130 consecutive games played before the debilitating disease robbed him of the ability to play. In two short years, the disease took his life and would forever after become known as Lou Gehrig's Disease.

DiMaggio's streak was not the only noteworthy feat baseball fans followed that summer. A young Red Sox slugger, Ted Williams, quietly

2: Off to the Minors

went about establishing his place in baseball history. While the major emphasis of reporters was centered on DiMaggio, Williams went most of the summer hitting at a .400 rate. For much of the season, Williams was able to play without the pressure of crowding reporters, as all eyes were focused on the Yankees and DiMaggio. The attention caught up with him after July 17, however, and for the remainder of the season baseball faithful watched anxiously to see if Williams could add his name to a small list of greats in the game. Only seven players had managed to hit .400 since 1900. The last had been Bill Terry, in 1930, while playing for the New York Giants. The last American Leaguer to attain the feat had been Harry Heilmann in 1923. Williams flirted with the .400 mark throughout the latter half of the season. He went into the final day of the campaign with an average of .39955, which would be rounded to .400 by statisticians. His manager, Joe Cronin, gave him the option of sitting out both games of a doubleheader that day to ensure he would finish the season with the lofty average. But Williams was too proud to attain the coveted mark by averaging upward. He chose to play and take his chances of earning the .400 average outright. In the first game, he went 4-for-5, and he added two more hits in the nightcap, finishing the season with an average of .406. Williams would become the last Major Leaguer to hit .400 in the twentieth century, and no player has seriously threatened to attain that plateau in the twenty-first century.

The New York Yankees finished the year by winning the World Series over the cross-town Dodgers in five games. Over the next 15 years, the two teams would face off against one another for the title six more times.

Ralph Kiner began his first year in professional baseball removed from the glitz and glamour of the Major Leagues. As a young player with loads of talent, he must surely have dreamed of the time when he could possibly set records of his own, but for now, he could only watch the accomplishments of stars like DiMaggio and Williams from afar, as a fan. His career started off hot enough when he reported the Pirates' big league training camp at San Bernardino, some 60 miles east of Alhambra. In those days, rookies were not treated the way they are today, regardless of their potential. In fact, they could not even get time in the batting cage unless a member of the regular squad gave up his time for them. In Kiner's case, a second-year member of the Pirates, Bob Elliott, finally gave him the opportunity by "handing me his bat and telling me to go hit."[1] Elliott was a budding young star for the Pirates in his own right. In 1939, the right fielder hit .333 in 40 games. He followed that up in his sophomore season by stroking a solid .292 in 148 games. He would have eight productive seasons with Pittsburgh before being traded to the Boston Braves in 1947. As a Pirates outfielder and third baseman, Elliott batted .292 with 50 home runs and was a three-time All-Star. Kiner would be a teammate of his during his last year in Pittsburgh, but for now, he was just a 19-year-old, fresh-faced kid that Elliott was giving a break by allowing him a few swings at the ball. Kiner made the most of these swings. He stated, "It didn't take long to see that I could hit the ball farther than anyone Pittsburgh had on its roster."[2] Kiner's ability to hit the ball hard impressed his peers, but more importantly, it caught the eye of Frankie Frisch, the tough manager of the Pirates. Frisch had been a member of the famous Gas House Gang of the St Louis Cardinals during the 1930s, and he quickly recognized the talent Kiner possessed. From that day on, Kiner got regular time in the cage during batting practice. Frisch was so taken with Kiner's ability that he even put him in the starting lineup of the team's first exhibition game, at first base.

The Pirates were playing the Chicago White Sox, a solid team that had finished fourth in the American League the previous year with a record of 82–72, and was led by future Hall of Fame shortstop Luke Appling. Kiner's debut could not have gone better. He went 4-for-5 that day, including two home runs. The first was hit off Bill Dietrich, a right-hander with a no-hitter to his credit. The second came off of left-hander Thornton Lee, who would go on to win 22 games in 1941 and be selected to the All-Star Game. Kiner would later write that he was "thrilled" over his performance against the White Sox in his first game played with Major Leaguers.[3] Frankie Frisch was paying close attention to the young rookie. His obvious power could add a great deal to the Pirates' lineup if it was not just a fluke.

Kiner continued to get chances to show what he could do, and by all appearances, he was on the fast track to making the big league club. Then, late in the exhibition season, the Pirates played the Chicago Cubs at Wrigley Field in Los Angeles. Pittsburgh got clobbered in this game, much to the dismay of Frisch. In a foul mood, the manager ordered his players to run laps following the game as punishment for their poor performance. Kiner had not played and he thus felt himself to be immune from the extracurricular activity Frisch had doled out. Instead of joining his teammates, Kiner found a seat in the bullpen, which is where an irate Frisch found him. The manager bellowed at Kiner, demanding to know why he was not out on the field with the rest of the players, running laps. Kiner responded, "I only have one pair of baseball shoes, and if I wear them out running, I won't have any for the games." The fiery Frisch must have nearly exploded at this answer. To be sure, Kiner's naïve response cost him the opportunity of spending more time with the team, and possibly the chance of breaking into the Major Leagues, that season. Frisch roared, "Well, that's fine. You can take those shoes to Barnwell, South Carolina, because that's where you're playing your next game."[4]

Barnwell, South Carolina, was the spring training site of the Albany Senators. For Kiner, that was a world away. For all intents and purposes, he had never been out of California. To be sure, he had been born in New Mexico, but he and his mother had moved from there when he was only four years old, and from that point on he was strictly a Californian. His experiences in South Carolina would be eye-opening, but his first order of business was getting there. Luckily, his friend, Lefty Johnston, had also been signed to a professional contract and was leaving to report to his minor league team. Johnston had been assigned to a Class D team in Louisiana and was planning to drive there himself. Kiner tagged along with his friend for about half of his journey. From Louisiana, he arranged to make the rest of the trip by train. He remembered that they made a leisurely journey to Louisiana. He and Johnston would stop every two or three hours to stretch their legs and play a game of catch along the side of the road. Obviously, Kiner was not nearly as worried about wearing out his baseball glove as his baseball shoes. His first trip away from home took the boy through vastly changing countryside, with vistas that should have made deep impressions on young Kiner, but baseball was all that was on his mind, and these vistas became merely scenic backdrops for their games of catch. Somewhere along the way, they picked up a hitchhiker who would add more than varied conversation to the trip. The extra passenger had a case of the measles, as it turned out, and

Kiner was unknowingly exposed to the disease for long enough to contract the illness. He would later recall, "When I finally reached South Carolina, I had two realizations: I couldn't understand the people because of their accents, and the hitchhiker had a contagious case of measles. So there I was away from home for the first time, miserable with fever and red bumps all over my body, and unable to communicate with anybody. It wasn't a great introduction to life as a professional ballplayer."[5]

It took Kiner about a week to recover from the illness and recoup enough of his strength to join the team. What he saw when he reported to the Senators was nothing short of culture shock. As he described it,

> In those days most people were unaware of the types of individuals who lived in other sections of the country because we never traveled and had no television to be our window to the world. Before I started to play pro ball, I had never been east of New Mexico, and I was only there till I was four, which was when my father died and my mother moved us to California. All of a sudden I was playing and living with guys from the Midwest, East, and South. They had different views and attitudes. Especially the Southerners who were biased against "colored" (which was the most common "acceptable" word used by players in those days) and ethnic people. During that eye-opening spring, I played in ballparks in Southern towns in which African American fans had to sit in their own sections of the bleachers. Everywhere, there were separate water fountains, bathrooms, and entrances for African Americans, and restaurants, hotels, and other places of business that prohibited them from entering at all. And years before Rosa Parks, it was the law that only whites could sit in the front of the bus. Schools were segregated, there was no dating between the races, and African Americans and whites did not play sports together. This was a whole new education for me.[6]

Kiner had not seen such things in California. He remembered that there were not many blacks in his school, but those who attended were permitted to play sports along with their white classmates, and no big deal had been made of it. Many times he had played baseball and softball on and against mixed-race teams in the Los Angeles area, and had faced some of the most famous black sports figures in his younger years. Jackie Robinson, who was three years Kiner's senior, was already one of the most renowned athletes in Southern California when the two met in competition. Kiner said,

> when I was about 13 or 14, I played a game or two of fast-pitch softball at Brookside Park in Pasadena against teams that included the most touted young African American athlete around. His name was Jackie Robinson. Jackie was in his late teens, and by that time I had read numerous articles about his achievements. In high school and then at Pasadena Junior College he was an unbelievable football

player, great basketball player, and fantastic track star. He played baseball on occasion, as an infielder, but it was his worst sport![7]

Kiner also remembered playing against all-black teams in his younger days, when Satchel Paige would bring his troupe of all-stars barnstorming through the area for exhibition games. He was only 17 when he got the opportunity to play on a team "with a few minor leaguers and many men who played ball only on weekends because they had to make a living." The opposition was Paige and a lineup that included such Negro Leagues stars as Willie Wells, Mule Suttles, Goose Tatum, and Biz Mackey. Kiner was impressed by Mackey, the first catcher he ever saw throw from his knees, but his greatest admiration was reserved for Suttles, who was, of course, a power hitter. "He was a Bunyanesque figure who stood 6'6", was a rock-solid 240 pounds, and swung a 50-ounce piece of lumber. The word was that he hit a ball in Cuba that traveled 600 feet, and I didn't doubt it." Despite his young age, Kiner got to start in the game.

> We had a few hitters with power, but I was the one who managed to homer off Paige! Wrigley Field was a bandbox, and I got lucky—he struck me out the next time up—but it was such a thrill because everyone knew about Satchel Paige, the slim and sly pitcher who took delight in throwing beebees anywhere he wanted. Of the pitchers, the great Paige was the leading man, but I also batted against Chet Brewer and "Bullet" Joe Rogan, who had a helluva fastball.[8]

Kiner was disturbed by the practices concerning blacks in the South. His own experiences back in California had caused him to have a much different opinion of blacks than many of the players he was now sharing so much time with. To Kiner, blacks were just teammates or competitors, and the color of their skin did not determine their worth as a person. His memories about how blacks had been treated back in California spoke more about the man then it did about the region he had lived in.

Actually, California was not as universally tolerant of blacks as he remembered. To be sure, the level of prejudice was not as extreme as was to be found in the South, but it was there nonetheless. Kiner recalled a more open society in California because the bigotry was not as pronounced as it was in the South, but more importantly, Kiner did not see it because he felt no such compunction himself. His personality led him to be kind to and accepting of all people, regardless of background, race, or any other consideration.

His favorite player, as a boy, had been Hank Greenberg, the star slugger of the Tigers. Greenberg was Jewish and had broken into the game at a time when fierce prejudice was aimed at players. Much of the same abuse and mistreatment that would later be hurled at the first black players in the sport were targeted toward Greenberg in his initial years in Detroit. But Kiner chose Greenberg to be his idol, not because or in spite of the fact he was Jewish, but merely because he was a great baseball player. The question of creed or race did not enter into it for Kiner.

Jackie Robinson painted a far different picture of life for blacks in Southern California than Kiner remembered. For Robinson, the open equality Kiner described was more fiction than fact. Like Kiner, he had relocated to California with his family at a very young age, and also like Kiner, he had been raised by a single mother. That is pretty much where the similarities ended. Robinson was born in 1919 in Georgia. His father, Jerry Robinson, labored as a share-cropper for a plantation owner, earning a meager living on which to support himself, a wife, and, with the arrival of Jackie, five small children. Shortly after Jackie's birth, Jerry Robinson made a trip to Memphis, presumably to seek work. He never returned. Abandoned, and without a way to provide for herself and her family, Jackie's mother, Mallie Robinson, decided that a change of scenery was in order. Her brother had previously moved to California and had written her that conditions were better for blacks there than in the South. Mallie decided that she would relocate her family to a place where her children might make a better start for themselves in life. Her brother sent her what little money he could spare, and she sold all of the family belongings in Georgia before buying bus tickets for the cross-country journey. Upon arrival, the family stayed in cramped quarters with Mallie's brother while she found a job and saved the money to get her own apartment. Mallie, with little education, was compelled to take menial labor washing and ironing other people's clothes in order to make a living. Jackie remembered his mother's labors from dawn to dusk in order to earn enough money to eke out an existence. Times were tough, and the family could not always afford two meals a day. "Even though she couldn't always give us enough to eat, my mother was determined that we should not starve for education. She was also determined that we should grow up with a sense of religious responsibility. Most important to her was the desire to keep the family together." Like Kiner, young Jackie had also sold newspapers, but it was not to learn a sense of responsibility. In Jackie's case, the papers were actually sold, not buried in the back yard, and the money derived from their sale went into the family's general fund.[9]

Jackie's memories of life in suburban Los Angeles were quite different from Kiner's. He recalled having racial slurs cast his way, and of "going to the YMCA and being told that Negroes were allowed to use the facilities of the Y only on a certain day of the week" or of going to the "municipal swimming pool and being told that Tuesday was the day for colored kids." Even when attending the local movie theater, he was "ushered to a special section on the right side of the theater or up above someplace. You don't forget these things easily. They create resentment in you. You are being discriminated against and segregated and you wonder why."[10]

Robinson had a love of sports, but he also had a desire to prove that he was the equal of any athlete, regardless of race. Luckily for him, California's prejudice did not extend onto the playing fields, as it did in the South. His opportunities were far better on the West Coast than they would have been in Georgia, but he and other blacks in California still faced far greater obstacles than Kiner observed.

When Kiner eventually got out of his sick bed and reported to the team, he was under the tutelage of Specs Toporcer, the manager of the Senators. Toporcer had been playing professional ball since 1921, but most of his 20-year career had been in the minors. He had divided nine years between the AA affiliate of the St. Louis Cardinals and the parent team, before being dealt to Boston. Seven of his minor league seasons he hit near or above the .300 mark, and he posted a .279 average with the Cardinals. Kiner and Toporcer were different kinds of players, however. Kiner hit for power, and Toporcer was a singles hitter. In the eight years he spent with the Cardinals, he went deep only nine times. In 1941, he was the player-manager for the Senators. Actually, he was much more manager than player, as he put himself into only four games and had only nine at-bats. The fact that he hit only .111 that season probably accounted for his limited time on the diamond.

The Senators were one of eight teams in the Eastern League. The others were the Binghamton Triplets, Elmira Pioneers, Hartford Bees, Scranton Red Sox, Springfield Nationals, Wilkes-Barre Barons, and the Williamsport Grays. Kiner described the Eastern League as "a pitcher's league. The parks were big, the lights were bad, and the ball was dead."[11] Among the promising pitchers who would make good in the big show that Kiner faced while at Albany were Sal Maglie, Lew Krausse, Allie Reynolds, Warren Spahn, and Early Wynn, the latter two going on to become Hall of Fame members. Big parks, dead balls, and good pitching notwithstanding, Kiner was able to clout a homer over the 440-foot left field fence in his first game.[12] It was as promising a start as had been his debut with the Pirates earlier that spring. Kiner played in 141 games that season with 509 at-bats. He led the Senators with 11 home runs and 212 total bases with a .279 batting average. His 11 home runs also put him among the league leaders. It was a great year, all things considered, for Kiner's first professional season.

When he returned to California, Kiner probably looked forward to seeing familiar sights and to an uneventful off-season while he prepared for his second year of getting paid to play the game he loved. Like most other Americans, once Thanksgiving Day had passed, the Kiners prepared for Christmas. Then came Pearl Harbor. On December 7, 1941, the Japanese made a sneak attack against the United States Navy's Pacific Fleet that resulted in more than 3,000 American lives being lost and crippled the fleet. Citizens across the nation gathered around their radios to listen in numbed silence to reports on the tragedy. Shock soon turned to outrage, however, as the people rose as one to avenge the atrocity that had been committed against the nation. On the West Coast, there was great fear that the Japanese might attempt to attack American soil. With the Pacific Fleet a shambles, many felt that there was nothing to stop the Japanese from carrying the war to our shores, and coastal residents of Oregon, Washington, and California kept a watchful vigil toward the western horizon for any sign of the aggressor's approach.

Kiner had a semi-pro baseball game scheduled for the afternoon of December 7, and the team played the contest, despite the somber news coming in from Pearl Harbor. The attack was the main topic of conversation, to be sure, as were individual plans to answer the threat and defend the nation. Many of Kiner's friends enlisted in the service in the

2: Off to the Minors

days immediately following Pearl Harbor. More were drafted as the country mobilized for war. Kiner and some of his friends signed up for the Navy's V-5 and V-12 programs to become naval aviators.[13]

The V-5 and V-12 programs were intended to increase the number of commissioned officers in the United States Navy. Candidates for the V-5 program were required to pass a physical examination and show a strong motivation to become a pilot. Successful applicants were required to complete two terms of college training before being assigned as aviation cadets. The V-5 program was eventually absorbed into the V-12 program, with the aviation cadets being given the designation of V-12(a).[14] There were 131 colleges and universities across the nation affiliated with these programs, and Kiner would not have to search too hard to find one close to his home. The University of Southern California as well as the University of California at Los Angeles both offered the courses and would be easy for him to attend during the off-season. A number of other notable personalities would join Kiner in selecting the V-5 and V-12 programs as a pathway into the service. Among them were Johnny Carson, Jackie Cooper, and Sam Peckinpah from the entertainment industry, future politician Robert F. Kennedy, and fellow baseball personalities Alvin Dark, Al Rosen, and Bowie Kuhn.

In the spring of 1942, as many young men in the country prepared to go to war, Kiner prepared for his second season with the Albany Senators. One big change from the previous year was that Specs Toporcer had been replaced by Ripper Collins as manager. Collins had spent eight years as a first baseman and right fielder for the Cardinals and Cubs before joining the Pirates for the 1941 season. Though he finished his career with a .296 batting average, he hit only .210 in limited play with the Pirates before taking the job as manager of the Senators. So far as Kiner was concerned, Collins would be a skipper more in tune with his power potential. During his career, Collins had been something of a deep threat himself. In his nine seasons, he had clubbed 135 round-trippers, with a high of 35 in 1934, leading the National League. The 38-year-old was born in Altoona, Pennsylvania, where most baseball fans rooted for the Pirates, but he had made his reputation as part of the St. Louis Cardinals' Gas House Gang in the mid–1930s, along with Frankie Frisch, Joe Medwick, Pepper Martin, Jesse Haines, and Dizzy Dean.

Collins was used to being around talented players, and Kiner displayed that same star potential that year with the Senators. Though his average dipped to .257 that season, Kiner swatted 14 home runs to lead the Eastern League. Bill Nagel, a utility infielder who would play parts of three seasons in the Major Leagues, was second on the team with 11 round-trippers, while the rest of the Senators combined to hit another 11. Kiner's power production in the pitcher friendly Eastern League that year earned him a promotion to the Toronto Maple Leafs of the AAA International League for the 1943 season.

The Toronto club had just recently become affiliated with the Pirates, in 1942, after being a top farm team for the Philadelphia Athletics in 1940 and 1941. The manager of the club was future Hall of Fame pitcher Burleigh Grimes. Other teams in the league included the Buffalo Bisons, Newark Bears, Syracuse Chiefs, Montreal Royals, Rochester Red Wings, Baltimore Orioles, and Jersey City Giants.

Outfielder Frank Colman led the team with a .312 batting average, and fellow outfielder Jimmy Ripple paced the club with eight home runs. Toronto had a great year in 1943, finishing first in the International League with a record of 95–57, winning the Governor's Cup. The team lost to the third-place Syracuse Chiefs in the Junior World Series, however, dropping the series in six games. Hank Sauer, a slugger destined to spend 15 years in the Major Leagues, showed glimpses of his potential by swatting 12 round-trippers for the Chiefs that season.

Kiner posted somewhat lackluster numbers with the Maple Leafs. He batted only .236 and hit a mere two home runs in his first campaign in the International League. But his time with the top farm club was too short to evaluate properly. Kiner played in only 43 games with 176 plate appearances before being inducted into another league. With World War II raging all over the globe, Ralph Kiner received notice that he was to report to the United States Navy for active service. Kiner was about to exchange bats, balls, and gloves for the life of a Navy pilot. But before doing so, he hit one of his two home runs for the season in the last game he played in 1943. It was an inside-the-park variety.[15]

CHAPTER 3

A World at War

The war in the Pacific was almost two years old by the time Kiner was called into the service, and the issue was still very much in doubt. The Battle of Midway was a huge American victory in June of 1942, and two months later, United States Marines landed on Guadalcanal. Fighting for possession of the island had been fierce, and it was not until February of 1943 that final victory was achieved. The march toward the Japanese homeland was underway, but the bloody battles of Tarawa, Saipan, Peleliu, Leyte, Iwo Jima, and Okinawa were still in the future, and thousands more lives would be lost before the war finally ended.

Baseball did its part for national defense during the war. More than 500 Major League players and 4,000 minor league prospects served in the United States Armed Forces during the conflict.[1] Quite a number of them were already in the service before Kiner's number was called. In fact, many had been drafted before the United States even became involved in the war. Hugh Mulcahy, a veteran pitcher with the Philadelphia Phillies, was the first Major League player to be drafted. He was inducted on March 8, 1941, nine months before the attack on Pearl Harbor. Mulcahy had earned the nickname "Losing Pitcher" Mulcahy by losing 76 games from 1937 through 1940, as a starting pitcher with the National League's worst franchise. When he reported for induction into the army at Camp Devens, Massachusetts, he was reported to have stated, "My losing streak is over for the duration. I'm on a winning team now." Kiner's boyhood hero, Hank Greenberg, was also an early draftee, inducted into the army in May of 1941. Greenberg was released from military service on December 5, 1941, due to an act of Congress exempting men 28 years of age and older. Two days later, on December 7, the Japanese bombed Pearl Harbor, and Greenberg made a quick decision.

"We are in trouble," he said, "and there is only one thing for me to do—return to the service." Greenberg, the American League's Most Valuable Player in 1935 and 1940, relinquished his $55,000 a year baseball contract for the $21 per month salary he received as a soldier.[2]

Many of the great names of the game postponed their baseball careers to fight for Uncle Sam during the war. Warren Spahn traded his Boston Braves uniform for one in the Army Combat Engineers. Spahn saw action in Europe and took part in the Battle of the Bulge. Another Boston product, Ted Williams, left the Red Sox to become a Navy pilot. Williams, like Kiner, had been enrolled in the V-5 Program and was called up in 1943. Dom DiMaggio, the Red Sox teammate of Williams, also joined the Navy. Bob Feller was in Chicago for a meeting with the general manager of the Cleveland Indians to sign a new contract for the 1942 season when news came of the attack on Pearl Harbor. Upon meeting the GM later that night, Feller informed his former boss, "I already called, and I am going to join the Navy." Hundreds of other Major League players went into the service, either by enlistment or through the draft, as baseball made its impression on the military. The game itself played a large role in the military success of the nation.

Ingrained as it was into the consciousness of the American people, baseball stats and terminology were used to fight the Germans in Europe. Soldiers would frequently ask baseball questions of those they were unsure of on the battlefield to help verify if they were Americans or not. During the Battle of the Bulge, English-speaking German soldiers infiltrated behind American lines to disrupt communications and sabotage American resistance to the Nazi offensive. Questions like "What's a Texas Leaguer?" and "Who does Bob Feller play for?" became common forms of distinguishing friend from foe on that frozen battleground, and served to bind the GIs together as only baseball could.

Kiner would not have to depend on baseball information to determine who his enemy was. As a Navy pilot, he served in the Pacific Theater, and above that, his service was performed in the air, where there were no infiltrators. Kiner's first posting was to the California Polytechnic State University at San Luis Obispo, where he began his pre-flight training for the Naval aviation program. From there, he was sent to Saint Mary's College, near San Francisco, to continue his training. While at

Saint Mary's, his instruction moved from the classroom to the cockpit. He obtained his pilot's license there after logging only eight hours of actual air-training time. While stationed there, he came in contact with one of the legends of the game. Charlie Gehringer, the Detroit Tigers star and future Hall of Famer, was one of his instructors. Gehringer also served as Kiner's soccer coach. Soccer was one of the many exercises the air cadets were subjected to.[3] Brooklyn Dodgers great Cookie Lavagetto was also there and had been placed in charge of passing out equipment to the cadets. From Saint Mary's, Kiner was sent to Livermore Naval Air Station in Livermore, California, also near San Francisco. The station had been built in 1942 in an effort to relieve the overcrowding at the Oakland Naval Air Station, and its primary function was to train pilots. Here, Kiner said, he learned to fly "bigger and faster planes" over the next few months. From Livermore, he was sent to the Naval Air Station at Corpus Christi, Texas, also known as Truax Field.[4] This was also a relatively new naval instillation, having been opened for pilots' training in May of 1941.

Corpus Christi Naval Air Station was a huge base. In fact, it was the largest naval aviation training facility in the world. Covering some 20,000 acres, it had 997 hangers, along with all the other barracks, halls and shops that make up a military base. There were also some 800 flight instructors who served to train the 300 or so student pilots who arrived there each month. Through the end of World War II, more than 35,000 aviators earned their Navy wings there. Potential pilots were trained to fly a number of aircraft at Corpus Christi. There were the T-6 Texan, the BT-13 Valiant, and the Naval Aircraft Factory N3N, all naval training craft. The Beechcraft Model 18, a light transport, light bomber, and air crew training craft was another plane potential pilots could be checked out in here. Given its proximity to the Gulf of Mexico, Corpus Christi also provided training for pilots who would fly sea planes during the war. The Vought OS2U Kingfisher was a single-prop observation floatplane, designed to be catapulted from cruisers and battleships. Lastly, the facility trained pilots to fly the Consolidated PBY Catalina, a twin-engine flying boat designed to serve in the capacities of patrol bomber, anti-submarine service, air-sea rescue, and convoy escort. The PBY Catalina was one of the most widely used seaplanes of World War II. It was the PBY that Kiner was assigned to learn to fly.

The PBY Catalina had a crew of ten: a pilot, co-pilot, flight engineer, radio operator, radar operator, navigator, bow turret gunner, ventral gunner, and two waist gunners. Its armament was three .30-caliber machine guns and two .50-caliber machine guns, and it could carry 2,000 pounds of bombs. The plane's maximum speed was 196 mph, and it had a range of 2,520 miles. While at Corpus Christi, Kiner attained the competency required to pilot the PBY, and on December 6, 1943, he received his Navy wings and was commissioned as an ensign.[5]

Kiner was so engaged by his classroom and applied training that there was little time for other activities. He almost never got to play baseball. In fact, Kiner remembered, "in the two-and-a-half years I served, I played only 12 games." That didn't mean others were not playing frequently. While at Corpus Christi, Kiner watched a baseball game between naval personnel. Ted Williams was on one of the teams. As a star player with the Boston Red Sox, everyone in the stands knew who he was, and the fans prepared to enjoy an offensive display by Williams at the plate. The game lasted 17 innings, but incredibly, Ted went 0-for-7 that day, possibly the only 0-for-7 stretch he ever had.[6]

From Corpus Christi, Kiner was sent to the Alameda Naval Air Station on San Francisco Bay and assigned to VPB-99, an operational training squadron that had just been formed in January 1944. This squadron provided relief crews to the Kaneohe Naval Air Station in Hawaii. Here, he received the final stages of his training before being sent himself to Kaneohe NAS for overseas duty. When he arrived in Hawaii, Kiner was assigned to the crew of a Martin PBM Mariner, a patrol bomber flying boat very similar to the PBY Catalina. The PBM Mariner only had a crew of seven, but it boasted a heavier armament of eight .50-caliber machine guns and could carry an increased bomb load of 4,000 pounds.

Initially, Kiner was not assigned as a pilot. "I was a navigator in the beginning," he later recounted. "The hardest part was celestial navigation. You got up in the hatch with a sextant and you identify the stars.... We had no landmarks—there was only the water. You'd check the waves, which gave you the wind actions.... You draw a fix, and if you were within ten miles of where you were supposed to be, you were doing a good job. Radar was just starting to come in. We didn't have it on our plane." The PBM Martin was constantly on or over the water. "All take offs and landing were on the sea. As you started down the runway of water you got on the hull and that got your tail off the water. We got on the step of the water and then we got going fast enough to take off."[7]

It wasn't long before Kiner was assigned to pilot a PBM Martin of his own. He and his crew were employed mostly in performing anti-submarine duty in the South Pacific. For the remainder of the war, he patrolled the South Pacific "looking for enemy subs and ships in an effort to keep our country secure."[8] While never actually in an active combat zone, the work done by Kiner and his crew was both laborious and difficult, not to mention tedious. Flights would go out up to 1,500 miles over the search areas, as the crew scanned the sea for signs of enemy activity. At an average cruising speed of just over 125 mph, this could equate to a round trip of nearly 24 hours. The stamina and endurance of the crew would be sorely tested on long-range missions, where continual concentration and vigilance were necessary. It took great physical and mental conditioning to perform these missions. The Navy saw that its pilots and air crews had plenty of both. Before entering the service, Kiner had been a slight 165 pounds. In fact, he was on the skinny side and somewhat fleet of foot. The inside-the-park home run he hit in his final game with the Toronto Maple Leafs before reporting for duty with the Navy bears testament to that.[9]

No one in baseball would take him for a speedster once he had been discharged from the service. Kiner remembered it had been "a tough life. You had to abide by the schedule, get up in the middle of the night and stand guard duty. It was work. It was an education. It was a different way of living."[10] Despite his many months away from the game, the Navy put Kiner in the best physical condition of his life. Traditional exercise was combined with swimming in an all-round training routine. One of the standard water workouts was swimming for 45-minute periods in the pool. Since Kiner and his crew flew constantly over the ocean, this training was vital should their plane ever have to ditch in the water. It was in the Navy that Kiner made the transition from a boy to a man. He went from the thin, baseball-playing boy to a muscular, well-toned man. His new physique would serve him well as a power hitter, and by the time he got out, there would be 30 more pounds of muscle added to his frame. There would also be a new-found element of mental and emotional maturity. Boys must grow up fast when they are in the military, especially during times of war. Discipline and being part of a team are constantly stressed in the training of a serviceman, and these qualities can readily be transferred to sports. Indeed, while Kiner managed precious little playing time during his service in the Navy, he was staying in shape and developing characteristics that would pay dividends on the diamond. He later reflected that "During that time as a flyer, I matured and learned what life was all about."[11]

Kiner was transferred to San Francisco shortly before the end of the war, but following the capitulation of the Japanese Empire in August of 1945, he was ordered back to Hawaii. With the war ended, there was no longer any need for patrol missions, so Kiner's flying days were, for the most part, over. The military personnel in Hawaii had much more free time on their hands and were able to take full advantage of the euphoria sweeping the land as a result of the conclusion of the long and bloody conflict. Kiner and his buddies prepared to make the most of their posting in the island paradise. "We figured we'd be in Hawaii for a long time—a year or more—when I got orders to go to Singapore. We were all set to go, then they changed my orders and I came back to San Francisco."[12]

The end of hostilities brought with it an immense outcry from the American people to demobilize the armed forces and return the soldiers, sailors and Marines once more to civilian life. At the close of the war there were some 12 million men and women in the armed forces of the United States, but that number would be reduced in slightly more than a year and a half to about 1.5 million. Service points needed for discharge were reduced several times, and by December 19, 1945, only 50 were required to be once more eligible for civilian status. Because of this reduced number, more than one million men were discharged from the military in December 1945, a Christmas present for the servicemen, their families, and loved ones.[13]

Kiner fell into this category. On December 5, 1945, he received his honorable discharge from the United States Navy. His duty to his country had been fulfilled, and he was once more free to pursue his career as a professional ballplayer. He was mystified by the fact that a large number of the Minor League players he had served with opted to stay in the service. "Amazingly, most of the guys I played with re-enlisted to get air pay (about $75 a month). I wanted to play baseball. I wanted to get out right then."[14] For many of his friends in the Navy, the monthly pay, along with the $75 air pay bonus, amounted to more than they were making as ballplayers. That was not the case for Kiner. While he had not given up the $55,000 salary Hank Greenberg had forfeited when he was taken into the Army, Kiner knew that he had the potential to make far more on the baseball diamond than he could earn staying in the Navy as a pilot. There was also the $5,000 bonus he had been promised if he ever made the Pirates roster to be considered. A lump sum of that amount must surely have looked like a fortune to a young man who had recently turned 23. The sky was the limit for this young prospect, and he was in a hurry to get back to the game he loved and try out his new muscles against opposing pitchers. He felt that he would probably be assigned to the Toronto Maple Leafs again, when he did return to the Pirates organization. After all, he had not exactly set the world on fire in his limited time there in 1943 before reporting for active duty with the Navy. By the spring of 1946, it would be two and a half years since he had played any organized ball, and the parent team's management would naturally feel that he had become rusty. To Kiner, it seemed only logical that he would have to go back to the minors, and the only question was whether he would be starting the 1946 campaign back at Toronto or back in the Eastern League to work on his mechanics and baseball timing. Regardless of where he ended up, he must surely have been thrilled over the prospect of swinging a bat and running the bases again.

CHAPTER 4

Breaking into the Bigs

The Pittsburgh Pirates had forged a reputation for competitive excellence through the majority of the 20th Century. Barney Dreyfuss owned and directed the team through the first three decades of the 1900s. A former owner of the Louisville Colonels, Dreyfuss had merged the best players of that club into the Pirates squad when he came to Pittsburgh in 1900, including the legendary Honus Wagner. The resulting team enjoyed enormous success. In 26 of Dreyfuss' 31 seasons guiding the Pirates, the club finished in the upper half of the National League. The team won six National League pennants and two World Series. Dreyfuss was credited as once stating, "I don't always win the pennant but I usually can make it close for the team that does. Why shouldn't a man finish in the first-division? It's a disgrace to finish in the second-division." When the Pirates owner was reminded that there were eight teams in the league, and four of them had to finish in the second division each year, he responded, "Yes, but not for me! Not for me! I'm a first-division man! Pittsburgh is a first-division town; it wouldn't stand for second-division baseball."[1]

Barney Dreyfuss was responsible for establishing a tradition in baseball that is now taken for granted by fans attending games. In the early days of baseball, it was customary that balls hit into the stands be returned. This was purely a matter of economics, as baseballs cost money and team owners didn't want to underwrite the expense for all the foul balls hit into the seats. Fans understood this and routinely threw back balls that ended up out of play. However, among other notable incidents, in a game during the 1921 season, three Pittsburgh fans refused to throw back a foul ball that one of them had snagged, and they were arrested. A police officer even wrestled one of the fans to the ground. The fan threatened to sue both the officer and the City of Pittsburgh over the incident, but Dreyfuss stepped in to make an out-of-court settlement. He then issued a statement that "Fans who attend games at the National League baseball park here may keep balls knocked into the stands without fear of being molested by policemen." Other teams quickly established the same policy in their parks, and the tradition of game souvenirs was born. True, it would cost the owners more money, but Dreyfuss reasoned that it would boost fan enthusiasm to be able to keep the game-used balls as mementoes of their trip to the ballpark.[2]

But Dreyfuss was not always so quick to concede to changes, especially when they concerned matters that he felt to be issues of morality. Once, when the team was in need of good players to bolster their lineup, he sent scouts across the country to scour the minors for promising prospects. One scout reported back that he had found an excellent outfielding prospect in Texas. The boy could do it all, and the scout thought that he was a sure thing to not only make it in the majors, but to become a star. Dreyfuss wired to inquire if the boy was the sort whose personal habits matched what he was looking for in ballplayers. "Does he drink, gamble and smoke?" The scout called his boss, gushing about the boy's talent and advising that the team sign him right away. Dreyfuss was adamant. He wanted to know the answers to his questions before he would even consider giving the lad a contract. The scout informed Dreyfuss that the boy did not drink and never gambled, but he did, on occasion, smoke a cigarette. Dreyfuss exploded, yelling that he wouldn't have a player on his team that smoked, before slamming down the receiver. The scout had been right. The boy would surely make a name for himself as a star in the majors, but Dreyfuss passed on signing Tris Speaker to a Pirates contract because he did not hold with smoking. Speaker became one of the greats of the game with a Hall of Fame career, but not as a Pittsburgh Pirate.[3]

When Dreyfuss died in 1932, management of the Pirates passed to his son-in-law, Bill Benswanger. Pittsburgh continued to be competitive under Benswanger, finishing in the first division in 11 out of 15 seasons. Though the Pirates won no more pennants under Benswanger, the club finished 2nd in 1938. Pittsburgh was in the thick of the hunt for most of the season, vying with the Giants and Cubs for the title. Though the

Pirates won 13 of 16 games in the stretch run, losses in Cincinnati in the final two games of the season eliminated them. Benswanger had been so certain of his team's final success that he had built a World Series press stand at Forbes Field and ordered press buttons for the reporters.[4] The gaffe proved to be a source of ridicule for Benswanger once the Pirates were eliminated, and he would have to buy tickets to watch the World Series.

Through the war years, while so many Major League players were away, the Pirates continued to field winning teams. In fact, they finished in the first division in three of the four years from 1942–1945, finishing in second place in 1944 with a record of 90–63. With the return of their regulars from the military, the Pirates seemed poised to embark on another period of winning baseball. Nothing could have been further from the truth.

The Pirates held their spring training in 1946 at San Bernardino, California, close to Kiner's home in Alhambra. He was invited to camp, though he was given little chance of making the big club. His thoughts of being sent to Toronto or Albany were unfounded, however. He was instead slated to become part of the Hollywood Stars, the Pirates' Pacific Coast League affiliate, once spring training was over. One of the obstacles to his making the Pirates' opening day roster was the Veterans' Act. For that season only, teams were allowed to increase their rosters to 30 players. The problem was that all players who had gone into the military were supposed to be given back their jobs with the teams, according to law. That meant that approximately 300 Major League roster spots were already taken out of the 480 available, even with the expanded numbers. For the remaining spots, minor league players, as well as those Major League players who had been given 4-F exemptions as being unfit for the military, would be in competition. Kiner remembered that "The vets were the best players, but many had lost their skills due to inactivity or had committed the unpardonable sin for athletes of reaching their mid-thirties. Consequently, despite the law, more than 140 players with big-league contracts when the war began were released or demoted to the minors by midseason—sparking a number of court cases."[5]

Kiner reported to camp determined to do his best and let the chips fall where they may. He was not the same ballplayer who had left for the

Navy, and the more muscular body his time in the service had molded was quickly noticed by those around him. "I really filled out in that time. I added about 30 pounds. Unfortunately, what I gained in strength, I lost in speed." Bob Lemon, the future Hall of Fame pitcher for the Cleveland Indians, had played against Kiner in the minor leagues. When Lemon saw him during spring training, he was amazed at his development. "I remember you," Lemon said. "I used to have to guard against the bunt when you batted. Now you can't run a lick." Kiner didn't think he had become that slow, but he was convinced that he would "go only as far as my bat would carry me."[6]

Among the Pirates players reporting to spring training that season were: 1st baseman Elbie Fletcher; shortstops Frank Zak, Billy Cox, Alf Anderson and Vic Barnhart; outfielders Al Gionfriddo, Maurice Van Robays, and Ben Guintini; catchers Hank Camelli, Bill Baker, Vinnie Smith, and Roy Jarvis; and pitchers Fritz Ostermuller, Ken Heintzelman, Ed Bahr, Jack Hallett, Ken Gables, Johnny Lanning, Ed Albosta, Lee Howard, Hank Gornicki, Junior Walsh, Al Tate, Lefty Wilkie, Jim Hopper and Bill Clemensen, all returning veterans with guaranteed jobs under the Veterans' Act.[7] That meant that 26 of the 30 spots on the extended roster would already be spoken for when Opening Day rolled around. The Pirates found themselves especially heavy at the shortstop and catcher positions, with four of each, and they had 14 pitchers.

Of the returning veterans, however, there were only three outfielders and one first baseman, and luckily, Kiner could play both positions. Elbie Fletcher was a dependable first baseman with nine years of Major League experience on his resume. In 1943, he had batted a respectable .283 for the Pirates, appearing in all 154 games, and was selected as an All-Star. Fletcher was then called into service with the U.S. Navy and missed the 1944 and 1945 seasons.[8] The first base spot would certainly be his at the start of the 1946 campaign, and the best Kiner could hope for in that regard was to be kept as a back-up. The outfield was another matter. Gionfriddo had started 122 games in 1945 before being called up, but that was the extent of his service with the Pirates. As for Guintini and Van Robays, they had seen limited or no action with Pittsburgh. The three of them may have had guaranteed roster spots, but they were definitely not guaranteed starting positions. Kiner would have ample opportunity to compete for one of the outfield spots that spring, and he made the most of chance.

Kiner's new, more muscular frame was built for power. He had always been capable of hitting the long ball, even as a boy, when his homers had broken out the school windows and gotten him in trouble. Now, he had the bulk and strength to complement his natural ability. Spring training would prove to be a coming out party for the Pirates' new power hitter, much to the surprise of team management. After all, Kiner had hit some home runs in the minor leagues, and though he had led the Eastern League at Albany, he had not exactly set the world on fire. In Toronto, against a better class of pitching, he had managed to swat only two round-trippers and had batted a mere .236. In all fairness, he had played only 43 games with Toronto before being called into the Navy, but his last impression made on the Pittsburgh brass before going to war had been one of a player struggling to compete at the higher level. If his numbers had dipped so dramatically when he was promoted to AAA ball, the Pirates organization would be hard to convince that he was indeed ready for the next step to the big leagues.

The rust accumulated through two and one-half years away from the game was quickly worked off as Kiner easily made the transition from Navy pilot back to being a ballplayer. In a time when physical conditioning was not actively promoted by the teams, Kiner established a pre-season ritual of his own, which he began immediately after being discharged from the Navy. Players were told not to swim or lift weights, as it was thought that would bulk up their chests and shoulders to the point where it would affect their swings. Kiner lifted weights regularly despite these warnings and also did exercises to increase the strength of his wrists and hands. He used a punching bag to improve his quickness, and, for a time, took fencing lessons from the man who often dueled with Errol Flynn in the movies. Kiner would later recall, "I was pretty fast with a sword." The hope was that it would serve to make him fast with a bat as well.[9] At 6'2" tall, and weighing a rock-solid 195 pounds, Kiner looked every bit the slugging star and presented an imposing site for most pitchers when he stepped into the batter's box. Another training ritual he had was watching film. Back in 1941 or 1942, he had gotten his hands on some footage of Babe Ruth swinging the bat, which he watched over and over again to see how he could emulate the Babe's mighty power stroke. Later, he would film his own swing in order to evaluate it for weaknesses. Kiner spent many long hours in this manner, watching film to improve his game and increase his power.

Maybe it was the fact that the Pirates' training facility in San Bernardino, California, was so close to where he came from that made him feel so at home in his debut, or possibly it was the new-found confidence he had gained in the Navy. One thing is certain, Perris Hill Park, the Pirates' home field, was where he started to open the eyes of team management and make a name for himself. Perris Hill Park had served as the spring training facility of the Pirates in 1935, and again from 1937 to 1942. It had been the home of the San Bernardino Stars of the California League in 1941, and by 1946 was the host of the San Bernardino Pioneers of the Sunset League. The park was originally built in 1934 and was named for Frederick T. Perris, a railroad developer who had been instrumental in the shaping of San Bernardino. A true baseball diamond, with no rounding off to the center field fence, the dimensions were 354 feet down the left and right field lines and 451 feet to dead center. Though it was a minor league park, Perris Hill boasted a most modern feature, lights for night games, which had been installed under the Works Progress Administration of Franklin D. Roosevelt's New Deal. The 3,500-seat stadium was a long way from the cavernous confines of Forbes Field in Pittsburgh, but Kiner was determined that when the team broke camp and headed east to begin the regular season, he would be on the roster and not left behind to play with the Hollywood Stars.

San Bernardino itself retained very much of a small town flavor, and the Pirates players were very accessible to the residents. Local boys would often hang out in front of the hotel where the Pirates stayed, in hopes of seeing their heroes and getting autographs. Kiner was not among the hotel crowd, however. With Alhambra in such close proximity to San Bernardino, he stayed at his home with his mother and commuted back and forth to the ballpark.

Florida had become the popular destination for most Major League teams as the place to practice and play in the pre-season, but from 1924 on, Pittsburgh made California its pre-season home. The Pirates were not the only Major League team to make southern California home for spring training that year. The St. Louis Browns held their training in Anaheim and played in La Palma Park. The Chicago White Sox were in Pasadena and played in Brookside Park. The other Chicago team, the Cubs, made Avalon their home.

Kiner got his chances in the early part of spring training and used them to catch the eye of manager Frankie Frisch. A hard-nosed veteran of 27 years in the game, with 18 of them spent as a player for the powerhouse New York Giants and St. Louis Cardinals, Frisch won four World Series crowns and played beside some of the top ballplayers in the game. He won the National League MVP Award in 1931 and was a three-time All-Star. As he began the 1946 campaign as the skipper of the Pirates, he could not know that the following year would find him elected to the Baseball Hall of Fame, placing him among the immortals of the game. For now, he was simply one of the game's greats from a bygone era. Frisch was fiery and combative, both as a player and manager. His squabbles with umpires were legendary and usually ended up getting him fined by the commissioner's office, as well as being ejected from the game. On one occasion, during a rainstorm, he came out of the dugout wearing rubber boots and sporting an umbrella to show his contempt for the fact that the umpires had not yet called the game due to inclement weather. He was immediately thrown out of the game, and a telegram soon followed from the commissioner informing him of the amount of his fine.[10]

Frisch was also tough on his players, demanding their best on the field at all times. Known for being especially hard on rookies, Frisch nevertheless paid special attention to Kiner. The 23-year-old had a great swing, and when he made good contact, the ball rocketed out of the ballpark. So Frisch continued to give him chances, and Kiner continued to make them count. In game after game he made solid contact in his at-bats, and his home runs began to add up and bring him notice. Pittsburgh sportswriter Charles J. Doyle followed Kiner's progress and gave Pirates' faithful a lot to hope for when he wrote that "Kiner can run like a deer, he can throw like a DiMaggio and when his bat clicks nothing but the fences will stop his line drives." Another article in a hometown Pittsburgh paper stated that Kiner "hits the ball longer and more consistently than either Vince DiMaggio or Johnny Rizzo." Vince was the

4: Breaking into the Bigs

older brother of Joe and Dom DiMaggio. Though not as accomplished a hitter as either of his younger brothers, he had some pop in his bat and hit 125 home runs during his career. Pittsburgh fans remembered him as a Pirate from 1940–1944. John Rizzo had also worn a Pirates uniform as an outfielder from 1938–1940. The comparison between him and Kiner would become almost ludicrous once Kiner started launching round-trippers on a regular basis at Forbes Field. Rizzo only hit 61 homers in his five years in the bigs. Kiner would come close to that total in a single year.

Doyle's appraisal of Kiner proved to be somewhat hyped, as he was not fleet of foot, nor did he possess an above-average arm. The part about his long line drives was true enough, however, and that alone might have biased the reporter's opinions about his other attributes. Kiner himself remembered, "I had a tremendous spring training. I hit, I believe the number was 13 home runs in spring training. I earned the job and opened up in center field for the Pirates in 1946."[11]

Though Kiner's story was of interest to the fans back home in Pittsburgh, another player was causing a stir in 1946, though he was still a year away from the majors. Jackie Robinson, a fellow Californian, was a year away from breaking the color barrier in Major League Baseball as a member of the Brooklyn Dodgers. Branch Rickey, the general manager of the Dodgers, was about to fulfill a promise he had made to himself a long time ago, when he coached the Ohio Wesleyan College team in 1904. It seems that the team had arrived in South Bend, Indiana, to play a game against Notre Dame. When the team attempted to register at their hotel, Rickey was informed that one of the players would not be allowed to do so. That player was Charley Thomas, the team's catcher, who was a black man. Rickey argued with the desk clerk and threatened to take the team's business to another hotel, though he knew no other hotel in town would be different. Finally, Rickey proposed that Thomas not be signed into the log, and that a cot be placed in Rickey's room for the catcher. The desk clerk agreed, and the incident was ended, on the surface. When Rickey went into his room, he found Thomas sitting on the edge of a chair, pulling at the skin on his hands as if he were trying to peel it off. The catcher was crying, and when he looked up he said, "It's my skin, Mr. Rickey, it's my skin. If I could pull it off, I'd be just like everybody else." Rickey tried to assure Thomas that the day would come when the color of a man's skin would not determine his right to play baseball, but he could not comfort his teammate, and he reported that Thomas sobbed throughout that night.[12]

By 1945, Rickey was ready to make good on the promise he had made himself to rectify the situation and make sure color was no longer a barrier for playing Major League baseball. He had recently been given the job as the Dodgers' general manager after filling the same spot with the St. Louis Cardinals. Rickey was a smart and innovative executive and had already made his mark on the game when he developed a farm system for the Cardinals, ensuring a steady stream of young talent to the parent club. All teams in Major League baseball eventually adopted this system, and Rickey hoped that that same trailblazing success would take place with his efforts to integrate the league.[13] Rickey's first step, after convincing the ownership of the Dodgers to support his plan, was to meet with longtime Dodgers announcer Red Barber, a beloved figure in Brooklyn and hailing from the South. Rickey wanted to get Barber's opinion of the proposed move. Barber was struck by the sincerity Rickey displayed when talking about integration, and he decided to stay with the team and lend the effort his support.[14]

Rickey sent out scouts to evaluate all of the top black talent. Their trips were not just to see players in the Negro Leagues, but also included junkets to places like Mexico, Cuba, and Venezuela, where some American black players had gone to earn a living playing the game. By the end of the 1945 season, one name kept appearing on the scouting reports handed in to Mr. Rickey: Jackie Robinson. Among those canvassed by Rickey was Wendell Smith, a writer for the *Pittsburgh Courier*, a black weekly publication that regularly reported on the Negro Leagues.[15] Rickey met with Robinson in August and offered him a contract for $600 a month to play for the Dodgers. The plan was for Robinson to start out with the Montreal Royals, the Dodgers' AAA farm team. Rickey asked Robinson to keep the arrangement a secret for the time being, but promised to make it formal by November 1, 1945. On October 23, a public announcement was made that Robinson was being signed by the Dodgers and assigned to the Royals. On that same day, representatives from the Dodgers and Royals met with Robinson to sign a contract.[16]

4: Breaking into the Bigs

The 1946 spring training in the Grapefruit League of Florida had more to offer than just the return of the veteran players from military service. It also featured Robinson, along with Johnny Wright, another black player signed by Rickey and assigned to the Royals, appearing on an otherwise all-white team. Much of the early coverage dealt with efforts to prevent Robinson and Wright from playing. Many whites in what was still very much a segregated country were not yet ready to tear down the barriers that prevented blacks from playing baseball. Some of the Royals' early games that spring had to be cancelled because the facilities at Jacksonville and DeLand became suddenly and mysteriously unable to host the visiting Montreal squad. On March 17, Robinson was finally able to make his debut at City Island Ballpark in Daytona Beach, the Royals' home facility. The game was against the parent team, the Dodgers. Robinson became the first black player to play against a Major League team since the color line had been implemented in the 1880s.[17]

Robinson played that season for Montreal, so after spring training the focus, for the time being, would shift away from him. A year later, Robinson would be back in the spotlight again when he was promoted to the Dodgers. For the remainder of the 1946 season, however, he played in the minors. Other stories would grab the headlines during the 1946 campaign, and none would be bigger, in Pittsburgh at least, than the handsome young slugger who was coming east with the team from California. Ralph Kiner had made it to the bigs, and it would be a rookie season to remember. Kiner would make a little history of his own that year and would set the stage for even greater accomplishments to come.

The Sporting News named Del Ennis of the Phillies as its pick for "Rookie of the Year" honors in 1946 and reported that Ennis had led all National League rookies in home runs and runs batted in. That was not the case. Ennis hit 17 home runs compared to Kiner's 23, and he had 73 runs batted in compared to Kiner's 81. The fact is that Kiner should have been given greater consideration for the award, as he bested Ennis in several categories and in many ways had a better season.

Chapter 5

Making a Splash in Pittsburgh

The Pirates opened the 1946 campaign on the road in St. Louis on April 16, in an afternoon contest. Kiner started in center field, with Johnny Barrett in right and Jim Russell in left. Elbie Fletcher was on first, Jimmy Brown on second, with Billy Cox at short and Bob Elliott on third. Fritz Ostermueller got the start in the season opener, with Vinnie Smith doing the catching as his battery mate. The Cards jumped on Ostermueller early, scoring three runs in the bottom of the first inning and chasing him after only three frames of work. Ken Heintzelman replaced Ostermueller in the bottom of the fourth and pitched five scoreless innings before surrendering a run in the bottom of the ninth. In the meantime, the Pirates did what they could to scratch their way back into the game. They broke onto the scoreboard with a single tally in the top of the third and tied things up with two runs in their half of the fourth. In the top of the fifth, they put another deuce on the board to take the lead. An insurance run in the top of the ninth capped the scoring for the Pirates and allowed them to walk away with a 6–4 victory. The season had started out on a high note for the team, and Kiner had done all right for himself as well. He went 1-for-4 with a walk. His hit, the first of his Major League career, was a single. He had also made two putouts in the field.

The Pirates were back at Sportsman's Park the following day for the second of a three-game set. Their starting lineup was the same as the previous day, and Ken Gables towed the rubber for his first start of the season. Max Lanier took the ball for the Cardinals in what proved to be a dominant performance. Gables kept it close through the first five innings, allowing single runs in the second and third innings. The Cardinals got to him for two more scores in the bottom of the sixth, including a home run by Enos Slaughter, making the score 4–0. Johnny Lanning

5: Making a Splash in Pittsburgh

replaced Gables in the seventh. He gave up one run in that inning and another in the bottom of the eighth, to give the Cardinals a commanding 6–0 lead. The Pirates were never able to mount any real threat against Lanier, who scattered seven hits, but no runs, in a complete game performance. Elbie Fletcher had two hits and was starting the season hitting a blistering .600, but he didn't have much offensive help. Kiner went 0-for-4, with two strikeouts, as his average in the young season dipped to .125. The Cardinals walked away with the 6–0 victory, and though Pittsburgh was 1–1 in the campaign, it was a sign of the misery to come.

The Pirates sent Ed Albosta to the mound in the final game of the series, opposed by Howie Pollet. The Bucs kept thing close through the first seven innings and trailed only 2–0. Johnny Barrett started the eighth off with a hit, setting the table for the next batter in the Pirates' lineup: Ralph Kiner. He stepped into the box and proceeded to smack the first home run of his Major League career, getting his first RBIs and run scored, tying the score. He would come to be known as a straight pull hitter. What was surprising about this first shot was "that the ball landed on the right-field roof, in Sportsman's Park, and, in my entire life, I don't think I hit more than seven or eight homers to the opposite field."[1] Opposite field or not, his swing was starting to catch up to Major League pitching, and though his batting average was still under .200, he was about to start exhibiting the power that had earned him his spot in the starting lineup. Nick Strincevich replaced Albosta on the hill in the bottom of the frame and gave up three runs before Al Gerheauser relieved him and put out the fire. Gerheauser surrendered another run before getting the two final outs, and the score was 6–2. Pollet got the final three outs to secure the victory, and Pittsburgh fell to 1–2 on the young season.

April 19 was an off-day. After the disappointing series in St Louis, the Pirates returned to Pittsburgh for their home opener against the Cincinnati Reds. The industrial city of Pittsburgh was a far cry from California, Hawaii, Toronto, or Albany. Kiner had never seen anything to prepare him for a city that thrived on coal and steel, and all the industrial pollution that came along with one of the great manufacturing centers of the country. "I couldn't believe it. I had come from California where they didn't have smog at that time. Mostly orange trees and orange groves, and things like that, and beautiful weather and everything." Kiner said that the team arrived in Pittsburgh "around 10:00 in the morning … and it was like midnight. I got off the train and couldn't believe it. There was so much soot in the air, from the burning of soft coal, and it was like midnight. And it was also very dirty."

As Kiner looked about, he developed a bad first impression of the city. "I went to the hotel and said I didn't like this." After checking into the hotel and putting his baggage away, Kiner decided to check out where he would be working. "Now, I went to the ballpark for the first time, never having seen Forbes Field. And I walked in the ballpark and looked down the left field line. It was 365 feet away. The center field fence was 465 feet away. I looked at that and that smog and the weather conditions and I thought, 'This is the worst thing I have ever done in my life.' I said, 'I'm on the wrong team.'"[2]

When Kiner first arrived in Pittsburgh, he was shocked by the pollution and dirt in the country's steel-making capital. He was also perplexed and a little awe-struck by the dimensions of Forbes Field, where he would play all of his home games with the Pirates. Though he had always been a power hitter, the distance to the fences in Forbes Field seemed overwhelming to the rookie, and he wondered if he would be up to the challenge.

5: Making a Splash in Pittsburgh

Kiner's performance on the field in the series with the Reds matched his depressing opinion of Pittsburgh and Forbes Field. Though the Pirates beat Cincinnati, 2-1, in their home opener, Kiner went 0-for-2 before being lifted for Al Gionfriddo. His average was down to .154, and Frankie Frisch was having his doubts about the abilities of the young rookie. An 0-for-3 effort at the plate in the second game against the Reds dropped Kiner's average to .125, and an 0-for-4 performance in the third game plummeted him to .100. Frisch had seen enough. When the Pirates opened a three-game set with the Chicago Cubs on April 24, Kiner was on the bench, and Gionfriddo had taken his place in center field. Luckily for Kiner, Gionfriddo provided no more offensive punch in the lineup, going 0-for-3 himself. On April 25, Kiner was back in the lineup in the first game of the series against St Louis. He managed only one hit in four plate appearances that day, it was a two run homer in the bottom of the third inning off Harry Brecheen. He drove in another run with an out and was responsible for three of the runs scored in the Pirates' 5-3 win over the Cardinals. Pittsburgh had raised its record to 4-5 and had handed the Cardinals their only two losses of the season. Kiner was back in the lineup for the final game against the Cardinals, as well as against the Reds in a two-game series in Cincinnati. He went 4-for-11, doubling his average, but it was still an anemic .200.

On April 30, the Pirates opened a series at home against the Philadelphia Phillies, hoping to gain some victories against the worst team in the league. Pittsburgh took two of the three games, but Kiner continued to struggle at the plate, and by the time the Phillies left town, he was batting .159. Once more, Frankie Frisch decided to sit the young outfielder down, and when the Boston Braves came to town on May 3, Johnny Barrett was penciled into the lineup to play center field. Barrett went 1-for-3, with a walk in the Pirates' victory, providing some doubt as to when Kiner would get back onto the field. Frisch decided to play him in the first game of a doubleheader against the Brooklyn Dodgers on May 5, and Kiner came through, going 2-for-4 and driving in a run in Pittsburgh's 5-4 victory. He started the second game of the twin bill in left field and went 1-for-2 with a walk, bringing his average back up to .200. Kiner struggled again in the first game of a two-game set against the New York Giants and found himself once more on the bench for the second game. He was still riding the pine on May 12, when the Pirates visited Chicago for a one-game set. Frankie Frisch was having trouble finding a consistent third outfielder for the team. Jim Russell was hitting a respectable .271, and Bob Elliott was holding on to his spot with a .240 average. The rest of the outfielders couldn't seem to stay above .200, which was providential for Kiner, as it seemed no one wanted to step up and lay claim to the third outfield spot. Frisch would continue to shuffle the lineup, looking for an answer, and Kiner would continue to get his chances.

Kiner was back in the lineup on May 14, when the Pirates traveled to Boston to play the Braves. His 1-for-3 performance at the plate earned him another start against the Dodgers on May 17, when the Pirates traveled to Brooklyn after two off-days. On May 22, Kiner had a big day at the plate, going 3-for-4 and finally getting over the .200 mark to an average of .224. He repeated the feat the following day, with two of his three hits home runs off of Tommy Hughes and Dick Mauney. He also drove in five runs in a 10–2 Pirates victory. Raising his average to .250, he was, for the first time since spring training, establishing a claim to the center field spot. When the Bucs returned home to open a set against the Cubs, Kiner was once more penciled in to play center field. He responded by belting another home run, off Hank Borowy, driving in three runs and pacing Pittsburgh to a 6–3 win. With his average now up to .265, he had settled all doubts in Frisch's mind, and there would be no more shuffling of lineups trying to determine who would start in center. The job would be Kiner's for the rest of the 1940s. By the All-Star break, Kiner had established himself not only as a regular starter, but also as one of the stars of the team. Halfway through the season, he was batting .274 with 15 home runs and 45 runs batted in. It was a solid rebound, considering his rocky start in the first quarter of the season.

By the All-Star break, the Pirates found themselves firmly in control of last place in the National League with a record of 29–44, 18.5 games out of first place, and three games behind the seventh-place Phillies. Their longest winning streak of the season had been four games, and they had gone on six losing streaks of three games or more. From June 19–23, they lost six straight games, surpassing the five consecutive contests they had dropped in May. Frisch's squad was having trouble putting it all together and playing consistent ball. New as he was to Major League play, Kiner looked around and came to the conclusion that the Pirates' lack of success was not primarily due to a lack of talent. While he genuinely liked his teammates and got along with all of them, on and off the field, he quickly diagnosed the cause of the team's lackluster performance. He noted that most of the players on the team "smoked, drank, chewed tobacco, and, particularly if single, prowled the bars at night in search of dates." He had already come to the conclusion that "superior teams had the most dedicated and disciplined players," and observed that his teammates exhibited little dedication or discipline.

> The Pittsburgh Pirates were a terrible team, and in my first two years, most of my teammates were crazy, card-playing, heavy drinking carousers who led the fast life and had good times after games and way past curfews. They were an all fun-and-games bunch. There was a record player in our clubhouse, and I think it's indicative of who these guys were that their favorite 78 was about how cigarettes, whiskey, and wild women will drive you crazy. They played it over and over. I liked most of the guys, but they were real characters and totally undisciplined. I know that a lot of what went on was the result of the players having just been in the service, where they had lived each day as if it were their last on Earth. Coming back to civilian life, they no longer wanted to follow orders and conventions, and their mantra was "eat, drink, and be merry." You often hear about how in those days, players on each team policed each other to make sure no one broke the team's rules or the town's laws and wasn't ready to play the next day. The Pirates didn't do this. So while management and members of the media gave nothing more than sidelong glances, everyone was free to get into whatever trouble they wanted to. And they did. It might have been easier to take if we won, but one reason we lost so many games is because of what was going on. Fortunately, I had grown up during the Depression, attended junior college (and would matriculate for three whole days at USC in 1947), and had been a pilot and officer during the war, so I was mature for my age and nothing fazed me. I may not have fit in with the older, veteran players, but I knew that I belonged in the big leagues. Still, it wasn't a good situation for a young man who wanted to become a good baseball player and play on a winning team.[3]

Kiner's assessment of the team's situation and morale was a stern indictment of the management of the Pirates, particularly Frankie Frisch, who had primary responsibility for ensuring that the players were following the rules, keeping out of trouble, and ready to play. What Kiner described was an unruly, poorly disciplined group of players, many of whom probably saw the games as an unwanted interruption in their otherwise fun-filled lives. To be sure, much of their raucous behavior could be traced to the fact that they had so recently been discharged from the service. After months and years of living day-to-day, fearing that death could come at any moment, these men had a great deal of pent-up stress and anxiety to get out of their systems. Military rations and canteens filled only with water were suddenly replaced by the full bounty of the nation and the availability of alcohol seemed endless. Lonely nights spent on the front line or at bases where male faces were the only ones to be seen were suddenly replaced with a stream of smiling, attractive women who were enamored by all ballplayers, and these veterans made up for lost time with a vengeance. While Kiner correctly stated that growing up during the Depression had given him a sound foundation of values and morals, he overlooked the fact that ALL of the teammates he described were of the same generation, and ALL of them had lived through the same Depression. This oversight sheds light into Kiner's personality and character more than he knew. The Depression was not responsible for making him the man he was. Every Pirates player had lived through those same years, yet their lifestyle was so different than was Kiner's. It was his own inner strength and his own sense of values that made him the man and player he was. Living through the Depression merely reinforced the life lessons he had been taught by his mother. Those lessons had taken root deeply, and his experiences during the Depression, and in the Navy, had only served to forge them into a core that defined his personality and the way in which he approached life. For now, however, he seemed to be in the minority as a right-thinking player on a wrong-thinking team.

    The second half of the 1946 season got underway with the Pirates hosting the Phillies in a three-game set. Pittsburgh lost the first game 4–1, with their only run coming via the long ball. Kiner wasn't responsible for the blast, however, as it was hit by Frankie Gustine, who was getting a spot start at third. The Pirates won the final two games of the series, including an 8–1 blowout in the rubber game. Kiner's bat was largely silent in the three games with Philadelphia, and he went hitless in the 8–1 thumping of the Phillies. A 2-for-12 performance in three games with the Braves meant that Kiner was starting the second half of the season the same way he had begun the first. He got his swing back in the first game of a series against the Giants which began on July 17. He went 3-for-4 in the game, but more importantly, he hit his 16th home run and drove in four runs in an 8–5 victory for the Pirates. Few fans were on hand, with just over 3,000 fans in attendance. With the team playing so miserably, and with almost no hope of the Pirates raising themselves out of the National League basement, most of the baseball fans in Pittsburgh had already decided that they were better off to save their hard-earned money and stay home.

Kiner was out of his short slump, and for the remainder of the month of July, he kept his batting average around .270. None of them were long balls, though, and he entered August stuck on 16. In fact, Kiner went more than five weeks before going yard again. He hit his 17th of the season off of Ed Wright of the Braves in the first game of a doubleheader on August 25. He had set out several games in the last few weeks and had seen no playing time during a Pirates' modest five-game winning streak. He added to his total in the second game of the twin bill by hitting a homer off Braves starter Si Johnson.

With only three home runs since the All-Star break, Kiner had seemed to cool off dramatically with his power stroke. Nevertheless, he still found himself among the leaders in the National League and was still in the hunt for the home run title. It was a full week into September when his next blast came, against Cardinals pitcher Howie Pollet, boosting his total to 19. Over the next three weeks, Kiner launched four more long-balls to finish the season with 23. Most years, that would not nearly be enough to claim a home run crown, but 1946 was not a normal year. Many returning veterans were rusty that year, having lost a bit of their timing while in the service. Kiner had trailed Johnny Mize, the power-hitting first baseman of the New York Giants, for most of the season. It looked as if Kiner would end the year as a runner-up, but fate stepped in to deal him a winning hand. Mize suffered a broken arm that ended his season a month early, when he was sitting on 22 homers.[4] With 19 round-trippers, Kiner needed three to tie and four to take the lead. He got that fourth home run on September 25, four days before the end of the season, against the Chicago Cubs. Pitcher Russ Meyer gave up the bomb in an eighth inning that saw Pittsburgh score four runs and scratch out a 6–5 victory. That was Kiner's last home run of the year. He finished the season with a less than enviable .246 batting average but drove in 87 runs, due in large part to having runners on base when he struck many of his 23 homers. Most importantly, he had accomplished something Pittsburgh fans had seldom seen in that franchise's storied history: he had won a home run crown. The title was the first for a Pirates player since Tommy Leach back in 1902, a feat accomplished with a grand total of six home runs. Pirates fans had never had a real contender for the home run crown before Kiner came to town, but that long drought had come to an end.

A generation of Pittsburgh faithful were about to be treated to many years of home run dominance, as Kiner became the pace-setting power hitter with 1946 the first of seven consecutive years in which he led the National League in home runs. Indeed, Kiner would become the Pirates' only significant drawing card through the late 1940s and early 1950s. The team left a lot to be desired throughout that period. They finished the 1946 season with a record of 63–90, 34 games behind the pennant-winning Cardinals. The Bucs had done reasonably well against St. Louis, which captured the National League Pennant in a two-game playoff against the Dodgers, but that was about their only claim to fame as a team in 1946.

The most notable event of the 1946 season for the Pirates happened off the field, much to the chagrin of the fans. That year, the Pirates became the first Major League team to attempt establishing a union in a quarter century. Robert Murphy, a Boston lawyer and management consultant for the National Labor Relations Board, had set his sights on professional baseball. World War II had lifted the country out of the Depression, and with the war ended, American workers were more than ready to see their paychecks increase. The problem was that most employers were not ready to share their post-war profits. Strikes paralyzed the country as union workers voted in numerous industries to take to the picket line. In Pittsburgh, known to be a strong union town, the coal and steel workers struck that year in search of higher wages.

Murphy, who knew several players from both the Red Sox and Braves, approached his acquaintances to sound them out about their willingness to join a union. Following this meeting, Murphy decided to form the American Baseball Guild, appointing himself as chairman. He began signing up players into his guild for 50 cents' dues per week. He also established a guild platform of six negotiating points that he planned to lay before Happy Chandler, the baseball commissioner. These points included a minimum annual salary if $7,500, the right to arbitrated salary negotiations, half of the purchase price on all player sales, and a vaguely worded plank that loosely attacked baseball's reserve clause. Murphy's demands were not outrageous. He feared that to demand too much, right up front, would doom his endeavor to failure. For a test case, Murphy selected the Pirates, mostly because of Pittsburgh's reputation as a strong union town. He felt the players would receive a great deal of support should they decide to go on strike. A deadline was set for the middle of the season for Pirates team management to come to terms with the guild, or Murphy assured Bill Benswanger that the players would refuse to play. Everything came to a climax on June 7. Pittsburgh was set to play the Giants, but before the first pitch was thrown, the players decided to take care of a bit of housekeeping in the clubhouse. A strike vote was called, and all management personnel, as well as Murphy, were asked to leave the room. A strike would require a two-thirds vote from the players, most of whom did not think that such a majority could be secured. Kiner was just a rookie, but he later stated that "none of us ever thought we would get out of" the reserve clause. Pitcher Rip Sewell spoke out against a strike, and he was able to win over a few undecided votes to his way of thinking. When the vote was taken, it was far short of the necessary majority. Several of the Pirates cited their respect for Benswanger as the reason they voted against the strike, but, regardless of the causes, the Pirates would not become unionized at this time.

The issue decided, the team ran out of the clubhouse and onto the field, ready to play the game. Third baseman Lee Handley stated, "We played a dirty trick on Murphy. We let him down, and I was one of those who did." Many fans in the crowd booed the players for not voting to strike, and one anti-union voter, infielder Jimmy Brown, got roughed up in the parking lot after the game. When word of what he had done became generally known, Rip Sewell received a gold watch from Happy Chandler for urging the other players to take the field. Murphy's dream of an American Players Guild was ended, but the seeds he had planted would continue to grow until the Major League Baseball Players' Association was formed in 1953. Murphy had been a little ahead of his time, but the movement he set in motion eventually paid dividends for the players.[5]

The other major off-field event of 1946 was a change in ownership for the team. For nearly 50 years, the Pirates had been owned by the Dreyfuss family, with Bill Benswanger, the son-in-law of Barney Dreyfuss, taking over administrative operations in 1932, following Dreyfuss' death. Labor rumblings, combined with the embarrassment of the lowly position to which the once-proud Pirates had fallen, led the family to consider selling the team. In August, Benswanger came to an agreement with a group of investors that included singer and actor Bing Crosby, realtor John Galbreath, banker Frank McKinney, and manufacturer Tom Johnson. It was reported to the press that the sale price for the Dreyfuss stock did not exceed $2,500,000.[6]

The new owners named H. Roy Hamey, president of the American Association, to serve as general manager. Ray Kennedy, a former Yankees executive, was recruited as the Pirates' farm director. Bob Rice was brought in to serve as road secretary, and, in a move to make the change in ownership as fan friendly as possible, the popular radio baseball broadcaster, Albert "Rosey" Rowswell, was hired as director of public relations.

The new owners were looking to make a clean sweep of things, and all agreed that a new approach was necessary. Frankie Frisch had lost control over the players he was supposed to be managing. Sensing that his head was on the chopping block, Frisch saved the new owners the trouble of firing him by resigning with three days to go in the season. Virgil Davis stepped in as interim manager as the Pirates held on to seventh place above the cellar-dwelling Giants.[7]

Money did not seem to be an issue for the Pirates' new owners, and they appeared willing to put some cash up front to improve the team on the field. That fact alone gave Pittsburgh fans reason to be hopeful for the future. The 1946 season had been an abject failure, but the Pirates' faithful looked forward to the 1947 campaign as one of promise.

Majority partner on an ownership group that included Bing Crosby, John Galbreath had made a fortune dealing in real estate. Galbreath would take Kiner under his wing and show him how to invest his money wisely.

CHAPTER 6

A Mentor for Ralph

Following the last game of the 1946 season, Ralph Kiner went home to California. He spent the off-season staying in shape, doing exercises to improve the strength in his hands and wrists and keeping tabs on all of the team's moves. In fact, the biggest news in baseball that winter was the Pirates' signing of Hank Greenberg, Kiner's old hero and one of the American League's top players. Greenberg had won the home run championship in the junior circuit in 1946, belting 44 round-trippers. His .277 batting average was the second lowest of his career, but it would have put him among the leaders on the Pirates' squad, and he had driven in over 100 runs. A feared slugger in the American League with 306 home runs already to his credit, Greenberg's addition promised to give the Pirates a power boost in the lineup. The team would also be able to boast that the defending home run kings of both leagues were on their roster. For Kiner, it would mean an opportunity to play with his boyhood idol and a chance to learn from one of the best in the game.

The signing of Greenberg had not been a simple feat. Indeed, there had been a great deal of behind-the-scenes manipulating before Hammering Hank inked his name to a Pirates' contract. Team management had to do some slick negotiating to bring the star over to the National League. Despite his great numbers in 1946, Greenberg had seriously contemplated retiring that year. He had a terribly slow start to the 1946 campaign, and it was speculated that he had lost the ability to play at a high level. Fans in Detroit began to boo him regularly, which was especially hard for Greenberg to take. Left off the All-Star Game roster for the first time in years, Greenberg began to think himself that maybe it was time to hang up his glove and walk away from the game. He missed the first game after the All-Star break because he was wrestling with the idea of quitting. After some soul searching, he rejoined the team in Boston on July 12, stating, "I have decided to stay the fifteen rounds."[1]

Greenberg caught fire in the second half of the season, boosting his batting average to a respectable level and clouting long balls at a pace that earned him the home run title. Greenberg beat out Ted Williams for the title, a great feat since Williams had already emerged as possibly the game's top power hitter. Famed sports reporter Grantland Rice wrote, "Only a great competitor could have rallied in this fashion in the sunset of his career. In my opinion, Greenberg's September surge was one f baseball's greatest achievements when you consider all the angles involved—the four years away from action, Greenberg's age, the handicap he faced in moving after such a power hitter as Williams has been."[2]

Despite his heroic finish, Greenberg seemed poised to walk off into the sunset following the 1946 campaign. He would be 36 years of age by the time spring training began for the 1947 season, considered old for a ballplayer, and he could feel that his body was starting to betray him in the field and at the plate. He had always been careful with the money he made from baseball and had invested wisely, so he didn't need the money. Finishing the 1946 season in the manner he had gave him the opportunity to walk away from the game while he was still on top and not undergo the embarrassment of becoming a has-been. The boos he had received from the fans at Tiger Stadium the past year had convinced him that was not the way he wanted to go out. Proud and competitive, he couldn't face the prospect of abuse that would come should he continue to play as a shell of his former self. It was at this time that fate stepped in to take the decision out of his hands. Sportswriter Dan Daniel wrote an article for *The Sporting News* in January of 1947, claiming to have inside information that Greenberg was about to be dealt to the New York Yankees. Daniel wrote that Greenberg had decided he would not play for the Tigers in 1947, but would be "delighted" to play first base for the Yankees. The apparent clincher to Daniel's article was a picture of Greenberg holding a Yankees jersey with a big smile on his face. Under the photo was the caption: "Hank Greenberg admiring Yankee flannels."[3]

Daniel's story had been a hoax, mere speculation on his part. The photo had been taken in 1943, when Greenberg had played in a War Bond game and had found himself without a jersey. The Yankees jersey

6: A Mentor for Ralph

had been loaned to him, and a photographer had snapped the picture when he held it up in the clubhouse. When it ran in 1947, few knew its origin, and it seemed to confirm Daniel's "scoop" that Greenberg wanted to end his ties with the Tigers. Greenberg was furious over the false story, but he was not nearly as angry as Walter Briggs, the owner of the Tigers. Known for his fiery temper, Briggs went wild when he saw the picture of Greenberg with the Yankees jersey in *The Sporting News*. Not waiting to find out if it were true or not, Briggs decided to take immediate action against the star player he now viewed to be a traitor. On January 18, Greenberg heard the news on the radio that he had been dealt to the Pittsburgh Pirates. The only notification he received from the Tigers was a terse telegram that simply said: "This is to inform you that your contract has been assigned to the Pittsburgh club of the National League. Trust you will find your new connection a most profitable one."[4]

When Hank Greenberg (left) joined the Pirates, he soon became a mentor for Kiner. Kiner learned all that he could from the slugging star, and the instruction paid off with dividends. The two became lifelong friends whose careers intersected several times.

Greenberg was devastated by this turn of events and felt severely slighted by the team he had been with since 1930. The abrupt manner in which he was treated did not equate to a star who had helped lead the team to four World Series appearances and two world championships, one who, along the way, had collected two MVP awards, four RBI titles, and four home run titles. Greenberg said, "I left Detroit with a very harsh, bitter taste in my mouth."[5] The whole affair left him deflated and depressed. His previous thoughts of retirement were only reinforced by the fact that he was now a part of the Pirates organization. There were too many variables to changing teams at this time. Greenberg had spent most of his adult life studying and getting to know the pitchers in the American League. National League pitchers were all unknown to him. Forbes Field had a much greater distance down the left field line than did Detroit's stadium, and that could ruin his reputation as a power hitter. National League umpires called more low strikes than they did in the American League, and he was not a low-ball hitter.

When Greenberg thought about all the detrimental differences to be found in the National League and weighed them against his own diminishing abilities, it did not provide a promising picture. He felt that he might destroy all that he had worked so hard to accomplish if he played for the Pirates, so he decided to retire from the game before his legacy was damaged. In a statement to reporters, he summed up his feelings: "I love the game and feel there is yet much good baseball in me as a player and executive. But after seventeen years and 1,150 games in a Tiger uniform, I always expected to finish my career at Detroit. Since it was decided for me this could not be, I do not desire to start anew in a strange environment."[6]

The Pirates' new ownership wanted to hear nothing about the pending retirement of their newly acquired star. Team president Frank McKinney reached out to Greenberg, with little result. Fellow owner John Galbreath then flew to New York to meet personally with Greenberg. Galbreath played on Greenberg's pride by telling him how much the Pittsburgh fans were looking forward to seeing him in the Pirates' lineup, and stoked the fears of his damaged legacy by informing him that those same fans would view him as an enemy if he failed to sign a contract with Pittsburgh. Galbreath addressed the objections Greenberg had to becoming a Pirate. The matter of the left field distance was erased when Galbreath informed Greenberg that the team intended to build a new bullpen in left field that would bring in the fence and make it the same distance he had been used to in Detroit. He was told that the team would fly him to away games instead of forcing him to ride the train, and he would have his own suite when the team was not in Pittsburgh. The team also intended to make him the highest paid player in the game by offering him $100,000 to play in 1947. To clinch the deal, Galbreath, who was originally from Kentucky and was a breeder of Kentucky Derby hopefuls, offered to allow Greenberg's wife to choose a yearling from his stables. Greenberg's wife, Carol, was a huge horse aficionado, and it was felt that this final inducement might be enough to tip the scales in favor of the Pirates. Fellow owner Bing Crosby and even National League President Ford Frick joined in on the effort to lobby Greenberg. Their efforts were fruitful. Greenberg thought about it for three days, then decided "Baseball was still in my blood" and agreed to sign a contract.[7] On a side note, though Greenberg would get most everything the Pirates had promised, one important offer was never honored. He never received the yearling promised to his wife.[8]

    Kiner was thrilled to have his old idol become a teammate, and there must have been a boyish reverence attached to his preparations to depart for spring training that season. After all, he was about to take the field with the player he had rooted for since he first developed a love for the game. In fact, Greenberg's signing with the Pirates had caused a stir of anticipation in people across the nation. *Life* magazine even ran a feature article in March of 1947 heralding the arrival of Hammering Hank with the team, and casting the Pirates as a team on the rise. "The New Pirates: Greenberg's Bat and Crosby's Cash Give Them a Fresh Start for 1947" was the headline that extolled all the moves the new management had made. It was placed beneath an almost full-page picture of legendary Pirate Honus Wagner, who had rejoined the team as a coach. The article stated that the Pirates "have not been a pennant contender for nine years. This season, however, they are undergoing the most thorough renovation a club ever had." The piece went on to say, "The Pirates have some valuable new assets: wealthy owners like Bing Crosby who plan to spend nearly $1 million in the first year; a popular new manager, Billy Herman.

The most exciting new asset of all is Pirates leftfielder Hank Greenberg, the home-run king of 1946."[9]

The Pirates moved spring training out of California for the 1947 season and held camp in Miami Beach, Florida. The first day proved to be a media circus, with reporters focusing most of their attention on Greenberg. As the current National League home run champion, Kiner was included in many of the photos snapped on the field. He could hardly comprehend what was taking place, remembering, "it was hard to believe that after all those years of admiring him from afar I was seeing him in the flesh. Because we had both won home-run titles in 1946, we were asked to pose together for a few pictures, but I don't think we said anything to each other. However, when the workout was over and I was following all the other players off the field, I heard him yell to me from the cage, 'Hey, kid, do you want to stay and take some extra batting practice?' Of course I was flabbergasted and eagerly said yes."[10]

After the workout, Greenberg asked if Kiner would like to go to dinner with him. Kiner jumped at the chance, and joined Greenberg and his wife, Carol, at one of the better restaurants in town. Greenberg was a class act who lived life large off the ball field, and Kiner was exposed to this lifestyle for the first time.[11] Kiner was impressed by Greenberg's way of living.

> Hank was different from any ballplayer I ever knew. He was well educated and cultured and spent a lot of time reading (particularly anything that might help him in business) and going to museums. Like debonair characters I saw in the movies, he wore great clothes, dined at the top restaurants, enjoyed steam baths, and knew the proper way to order wine and champagne (which I tasted for the first time). He wanted to be top dog and tried to learn everything he could from people who could help him be successful. I went with him to art museums, to see big bands, and to dinner at such swank places as the "21" Club and Copacabana. He was well aware of his public image and his special responsibility of being the greatest Jewish player ever, and he was very careful about what he did and where he did it. He lived with dignity and class and taught me to do the same.

Indeed, Kiner was learning that there was a great deal more to admire about his idol than simply his feats on the ball field. For his part, Greenberg took a shine to the young power hitter and decided to take him under his wing. As Kiner remembered, it "was the beginning of a beautiful friendship. I say 'friendship,' but in truth Hank Greenberg became the brother I never had."[12] In Greenberg, Kiner found a perfect

6: A Mentor for Ralph

example of how the best stars were dedicated to their craft, and the amount of extra effort necessary to stay in top form. Greenberg may have lived a posh lifestyle off the field, but once at the ballpark, he was a hard-nosed and hard-working competitor. A consummate student of the game, he spent endless hours studying opposing pitchers and making adjustments to the way in which he approached them. A power hitter himself, he took special interest in Kiner's development and gave the youngster a great deal of personal attention. Kiner had been working in the off-season, practicing hitting the ball to right field in order to cut down on the strikeouts he had in 1946. Greenberg advised him to forget about hitting to right. Instead, he told Kiner to move closer to the plate so he could pull any pitch, even those on the outside corner.

"The theory was excellent," Kiner recalled. "My execution was something less." He struggled with the new position in the batter's box, but decided to stick with it because his new mentor had told him to do so. Seven weeks into the 1947 campaign, Kiner had hit only three home runs, and his confidence was shaken. Pirates manager Billy Herman felt that the kid's performance the previous year had merely been a flash in the pan and was on the verge of sending Kiner down to the minors. Greenberg intervened on Kiner's behalf. Going to team president Frank McKinney, Greenberg argued that Kiner belonged with the Pirates and asserted that he would turn things around before the end of the season. He even bet McKinney a new suit of clothes that Kiner would finish the year with at least 30 home runs. Management bowed to Greenberg's assessment and decided to give Kiner a little more time to prove that he belonged.

Kiner started doing so almost immediately. In the second game of a doubleheader against the Braves on June 1, he exploded for two home runs. In the four months from June 1 to the end of the season, he hit an amazing total of 48 round-trippers, a record-setting stretch that topped anything in the Major Leagues to that time. Finishing the year with a batting average of .313, 123 runs batted in and 118 runs scored, Kiner's season numbers placed him among the leaders in each category and earned him strong consideration for MVP honors that year. More importantly, his 51 homers earned him the home run title for the second straight year, though he had to share the honor with Johnny Mize, who also had a terrific season. The two had not only tied for the title, but also for the second-most home runs ever hit in the National League.[13]

To Kiner, the season was indeed memorable.

> I think the biggest day I ever had in baseball came when I hit my fiftieth home run at Ebbets Field. It was a bigger kick than any I've had in baseball and probably will remain my biggest thrill until the Pirates get into the World Series or I hit sixty homers. I'd already hit four home runs in a double-header against the Braves but that was nothing compared to hitting my fiftieth against the Dodgers. I even forgot about my chances of tying the Babe then, for No. 50 meant to me that I had arrived in a very exclusive club. Outside of the big fellow (Ruth), only Greenberg, Foxx, Wilson, and, of course, Mize had ever reached fifty.[14]

By the end of the season it became almost amusing that Greenberg had to intercede to keep Kiner with the Pirates. In retrospect, it might have been the other way around. Greenberg had experienced the worst full season in his career in 1947. Though his 25 home runs would have been enough to capture the National League title in 1946, it was the second lowest of his career. His .249 batting average was the lowest in his career, as was his 74 runs batted in. The offensive punch he had provided for the Tigers for more than a decade had declined to a shell of its former self. His appearance in the Pirates' lineup had still been a huge success for the team, however. Fans came out in droves to watch the star player, just as team management had hoped when they signed him to the big contract. The fan excitement enabled the Pirates to top the one million mark in attendance for the first time in team history, even though they finished a disappointing seventh with a record of 62–92. In fact, more than one and a quarter million Pirates faithful came through the turnstiles in 1947, topping the 1946 attendance by more than half a million. The Pirates' investment had paid huge dividends. There was a buzz around the city for the team once again, and revenues rose dramatically from what they had been. More importantly, there was the effect of Greenberg's presence on Kiner, and his influence on the young slugger would go a long way toward providing Pittsburgh a star attraction for many years to come.

Greenberg and Kiner were a big sports story in Pittsburgh in 1947, but baseball was undergoing a transformation that season that reached far beyond the ball fields and touched the very fabric of American society. Jackie Robinson's debut with the Brooklyn Dodgers had broken the

6: A Mentor for Ralph

color barrier in Major League baseball and had become one of the greatest stories in baseball history. Despite prejudicial harassment from both players and fans that would have caused a lesser man to quit, Robinson put together a stellar season in 1947 with a .297 batting average, 12 round-trippers, and 125 runs scored. He earned the Rookie of the Year Award and finished 5th in the balloting for the National League Most Valuable Player Award, one spot ahead of Kiner. Kiner remembered when Robinson first came to town to play the Pirates.

> His first game in Pittsburgh in May drew a small crowd. This wasn't surprising in that his momentous first game in the majors drew only about twenty-six thousand fans, even though it was at Ebbets Field. Attendance for the Dodgers at home and on the road would increase dramatically as the year progressed and Robinson turned into a bigger story than anticipated. No vote was taken by our players about whether to play of not. We considered it just another game. In fact, I can't remember there being much publicity surrounding the game or extra media presence, other than Wendell Smith, Sam Lacy, and other members of the African American press who followed Robinson during his rookie season. I met Smith, who was a very nice man, and we talked baseball but not about Robinson. He didn't want to stir up any controversy because there was enough of that already.
>
> I also introduced myself to Robinson before the game. I told him I'd grown up in Alhambra and had played softball against him. He didn't know me from a hole in the ground and didn't say much.

Kiner and Robinson would become friends over the course of time, and Kiner considered Robinson to be an exceptional player and man. "What Jackie Robinson did changed more than sports, it changed society as a whole. It was a major step in the integration of America that had to happen, so I wasn't surprised by its impact or that Robinson justifiably became a hero and symbol of social change."[15]

Kiner's greeting of Robinson seems to have been cordial and very sportsmanlike, as opposed to that offered by some of his teammates, who launched racial epithets at the rookie. Greenberg showed the caliber of his character in his first encounter with Robinson, for, as he later wrote, "I had feelings for him because they had treated me the same way. Not as bad, but they made remarks about my being a sheeny and Jew all the time." During the game, Robinson laid down a bunt and sped for first. The Pirates pitcher, Ed Bahr, threw wide of the bag, and, as Greenberg reached out to try to catch the ball, he and Robinson collided. Robinson fell to the ground, and the crowd went silent. The sight of a black man running into a white man, especially a star of Greenberg's status, was something foreign to fans, and everyone waited and watched to see how Greenberg would react to it. For his part, Greenberg did nothing out of the ordinary. Robinson bounced up and raced to second, and the matter was ended for the moment. The next inning, Greenberg walked, and while standing on first base, he had a chance to talk to Robinson. "Hope I didn't hurt you, Jackie," Greenberg said. "I tried to keep out of your way but it was impossible." "No, I didn't get hurt," Robinson responded. "I was just knocked off balance and couldn't stay on my feet." Then Greenberg did something that endeared him to Robinson: he offered encouragement. "Listen," he said, "I know it's plenty tough. You're a good ballplayer, however, and you'll do all right. Just stay in there and fight back. Always remember to keep your head up."

Greenberg's comments did a great deal to shore up Robinson's confidence, not just in his own game, but in humanity in general. Robinson remembered, "I found out not all the guys on the other teams are bad heels. I think Greenberg, for instance, is pulling for me." Later, when he told others about the incident, Robinson concluded, "Class tells. It sticks out all over Mr. Greenberg."[16]

Though already possessed of the right sort of stuff himself, it is obvious that Kiner could not have picked a better role model to serve as his friend and mentor. His relationship with Greenberg would provide him with lasting examples of class and dignity, and how to approach baseball and life in a manner that brings honor and respect.

CHAPTER 7

The Assault on Ruth's Record

Following his dramatic 51 home run season in 1947, Kiner became a bona fide star in the National League. His celebrity status extended beyond baseball, and he remembered that "By the end of my second year, I no longer had to stand in line anywhere." His status as a home run hitter meant that "I was treated much differently. When I'd go to nightclubs I'd be given the star treatment. That meant I'd be whisked past the line and escorted directly to a front-row table, and then whoever was headlining the show would acknowledge me to the audience during their acts."[1] It must have been a great thrill for the young ballplayer to be treated in such fashion and receive such accolades. It also must have been quite ego-inflating to the young bachelor to have adoring female fans express their adulation in no uncertain terms, especially when they held celebrity status of their own. One such example was Monica Lewis, a singer and actress who had become famous as the singing voice of Miss Chiquita Banana in a cartoon television commercial. Known as "America's Singing Sweetheart," she was a beautiful and well-known celebrity in the late 1940s. Once, when Lewis was being interviewed, she happened to mention that Ralph Kiner was her favorite baseball player. Kiner heard about the interview and called her at the theater where she was performing to introduce himself. "After that we saw each other for a while," he remembered, but the relationship never blossomed into anything and the two would shortly go their separate ways.[2]

Celebrity status seemed natural to Kiner, and his kind nature and easy-going manner lent itself well to his new-found fame. It also attracted other celebrities to him like a magnet and forged bonds of friendship that would last throughout his lifetime. Tim McCarver, All-Star catcher and long-time fellow broadcaster of Kiner's, remembered him as being "a thoroughly polished man." McCarver remembered Kiner's greatest trait, and the one that endeared him to most everyone he met, was that "what Ralph learned was how to treat people, and he evidently learned it at an early age because he was across the board nice to everybody."[3] The combination of talent on the ball field and genuine humility and sincerity in private life made Kiner a prime candidate for hero worship as well as a person others wanted to get to know. And get to know him they did.

Pirates owners also took notice of their up-and-coming star. Kiner's salary in 1947 had been $10,000, plus a $5,000 bonus, for a grand total of $15,000. For the 1948 season, he was given a big raise to $35,000, more than double what he had made the previous year. Team owners took Kiner under their wings in other ways as well. Bing Crosby had gotten close to Kiner and the two frequently played golf together. One day, Kiner was on the set of a movie Crosby was filming, and the two were talking about sports. Out of the blue, Crosby asked, "How would you like to have a date with Elizabeth Taylor?" Kiner thought he was kidding and said, "Well, why not?" Crosby wasn't kidding. He told Kiner, "Well, I'll set it up for you," and arranged for Kiner to contact the young starlet.

The date turned out to be the premiere of the movie *Twelve O'Clock High*, a World War II film starring Gregory Peck and Dean Jagger. Kiner remembered that it was "an old fashioned premiere. They had people sitting on the street on Hollywood Boulevard in bleachers and they had klieg lights going all around the sky." He drove to pick Taylor up "in a Cadillac with the top down. I thought I was going to really impress her." At the time, the starlet was still living with her parents, so he had to meet her mother and father. Taylor was running late and was not ready to leave when he arrived, so he "sat there talking with her father for about half an hour." The couple ended up being the last to arrive at Grauman's Chinese Theater, where a valet took his keys and parked the car. After the movie ended, they came out of the theater, and Kiner watched as the cars of various stars were paged and driven out of the parking area. Finally, he went up and asked for his car to be paged. The couple waited for a long period of time, with no car forthcoming. He was getting a little heated and undoubtedly felt a bit awkward in front of his famous

7: The Assault on Ruth's Record

date. He approached the valet and tersely asked that his car be paged again. "Well, your chauffer must have fallen asleep," the valet said. "Chauffer! I don't have a chauffer," Kiner gasped. "Well, then your car is out there," the valet directed, pointing to a vacant lot about 100 yards away. The couple had to hike out to the car, Taylor in her gown and high heels. Kiner's sense of humor allowed him to poke fun at himself over the ludicrous way in which the date had transpired. "Needless to say, that was my last date with her," he would later quip.[4]

John Galbreath, another of the Pirates' owners, also took a personal shine to Kiner. "He asked me to visit his home in Columbus, and we went duck hunting on his preserve. More important, he also came up with a contract that helped me offset the tremendous taxes I was paying." Kiner stated that most people assumed that he was getting the lion's share of the money he was making, when in fact "I was paying out an astronomical 91 percent in taxes! Even with write-offs such as entertainment, I was only able to get it down to 50 percent. So Galbreath put me onto real estate, and took my profits out of that instead of a straight salary. It was never publicized, but I was probably the first player to do that."[5]

One of Kiner's real estate investments was at Rancho Mirage, California, where he would build his home. Located near Palm Springs, the popular resort for many of the in-crowd from Hollywood, Rancho Mirage owed its claim to fame to its many golf courses and racquet clubs. Kiner bought a lot adjacent to the seventh hole of the Thunderbird, the area's original 18-hole course. His neighbors included such celebrities as Lucy and Desi Arnaz, Phil Harris and his wife Alice Faye, Bing Crosby, and Bob Hope. Of the many celebrities who frequented Rancho Mirage, Kiner became friends with Esther Williams, Jack Benny, Randolph Scott, James Garner, Frank Sinatra, Forrest Tucker, Johnny Weissmuller, and Jack Lemmon, to name a few. Friendships were formed with many of these on the golf course, a place where Kiner spent a great deal of time during the off-season, hitting a different type of ball.

Bob Hope was a frequent golf partner of Kiner's. For the millions of fans who watched him on the silver screen, it was difficult to imagine Hope being anything but a comedian, but comedy and acting had been well down on the list of his chosen professions. Hope's greatest aspiration had been to become a professional baseball player. When it became evident that he did not have the talent to make that dream come true, he cast about for another way to be an athlete and earn a living in sports, and he vowed that even if he couldn't become a big league ballplayer, someday he would own a team. Since the only other sport that paid any real money in those days was boxing, he tried to make a living in the ring. Taking the name Packey East, Hope became a fighter and did reasonably well in the amateur circuit. In his first professional match, Hope was paired against a fighter who was much too good for him, and he ended up getting pounded all around the ring. The experience convinced Hope that he would have to look outside of sports to earn a living. He began a career in show business, and the rest is history. He never forgot his vow to own a baseball team someday, however, and would later become a minority owner of the Cleveland Indians.[6]

As Kiner's celebrity status increased at the ballpark, so did his celebrity status outside of the game, aided greatly by the many friendships he had already established with the who's who of the Hollywood set. In 1951, MGM filmed the movie *Angels in the Outfield* largely in Pittsburgh, using Forbes Field as the home stadium for the fictional team and many of the Pirates as extras. The movie starred Paul Douglas and Janet Leigh. Douglas played the role of manager of a hard-luck team that had to be helped to win by angels. Leigh played a local reporter who befriended Bridget White, an eight-year-old orphan who was the team's biggest fan. Bridget prayed to the Archangel Gabriel to help the team, which brought angels to the aid of Douglas' character. When the team started winning and Leigh's character reported that little Bridget had seen angels helping the players, both the team and the town were turned on their ears. Ty Cobb had been instrumental in getting MGM to film the movie in Pittsburgh. The players received nothing for being in the film, however. Kiner remembered that "Filming took place during the regular season, and the baseball scenes in the movie of the Pirates and their opponents are from real games. Janet and other cast members were planted in the stands and filmed while watching us." All those connected with the movie got paid, but "we had to do our cameos for free."[7]

The players were naturally distracted by Leigh's presence at the ballpark, not being used to having a beautiful starlet in such close proximity.

7: The Assault on Ruth's Record

For his part, Kiner had become accustomed to being around celebrities, even beautiful ones like Leigh. But she caught his eye. "She certainly got my attention, and one day prior to a game, during a break in filming, I went up to her near the batting cage and introduced myself. We just started talking. I wasn't intimidated by her stardom, and what made it easier was that she was a real down-to-earth girl who even knew who I was. Maybe she followed baseball closely, but it's more likely she simply took the trouble to get some personal information on the Pirates." He decided to take a chance and ask her out to dinner, and she accepted. "And that was the beginning of our brief romance—a good romance. We went to private clubs, out of the public eye, but even so we made the headlines. Fortunately, there was nothing derogatory written about what was going on, perhaps because we were both single and enemy free. We were together about three weeks." He confessed that "it was serious—at least on my side—and I thought there was a good chance it would continue."[8]

Leigh had been dating Tony Curtis, who was out of the country filming a movie, at the time she and Kiner started dating. When filming on *Angels in the Outfield* concluded, the couple made plans to get together again, but that never came to fruition. As Kiner said, their romance had been reported in all the movie and gossip magazines. A picture of the burly Kiner with Jan Sterling, the actress wife of Paul Douglas, contained the caption "Home run king Ralph Kiner, who wooed Liz Taylor and Janet Leigh, gives Jan some expert advice on correct bat grasp."[9] Many such reports were made of the good-looking couple being seen here or there, and eventually they were brought to the attention of Tony Curtis, who left his filming to make an unexpected flight back to the states. The next thing Kiner knew, it was being printed in the papers that Curtis and Leigh had announced their engagement.

Some 34 years later, Kiner happened to be in the same room as Jamie Lee Curtis, Janet's daughter. He went over to introduce himself and informed her that he had dated her mother long ago. "I expected her to look at me with puzzlement. Instead, she leapt to her feet and threw her arms around me, and exclaimed, 'Daddy! I've been searching for you all my life! At last I've found you!'" The incident gave Kiner a good chuckle, but it wasn't the end to Jamie Lee's prankster antics. Shortly thereafter, he happened to be flying on a cross-country trip.

Unknown to him, Jamie Lee was on the same airplane. At one point during the flight, the stewardess handed him a note. When he read it, he knew exactly who it was from. "Mom says you're behind in child support payments. Send money!" On another occasion, she sent him some pictures her mother had given her of her mother and Kiner many years before. The pictures came with a note from Leigh which said, "It's been a long time, hasn't it?," prompting Kiner to speculate "maybe I did make an impression after all."[10]

At that time, Kiner was considered to be one of the best "catches" available. One writer described him by stating,

> In the sense that the adjective "colorful" was applied to Babe Ruth or Pepper Martin, Kiner is not colorful. He has a pleasing appearance, a friendly personality but is more engaging off the field than on it. As a bachelor, Kiner is the most eligible since the Duke of Windsor was a boy but even his romances rarely make the press, save on such occasions as he squires Elizabeth Taylor or some other "name" cutie-pie. And then it is the young lady who makes the headlines, not Ralph. Kiner's color is strictly in his bat. He is not only a good home run hitter, the best of the current generation, but he is a good clutch hitter. Ralph breaks up many tight ball games with his distance clouts. He isn't the sort of hitter who belts one nine miles when the game is irretrievably lost. Ralphie can hit 'em when the chips are down, too. His clutch hitting, of course, enhances his box office pull.[11]

Kiner rebounded quickly from his romance with Janet Leigh. He was soon reported to be making the rounds with Nancy Chaffee, a tennis star ranked fourth in the world and considered the glamour girl of the sport. The two had gotten together after Chaffee had stated that Kiner had caught her eye. In an interview, she was asked about her love interest. She had been leafing through a newspaper at the time, and when the question was asked, she had reached the sports page, which contained a picture of Kiner. She pointed to the picture as her answer. Her response was promptly reported, and she followed it up by sending Kiner a telegram wishing him luck on his newly opened sporting goods store in Alhambra. A few days later, ex-football player Tom Harmon arranged to secretly have Kiner appear on a TV show that he and Chaffee hosted. When she arrived in the studio, there was Kiner to greet her. The two hit it off, and by June 10, they announced their own engagement.[12] He had wanted to surprise her with her engagement ring, but he was deprived of that opportunity when Walter Winchell beat him to the punch by announcing his intentions on Winchell's radio show.[13]

7: The Assault on Ruth's Record

The couple were married in October and made their home at Kiner's house in Rancho Mirage. The marriage would last 17 years and produce three children: Michael, Scott and Kathryn Chaffee, called K.C. by her parents.[14] When Kiner walked down the aisle, a now familiar friend and mentor was there to stand by his side. Hank Greenberg, his old idol and the man who had taken him under his wing like a little brother, served as his best man. Greenberg, who had taught him so much about baseball and life, was there to share in one of his most important moments.

With so much going on in his personal life, one wonders how Kiner had the focus to concentrate on his career as a baseball player, but concentrate he did. The 1948 season was somewhat marred by the fact that Hank Greenberg had decided to retire from baseball and had left the team. The Pirates had lost their biggest star attraction, and Kiner had lost a mentor and friend. Not completely, though. The two would remain close for the rest of their lives. It was up to Kiner now to pick up the mantle of leadership and serve as the team's new star. The transition would not be a difficult one, however, for as one astute biographer put it, the multitude of fans who had come to the Pirates' games the previous season had "paid to see Greenberg; they stayed to watch Kiner."[15] Another new face with the Pirates was the manager, Billy Meyer,

When Kiner married tennis star Nancy Chaffee, the pair became sports darlings to the nation. Though he had dated the likes of Elizabeth Taylor and Janet Leigh, his relationships were largely kept out of the news because he was respected as a wholesome and respectable sort.

who took over for Billy Herman. A long-time minor league catcher with two seasons of Major League experience with the Philadelphia Athletics, Meyer had managed in the Yankees' minor league system for nearly two decades, under the direction of Joe McCarthy, before being signed to take the helm of the Pirates.

Kiner's 1948 campaign was not quite as good as 1947, but then again, it also lacked the inconsistency that had marked the first two months of the previous year. By the end of May 1948, Kiner had already hit 11 home runs and was batting a solid .307, a far cry from the three homers he had swatted during the same two months in 1947. There was no longer any talk of sending him back down to the minors for seasoning. The problem was that the Pirates didn't have anyone in their lineup to protect Kiner and keep the opposing pitchers honest. Greenberg had provided that support in 1947, but his departure left a huge void in the Pirates' batting order. No one else on the Pittsburgh roster put fear in National League hurlers that if they pitched around Kiner they might pay the consequences. Subsequently, Kiner often got little or nothing to hit when he came to the plate. This sometimes frustrated the star, causing him to press for hits when hittable pitches just weren't there. As a result, his batting average suffered, and he ended the season at .265, one of the lowest averages he would post in his entire career, just .018 above his rookie season.

The adjustment made toward pitching to Kiner meant that he would get more walks if he remained disciplined at the plate, however, and he ended the season with 112 base on balls, the first of six consecutive seasons in which he had over 100 walks. When he did get a pitch to hit, he usually gave it a good ride, and 40 of them cleared the outfield fences that year. That was good enough to tie him with Johnny Mize, once more, as home run champion of the league for his third consecutive season. Stan Musial of the Cardinals fell just short of making it a three-way tie by hitting 39 round-trippers. The year 1948 also marked the first time that Kiner was named to the All-Star team. Stan Musial, Enos Slaughter, and Richie Ashburn got the starting spots in the outfield for the National League that year, but Kiner managed a late-inning plate appearance, in the ninth inning when he grounded out to third.

All in all, it was a good year for the slugger, and a three-time home

7: The Assault on Ruth's Record

run champion was nothing to be sneezed at, especially in Pittsburgh. He also broke the Pirates' record for career home runs, set by Paul Waner back in 1940. In 14 seasons with Pittsburgh, Waner had tallied only 109 home runs. Kiner amassed 114 in three short years and seemed poised to achieve even greater feats in the coming years. After all, at just 25 years of age, he was just coming into his prime. Little wonder that Pirates fans held great expectations for the player who was like no other in Pittsburgh history. Other teams had been blessed with home run threats to thrill their fans, but in Pittsburgh this was a first. No one in franchise history had been able to generate the excitement in the stands that Kiner could with one powerful swing of his bat.

He was indeed a fan favorite, and he was constantly in demand to sign autographs. This he never refused. The only demand he ever made of autograph seekers was that they line up in an orderly fashion, instead of mobbing him. He explained that his willingness to sign autographs for all fans who requested them stemmed from his boyhood days and a bad experience he had with a star of the time. He had gone to the St. Louis Cardinals' spring training camp and approached Dizzy Dean with a baseball, hoping to get the star pitcher's autograph. Dean curtly brushed him aside and refused to sign, crushing the boy. Kiner said, "At that moment, I vowed that if ever I became a major-league ballplayer, I would never, ever, make a kid feel as bad as I felt right then." He never forgot that moment and always made good on his promise to treat youngsters better than he himself had been treated. He would always sign, and he did so with a grace that endeared him to the fans.[16]

The team finished the 1948 season with a winning record of 83–71, but that was good enough for only a fourth-place finish, 8.5 games behind the front-running Boston Braves. Attendance surged past the record-setting level of the previous year, to over 1.5 million fans. Pittsburgh faithful were coming through the turnstiles in record numbers to see their hitting phenom launch majestic shots over the left field bullpen that had now become commonly known as Kiner's Korner. That was a good thing for management. The 1948 season was the only year of Kiner's time with the Pirates when the team had a winning record. Ownership would have to rely on him to keep fans coming out to the ballpark, as the frenzy of pennant fever would not come to town for more than a decade.

Billy Meyer won "Manager of the Year" honors in the National League for the turn-around the team had made in becoming competitive after the dismal 1947 campaign. The team had 21 more victories in 1948 and finished only two games out of second place. Fans in Pittsburgh felt that the Pirates had turned the corner and wondered, "could a World Series be far away?"[17]

In 1949, Kiner improved on his performance of the previous year and created something of a sensation throughout the baseball world. Billy Meyer had the opposite turn of fate. After leading the team to a marked improvement in the 1948 campaign, Meyer saw the Pirates slip once more to the second division, a position they would remain in during Meyer's tenure in Pittsburgh. Kiner got off to a hot start that season, and by the end of May he had equaled the 11 home runs hit the previous year. In 1948, however, he had hit only 29 more over the final four months of the season. The 1949 campaign would see him stay hot and average nearly 11 home runs per month during that same period of time. He was following the formula he himself had advanced for hitting a lot of home runs and possibly challenging Babe Ruth's single season record. "It takes a good start, lots of home runs in April and May, the first six weeks of the season, a good closing rush in September, a good hitter behind you in the lineup, as Ruth had Gehrig, so the pitcher can't walk you without running into real trouble."[18]

In 1949, fellow outfielder Wally Westlake batted behind Kiner and did a pretty good job of protecting him. Westlake hit a respectable .282 and was second on the team with 23 home runs. His 104 runs batted in were also second on the club. While Westlake performed his job of protecting Kiner well, he also derived immense benefits as the recipient of many pitches opposing hurlers were afraid to throw to Kiner. Indeed, National League pitchers needed to be cautious when Kiner was in the batter's box. He topped the league that year with 117 free passes issued by pitchers who knew better than to make the mistake of giving in and throwing a hitter's pitch when they were behind in the count. Kiner had a way of driving pitchers' mistakes out of the ballpark, and his fourth year with the Pirates proved to be his best yet, as he slugged 54 home runs and drove in a league-leading 127 runs. His .658 slugging percentage was also tops in the league. The final months of the 1949 season were

7: The Assault on Ruth's Record

spent in speculation, as baseball fans followed the Pirates' box scores and wondered if Kiner might be able to beat Hack Wilson's National League record of 56 home runs in a season, or possibly overtake Babe Ruth's magical number of 60.

Kiner noted how fans expressed differing opinions of his assault on the Babe's record, as well as his own mixed feeling on the subject.

Kiner rounding the bases after a home run at Forbes Field became a familiar sight to Pirates fans. Here he is greeted by teammates following a shot that went out of the park.

> If I am ever fortunate enough to hit that magic "sixtieth" I don't know whether I'll be glad or sorry as I watch it sail out of the lot. You see, Babe Ruth was a great idol of mine, as he was to most fellows in my boyhood. So, while I'm trying my best, I must say that my feelings are mixed. And the fan mail I get doesn't help to unscramble my emotions. This mail is heaviest during seasons when I seem to be threatening the Bambino's tremendous total. The letters are by no means all from well-wishers. At least half of them beg me not to break that record. But baseball is my business, as well as my favorite sport, so I try not to pay too much heed to the fans and get as many homers as the baseball fates (and pitchers) will allow.[19]

In the end, he finished the year with 54 home runs, two behind Wilson's mark and six short of Ruth's. It was still good enough to earn him his fourth consecutive home run title, and 18 more than Stan Musial, the second-place finisher. For the first time in three years, he did not have to share the title with Johnny Mize. In fact, it was his first title without Mize being his main competition. The season also saw his second straight selection to the National League squad for the All-Star Game. This time, however, he was a starter and not a backup. Kiner came to the plate five times in the summer classic, managing only one hit. But that hit was a big one. In the bottom of the sixth inning with a runner aboard, he launched a pitch from Lou Brissie deep over the left field fence at Ebbets Field for a two-run homer. The National League squad ended up losing the game by an 11–7 score.

Kiner was used to being on the losing side of things this season. The Pirates finished with a record of 71–83 and slipped to sixth place in the league, 26 games behind the pennant-winning Brooklyn Dodgers. Despite that fact, the team still managed to draw nearly 1.5 million fans out to the ballpark, mostly to see Kiner come to the plate. As one old fan told me, people went to the park to watch Kiner play. In most cases, with the Pirates trailing, they would stay only until Kiner's last plate appearance, and after that there would be a mass exodus from Forbes Field. Kiner had become more than merely the face of the Pittsburgh Pirates, he had become the team's sole star attraction and its cash drawing card. Management knew it, too. That's why they tried to keep their star happy by increasing his salary for the 1949 season. That year, Kiner's salary was commensurate with the All-Star status he had earned on the field, and the team paid him $50,000. Ownership probably felt that it was good business to give Kiner a slice of the income he was bringing through the turnstiles, a practice they would employ for the next few years.

7: The Assault on Ruth's Record

Kiner had the distinction of being one of the top ten home run hitters in all of Major League baseball in the 1940s. Though he played in only four of those years, he amassed a total of 168 round-trippers, good enough to earn him ninth place on the list. In front of him were such noted sluggers as Ted Williams, Johnny Mize, Joe Gordon, and Joe DiMaggio. Bobby Doerr finished behind Kiner as the tenth slugger on the list.[20]

Billy Meyer and his squad reported to the 1950 spring training camp in the familiar confines of San Bernardino, California. It was the team's third consecutive spring training held in California, which worked out well for Kiner as he didn't have far to travel. The majority of players report to camp with a feeling of optimism for a new campaign and with hope that their team has a chance to compete for their league's pennant. Such was not the case with the players on the Pirates' roster. Most of them knew that they were on a bad team and had little if any chance of a pennant. Reporters assigned to cover the team knew it as well, but that was not the story they were seeking. Instead, they wanted to get an interview with Kiner, the National League's most feared power hitter. With 168 home runs to his credit in just four years of play, he had become the greatest long-ball threat in the game, and the question that was at the top of the list for most reporters was whether Kiner felt he could continue his home run streak going into his fifth season.

The 1950 edition of the Pirates was actually not that bad of a team, offensively. What they lacked to be competitive was pitching. Pittsburgh pitchers posted a league-worst 4.96 earned run average that year, more than .6 runs per game higher than the next worst team. Of the starting position players, catcher Clyde McCullough had the worst batting average, hitting at a .254 clip for the season. Kiner posted the third lowest average, ahead of shortstop Stan Rojek's .257, closing the year at .272. All the other starters posted averages of .282 or better, with first baseman Johnny Hopp leading the way with a torrid .340. Wally Westlake continued to bat behind Kiner and provide protection for him in the lineup. Batting .285 and swatting 24 home runs, Westlake did his job effectively. The Bucs started the season out well enough, winning five of their first six games, with Kiner batting well over .350 and hitting two home runs. Then the wheels fell off the wagon. They won only 11 more games through the end of May, when their record stood at a dismal 16–23.

Pittsburgh went on numerous extended losing streaks, including two of five games, one of six, one of seven and a season high of nine games lost in a row twice. By the All-Star break, the team was 27–47 and for all intents and purposes out of the race. Pittsburgh fans had also given up by the time the summer classic was played. Attendance at Forbes Field dropped to its lowest level since 1945, and just over 1.1 million came out to the park to watch the games.

Despite the gloomy aspect of another losing season, Kiner was once more on top of his game. His batting average was not up to the level it had been the year before, but he was still launching mammoth shots out of ballparks around the league and finished with a total of 47, driving in 112 runs. His walks were up slightly over the year before, with 122 free passes, a sign of respect from opposing pitchers who were unwilling to give him a chance to win games for the Pirates with one mighty swing of his bat. For the fifth straight season, Kiner was crowned the home run king of the National League, finishing 11 above Andy Pafko of the Chicago Cubs. In five years in the league, he had stroked an amazing 215 home runs, and talk among baseball fans across the country went from speculation over whether he would be able to break Babe Ruth's single season record to the possibility that he could eclipse the Bambino's career mark as well. It wasn't a stretch for fans to consider the possibility. At Kiner's current rate, he would have 645 home runs in just 15 years of play. Ruth had hit 714 in his 22 seasons in the game. It was not unreasonable for baseball fans to project that Kiner was on a pace to beat that mark if he could play the same number of years. After all, Kiner seemed to be in much better physical condition than Ruth had been, even in his prime. And then there was the matter of lifestyle. Kiner took much better care of himself and did not partake in the wanton excesses that had been such a large part of the Babe's legend.

This clean-cut, all–American youth of 26 years seemed the likely heir to baseball's most lofty throne. Babe Ruth himself was impressed by Kiner's power and had predicted that if any player could beat his single season record, it would be Kiner. He reserved any comments about his career record, though. The 1950 season also saw Kiner join some exclusive company in another statistic. Stan Musial, Duke Snider, and Kiner were the only players in the National League that season to post

100-plus runs scored and runs batted in. That, along with his home run accomplishment, led *The Sporting News* to name Kiner its "Player of the Year."

Kiner, by this time, had become more than a baseball hero to the fans in Pittsburgh. Always affable and approachable, he made numerous personal appearances throughout the city and lent his backing to a great many charitable events. Pittsburgh fans felt as if he was one of their own and cheered for this local idol. With the advent of television, Kiner became one of the first Major League players to host his own local TV show, which brought him into the living rooms of many Pittsburgh homes, just like family. Indeed, he was looked on as family by many of the Pirates' faithful.[21]

Kiner made it to his third straight All-Star Game in 1950. For the second consecutive year, he was a starter in left field. In the top of the first inning, he came to bat against Vic Raschi with one out and nobody on base. He got hold of one of Raschi's offerings, driving it deep to left field, and it looked as if the National League was going to take an early lead. Ted Williams, playing left field for the American League, ran hard to try to track down the fly ball, catching it just before slamming hard into the fence. Williams was shaken by the collision, but managed to keep the ball in his glove to make Kiner's blast just a long out. Teammates could tell that Williams had been hurt on the play, but he refused to come out of the game. He played eight innings before asking to be relieved. Tests later determined that he had broken his elbow making the catch and had played from that point on in excruciating pain.[22]

Raschi gave up two runs in the top of the second inning to give the National League squad the lead, but the American League came back with a run in the third and two more in the fifth to surge ahead. The game settled into a pitchers' duel for the next three innings. Kiner led off the top of the ninth against Art Houtteman and launched another majestic fly ball to left field. No one was catching this shot, as it sailed over the fence to tie up the score. The American League failed to score in their half of the inning, and the game went to extra innings. Kiner's one out double in the 11th started a rally, but his teammates were unable to bring him home. Finally, in the top of the 14th, Red Schoendienst led off with a home run off Ted Gray to break the tie. Ewell Blackwell set down Dom DiMaggio, Ferris Fain singled and Joe DiMaggio then hit into a double play to give the National League the 4–3 victory. Kiner had finally gotten to experience a win in a big game, and what's more, he had played a huge role in securing the win.

Kiner was particularly proud of the home run he hit in this game because he considered that particular All-Star Game to "have been the best in the history of the event." As he later recalled, "It was a scorching day. The temperature reached 103 degrees." When he took his big swing in the top of the ninth, "I hit the ball nine miles into the air, which was the way I hit most of my home runs. This one looked like a routine fly ball to left field, but it kept carrying and carrying until it landed in the upper deck."[23]

CHAPTER 8

Earning a Tie with the Babe

By 1951, Kiner had become one of the most recognizable and most respected players in the game. His $65,000 salary was testament to that, as were the frequent stories about him in baseball and sporting publications. Team ownership was doing its best to turn things around and bring winning baseball back to Pittsburgh. They doled out lots of cash in an effort to bring players into the fold who they thought could benefit the club and put it on the road to winning. The problem was that their investments were largely ill-advised or unfortunate. One of their expensive moves that proved to be a bust was the signing of a high school pitching sensation named Paul Pettit. The Los Angeles native was given a $100,000 bonus to sign with the Pirates, amid great expectations of his becoming the next Bob Feller or Lefty Grove, who was also a southpaw, like Pettit. While still in high school, Pettit had pitched for the semipro Signal Oilers, for whom he had thrown six no-hitters, three of them in a row. In 549 innings with the Oilers, he had struck out 945 batters.[1] In 1949. Pettit signed a contract with Frederick Stephani, a movie producer, to be featured in a film he wanted to make about baseball, for the sum of $85,000. The Pirates, feeling Pettit to be the next pitching sensation in the game, bought out his contract from Stephani for $100,000, a record amount at the time.[2] Pettit was assigned to the New Orleans Pelicans for the 1950 season, and he was a highly anticipated call-up for the 1951 campaign. But Pettit was a bust for the Pirates. Suffering from arm soreness, he threw only 22/3 innings in Pittsburgh before being sent back down to the minors with the Hollywood Stars of the Pacific Coast League. He returned to the Pirates, briefly, in 1953, but was able to work only 28 innings, gaining a record of 1–2 with an earned run average of 7.71. Back in the minors, his arm trouble eventually forced his conversion to a position player, but he never returned to the majors. The huge signing bonus the team had paid to attain him had all been a waste.[3]

Another highly touted pitcher recruited by the Pirates was Vernon Law, a right-hander fire-baller from Idaho. The Pirates' signing of Law was a perfect example of the lengths scouts would go to in order to secure a prospect for their team. Law and his family were Mormans, faithful members of the Church of Jesus Christ of Latter Day Saints, and as such were very pious. When other scouts went to the Law home, they were smoking cigars and carrying cigars as a gift to Vernon's father. The Laws abhorred smoking, for both health and religious reasons, and these scouts made a bad impression on the family. Babe Herman and Herman Welker, the Pittsburgh scouts, knew about the Laws' stance on smoking, but they had deviously passed the rumor around the scouting community that Mr. Law was a big fan of cigars. When Herman and Welker went calling at the Law home, they carried with them a box of candy for Mrs. Law, posturing themselves in much better light to the family. During the course of negotiation, a phone call came for Mrs. Law from Bing Crosby. "She almost fainted on the spot." That was it, Vernon Law would become a Pirate.[4]

Law's first season with the Pirates was in 1950. He finished the campaign with a record of 7–9 and an earned run average of 4.92, miserable, but still slightly better than the 4.96 earned run average posted by the team. Law eventually became a star pitcher for the Pirates and led the team to a World Series victory in 1960, but at the outset of the 1951 campaign, he was still a youngster learning the ropes and struggling through the problem of figuring out Major League hitters.

Yet one more future Pittsburgh pitching star made his debut in a Pirates uniform in 1951. Bob Friend was a hard-throwing right-hander from West Lafayette, Indiana. Though Friend would later become a workhorse for the Pirates and was the first pitcher to lead the league in earned run average while playing for a last-place team, his days of dominance on the mound were still several years in the future.

One of the biggest changes for the 1951 season was the hiring of Branch Rickey as general manager of the Pirates in November of 1950. Rickey had guided the St. Louis Cardinals to four World Series titles from 1919 to 1942, and had most recently been at the helm when the

Brooklyn Dodgers won the National League pennant in 1947 and 1949. A proven executive, he had been responsible for establishing the farm system in baseball and had also advocated innovations to the game such as permanent spring training facilities, batting cages, pitching machines, and batting helmets. A pioneer in statistical analysis, he also was one of the first in the game to promote the idea that on-base percentage was more important that batting average. Pirates ownership once more showed that they were willing to spend money to win by offering Rickey a five-year contract for $100,000 per year. Over and above the salary, the Pirates had a huge connection with Rickey because he and team president John Galbreath had been fraternity brothers at Ohio Wesleyan University.[5]

One sports columnist predicted,

Branch Rickey takes command of Pittsburgh this year, and that means any appraisal of the squad when he took over may mean little at mid-season and nothing at season's end. Rickey has Ralph Kiner, a great batsman, and one who delivers in the clutch, and he has two pitchers everybody admires, Willie Werle and Cliff Chambers. That's enough for Rickey to start with. The rest of the players may not matter much. There is certain to be unending experimentation, because that is Rickey's way with any squad new to him. There will be many shifts and seeming confusion, because Rickey is a showman, and it will not be long before he has the ballyhoo going to create numerous phenoms in Forbes field, as he did at Sportsman Park and in Ebbets Field. The Mahatma's estimate of the Pirates when he became general manager was: "The outfield is the best, the pitching is next, and the infield is the worst."[6]

Rickey announced that he intended to put the Pirates on a five-year plan, and by the end of that time he predicted they would once again be a solid Major League team. The thrust of Rickey's plan was for the Pirates to stockpile young talent, which they could bring along over the next few years until they became legitimate stars. The team invested in Rickey's scheme heavily, spending some $496,000 in the open market in 1951. The emphasis was on youth, and touted prospects like Tony Bartirome, Bobby Del Greco, Dick Hall, Eddie O'Brien, Felipe Montemayor, Dick Cole, and Dick Groat were brought into the fold.[7] Pirates fans had to do double-takes at their scorecards to learn the names of these unknown youngsters when they were inserted into the lineup. Regrettably, most of the young talent Rickey stockpiled turned out to be busts. The exception was Groat, who would go on to an all-star career and became a staple of the Pittsburgh lineup for several years.

Amazingly, one of the significant changes Rickey wanted to make with the Pirates roster was the elimination of Ralph Kiner. Rickey felt that Kiner would be worth a lot of money if the team sold him, and that money could then be invested in acquiring more young talent for the future. This was one decision that he could not make on his own as general manager, however. Pirates ownership liked their home run-hitting star, and he couldn't be moved without their consent. When Rickey was asked if he'd trade Kiner for three infielders, he showed his intentions by replying, "I'd trade anybody for three infielders." His hands were tied without the approval of the owners, so he started a smear campaign against Kiner with John Galbreath, the team president and majority owner. Rickey spoke ill of Kiner to Galbreath every opportunity he got, and tried to make him the scapegoat for all the misfortune the team had been having. He even went so far as to draft a letter to Galbreath enumerating 20 reasons why Kiner was a detriment to the Pirates and should be cut loose. At the close of this letter, he wrote a personal note about Kiner that must have been intended to show Galbreath that his conclusions about Kiner's worth to the team were purely business. "This relates only to his baseball value and certainly not to his personality. He is one of the nicest boys I ever met, but Ralph satisfies my requirements in only one respect—as a home run hitter. To me that isn't enough."[8] The fact that Kiner was making $65,000 a year and was one of the highest paid players in the National League must have certainly irked Rickey, who was itching to have that much extra capital to sign new players.

The team started the year off well. In fact, there was reason for hope on Opening Day. Pirates pitching had been a major weakness during the past two years, but Cliff Chambers started the new season off with a strong pitching performance in a road game against the Cincinnati Reds, winning 4–3. The following day, the Pirates had their home opener, and Murry Dickson allowed only two earned runs in six innings on his way to a 5–4 win over the visiting Cardinals. Dickson even helped his own cause by hitting a home run in the fourth inning that gave the Pirates the lead. Six games into the season, the team was 4–2, though Kiner had yet to hit his first home run of the campaign. Pittsburgh faithful started to feel optimistic that maybe Rickey's moves might pay dividends. After all, everyone knew that Kiner was going to get more than

8: Earning a Tie with the Babe

Kiner's assault on Babe Ruth's consecutive seasons with home run titles resulted in his setting a new record by leading the National League for seven straight years. This record has never been broken. A large number of his home runs sailed over the left field fence at Forbes Field, pictured here. This picture shows the fence after Kiner's Korner had been removed.

his fair share of home runs once he got going, and Kiner's extra power might just be enough to keep them in contention. On May 3 the team was 8–5 and in third place. By the end of that week, they had managed to improve their record only to 9–8, still good enough for third place, only two games back of first place. Kiner had started to get hot and hit his fourth home run of the campaign on May 8. By the end of May, however, the team had gone on a losing binge that found them at 15–23, firmly in possession of last place. The slide would continue for the remainder of the season, with the Pirates finishing with a disappointing 64–90 mark. At 32.5 games back of the front-running Giants, they finished seventh, just ahead of the Chicago Cubs.

One of the big moves of the year came when Rickey decided to trade Wally Westlake and Cliff Chambers to the St. Louis Cardinals for catcher Joe Garagiola, pitchers Howie Pollet and Ted Wilks, outfielder Bill Howerton, and Dick Cole in a mid-June deal. Westlake had become very popular with the Pittsburgh fans, and Chambers had been pitching well that year. When asked if his decision to trade these two well-liked players might not cause problems for the team, Rickey responded, "Problems are the price you pay for programs," referring to his five-year plan.[9]

But the trade caused more than just resentment among some Pittsburgh fans, it left Kiner without a stable bat behind him in the lineup. Bill Howerton was slotted into the batting order behind Kiner. His rookie season had been the year before, when he batted an impressive .281 and hit ten home runs in 110 games with the Cardinals. Batting behind Kiner, he proved to be a slight downgrade from Westlake, but he still managed to bat .271 and swat 12 homers that year in a Pirates uniform, largely due to the fact that he got some good pitches that opposing hurlers did not want to serve up to Kiner. It would prove to be his only great hurrah in baseball. The following year, he played only three weeks with Pittsburgh before being waived to the New York Giants. In 11 games with the Giants, he hit only .067, and was soon out of baseball.

The 1951 campaign must have been especially disappointing for Kiner. By the All-Star break the team was 31–45, last in the league, and it seemed probable that the Pirates would finish yet another year at the bottom of the heap. Even the All-Star Game was something of a letdown for Kiner. True, he was selected to represent the National League for the fourth straight year, but he would not be a starter. The home run champion for the past five seasons was delegated to ride the bench while Stan Musial, Richie Ashburn, and Del Ennis took the field. Kiner would find a familiar face and friend with whom he could chat, however. Wally Westlake had also been named to the team. Kiner got into the game in the fourth inning. In the top of the eighth, he stepped into the batter's box, facing Mel Parnell. Kiner greeted the Red Sox star with a deep drive that cleared the left field fence at Briggs Stadium, the home of the Detroit Tigers. The National League squad went on to win the game, 8–3, in a lopsided victory that must have been a high point for Kiner that season. It must have also provided him a few retrospective moments to ponder that fact that the game was played where his idol, Hank Greenberg, had risen to stardom, and swatting one over the same left field fence where so many of Hammering Hank's drives had ended up must have been especially satisfying.

Kiner managed to put together another stellar year despite the overall poor performance of the team. He ended the season as the league leader in numerous categories, including 137 bases on balls, 124 runs scored, an on base percentage of .452, and a slugging percentage of .627.[10] He also hit for a .309 average, the third highest of his career, and drove in 109 runs. Most importantly, he managed to power the ball out of the park 42 times for his sixth consecutive National League home run crown, beating out the Brooklyn Dodgers' Gil Hodges, who hit 40 round-trippers. It was a momentous accomplishment for the 28-year-old Pirates star. The only other player in baseball history to lead his league six consecutive years in home runs had been the immortal Babe Ruth, who accomplished the feat from 1926 through 1931. In Ruth's first six years in the majors, he had hit only 49 home runs. To be fair, during this time he was employed mainly as a pitcher. Still, Ruth was 31 years old when he won the first of his six consecutive crowns. Kiner was three years younger than that and had already accomplished the feat. His 257 home runs were also ahead of the 238 Ruth had hit by the time he was 28 years old. It was little wonder that he was being compared so favorably to the all-time slugger. Pittsburgh fans were wont to wonder how many long balls Kiner might have already launched if he were playing on a better team, or if there was another power threat hitter in the lineup to cut down on his walks and give him more good pitches to hit.

Comparisons to Babe Ruth were common for any power hitter that showed potential or put together a good season, and Kiner was merely the latest in a long line of sluggers anointed to become the next great home run king. The string had begun with Ruth's first main rival, Ken Williams, who had played with the St. Louis Browns and Boston Red Sox from 1915 through 1929. Williams had been one of the hitters who benefited greatly from the end of the Deadball era, when he started launching home runs at a prodigious rate. In 1922, he stroked 39 long balls to capture the home run title from Ruth, who had won the crown the four previous seasons. Baseball fans and analysts were quick to speculate that Williams might be the player to take away the Babe's crown as home run king. Then, in 1925, with a .331 batting average and 25 home runs already swatted for the season, Williams was hit in the head by a pitch thrown by Cleveland's Byron Speece. He spent ten days in the hospital before being sent home for the remainder of the season. Though he returned to baseball for the 1926 campaign, he was never again the same player. Headaches and dizziness plagued him for the rest of his career, and though he played four more seasons in the Major Leagues, he never regained his former dominance.[11] It was a lesson to be repeated many times over the decades. A player had to be more than talented in order to challenge for the king's crown. He also had to be lucky. He had to be able to somehow remain in good health for an extended period of time in order to challenge the Babe. Luck, or lack of it, would be a major story with Kiner, the latest heir apparent to the Bambino.

For the Pirates, the just-concluded season was one that left ownership probably more dejected than Kiner. Attendance had dipped to below one million fans, as more and more Pittsburgh residents opted to save their money and stay away from the ballpark. Most who still went were there to see Kiner, but he couldn't make the team a winner all by himself, so enthusiasm for the team ebbed for the second straight year. More importantly, the reduced gate revenue, along with Rickey's excessive spending, meant that the team was losing money, big money. By the end of the 1951 season, the Pirates were one million dollars in the red, and President Galbreath was forced to dip into his own finances to keep the team moving forward.

In 1951 baseball was visited by a new medium. Television was becoming affordable for many Americans, and games were beginning to be broadcast in some markets. In the years to come, television would eclipse radio as the way in which most people kept up with the team when they were not able to go to the park, and it would become a major source of revenue for the sport. Television would later provide Kiner with a vehicle to stay close to baseball and win over a whole new fan base. For the present, however, most Pittsburgh fans kept tabs on the games by listening to Pirates announcer Rosey Rowswell on the radio. Rowswell was an innovative personality with a distinctive way of calling games. Whenever a Pirate hit a home run, he would cry out, "Raise the window, Aunt Minnie, here she comes!" After a brief pause, he would

8: Earning a Tie with the Babe

point to an assistant, who dropped a pan filled with nuts, bolts, broken glass and the like onto the floor, to simulate the sound of a shattering window pane. Rowswell would sigh and say, "She never made it." Kiner gave Rowswell the opportunity to make many such calls.

Rowswell also came up with phrases like "he got him with the old dipsy doodle" when a Pirates pitcher struck out an opposing batter, or would cry out "it's a doozey marooney" when a Pirate got a hit for extra bases. Beloved by Pirates fans, his use of personal phrases and sayings were almost a foreign language to people from out of town who attempted to listen to the games. A well-known figure around Pittsburgh, Rowswell was constantly seen visiting hospitals and nursing homes, as well as shut-ins who loved the Pirates but could not get out to a game.

His one great quirk was that he refused to accompany the team on road trips. One would think that meant there were no broadcasts of Pittsburgh games when the team was on the road, but such was not the case. Instead, Rowswell, along with his assistant, Bob Prince, would re-create the action for the listening audience. From a studio located at WWSW radio station, Rowswell would get up-to-the-minute reports on the game that was being played via a Western Union relay. He and Prince would announce the game exactly as if they were in the stadium watching it being played. This system called for a great deal of imagination, as well as an array of sound effects. Taped crowd noises could be played in the background when a home run was hit or there was any other noteworthy event. When it came to the sounds of balls being hit or caught, Rowswell and Prince usually replicated the noise with props they had in the studio. Naturally, the tray of nuts, bolts, and broken glass was thrust to the floor when a home run was hit. It all worked wonderfully, and for those who were not privy to the secret of what was going on, sounded just like a broadcast from the ballpark. Bob Prince, who would go on to become the voice of the Pirates for later generations of Pittsburgh fans, was himself a colorful and distinctive announcer. He credited the time he spent with Rowswell as being the fundamental basis for his style and technique. When Rosey Rowswell passed away in 1955, a local newspaper ran an editorial that stated, "To the hundreds of thousands of district baseball fans, he was the symbol of the Pirates."[12]

CHAPTER 9

Best Player on Bad Teams

The 1950 and 1951 seasons had been terribly disappointing to everyone associated with the Pirates. Most of the enthusiasm to be found in camp when the team reported to San Bernardino for spring training in 1952 came from the surplus of young players on the roster. Why not? The majority of the youths were thrilled to be attending a Major League camp, and still optimistic over their abilities to make the grade and prove themselves worthy of being on the team. Then again, most of them had reason to be optimistic. They were trying out for one of the worst teams in the game, which only increased their chances of playing in the majors. Truth is, most of these hopefuls had more than an even chance of making the team. Branch Rickey went for his youth movement that year with careless abandon, and the roster was stocked primarily with rookies. Nine different players would be tried at third base in a season that saw 45 different players on the Pirates' roster. Bobby Del Greco and Tony Bartirome were among the youngsters to make the team. Both were Pittsburgh natives who had grown up in the Hill District, playing ball and rooting for the Pirates. Both were signed right out of high school by former Pirates great Pie Traynor, who was a scout for the team. Both almost immediately found themselves in the majors, whether they were ready for the transition or not. At 18 years old, pitchers Jim Waugh and Bill Bell were the youngest players on the team, but they had plenty of other teammates who were too young to drink or vote with whom they could hang out on road trips. Rickey's youth movement was in full swing. The thing was, youth did not necessarily mean these players were talented but merely inexperienced. It was not just that they had a lot to learn. For several, it meant that they were not, and never would be, Major League talent. In many respects, the Pirates became a minor league team in 1952. The problem was that they were still playing against teams that were stocked with Major League talent. The result was predictable.

The 1952 Pirates set a record for futility and would earn the dubious honor of being one of the worst teams in the history of the game. Posting an agonizing record of 42–112, they served as the brunt of jokes and barbs from baseball fans all over the country. Whenever anything was said to be bad, a rejoinder would be added that it was still not nearly as bad as the Pirates. Joe Garagiola, who caught 118 games for Pittsburgh that year, went so far as to proclaim, "if there was a way to lose, we would discover it. We had a lot of triple-threat men—slip, fumble, and fall. They talk about Pearl Harbor being something; they should have seen the '52 Pirates. George Metkovich, our first baseman, who had been around the big leagues, would holler at the umpires, 'For Pete's sake, grab a glove and help me out.'"[1] Ralph Kiner was not immune to seeing the humor in things. In fact, he was known as something of a prankster with the Pirates. Joe Garagiola remembered that the Pirates' trainer, Doc Jorgensen, was a frequent victim of Kiner's pranks. Once, Kiner took all of the bottles and bandages out of Jorgensen's medical kit. Later, when a player got spiked during a game, Jorgensen ran out onto the field to assist him. When he opened his kit, what he found inside was more suited to a picnic than a medical visit. Kiner had filled his bag with sandwiches.

For all appearances, if Kiner was to have any fun this season he would have to do so during spring training. In those days, it was quite common for players to be entered into home run contests before exhibition games were played. Kiner had been participating in these contests for years, since he had first emerged as a legitimate home run threat. "We staged a lot of home-run contests before exhibition games in those days in an effort to increase attendance. I don't think I ever lost one, including the contest against [Ted] Williams and the Red Sox before that '48 game. In fact, Williams finished third, behind teammate Walt Dropo." One particular contest between Kiner and Cleveland Indians slugger Luke Easter held a special place in his memory. "Now Easter was a massive man who hit awesome home runs. I had first seen him play in California and I was impressed. The rule for this contest was that I, as the visitor, was to hit 10 balls, and then he would hit 10 balls. Well, I hit nine out of 10 over the fence, including six into the upper deck. And Easter wouldn't come out to hit. I won the trophy by default, and I still have it at home. Now, of course, they give players money for their participation. In those days, you performed for the glory."²

Personal glory was one thing, and Kiner had certainly earned a great deal of that since he first donned a Pittsburgh uniform in 1946. Like most competitors, though, Kiner yearned to be on a winning club that had a real shot at post-season play. Dreams of playing in a World Series must have seemed nothing more than passing fancies. A lesser man might have pouted and felt sorry for himself, or griped and complained until he received a trade to a contending team, but that was not the sort of individual Kiner was. Instead, he continued to perform at a high level, doing the best he could, day in and day out, to try to help his team win. It was an insightful measure of the man, how he remained one of the hardest working players on the team, still taking extra batting practice and going full tilt for a team that never threatened to get out of the basement in their league. Hank Greenberg would have been proud of him. It was just the sort of class that his old mentor had displayed throughout his career, and it was obvious that Jackie Robinson's comments about class applied to Kiner the student, as well as to Greenberg the teacher.

Joe Garagiola was a catcher for the Pirates during some of the worst seasons in franchise history. His quips about how bad the 1952 team were became a regular part of his broadcasting routine after his playing days had ended.

The year could not have been worse for the team. Opening Day of 1952 started out well enough. Murry Dickson, the Pirates' 20-game-winner from the previous year, got the start on the road against the St. Louis Cardinals and pitched well. Dickson gave up three runs in seven innings of work. The Pirates staged a late-inning rally, kicked off by a seventh-inning solo home run by Kiner, but the team fell short in the 3–2 decision for its first loss of the year. Losing would become a part of the team's mantra, and regrettably, most of the losses would not be nearly as close as that opening contest. By the end of April, the Pirates' record stood at 3–11, and things went downhill from there. They went 2–12 in their next 14 games, and by the All-Star break were 21–59. When the campaign mercifully ended, on September 28, they had compiled a record of 42–112, one of the all-time worst. The Pirates finished last in the National League in runs, hits, doubles, triples, home runs, runs batted in, batting average, slugging percentage, complete games, earned run average, walks allowed, home runs allowed, fielding percentage, and errors committed.[3] The team was so bad that it finished 54.5 games out of first place and 22.5 games out of seventh place. Joe Garagiola quipped that the Pirates had finished ninth in an eight-team league.[4]

It was amazing how many different ways the Pirates came up with to lose games that season. In one contest against the Dodgers, Bobby Del Greco hit a two-out single. George Metkovich then slapped a grounder through the infield that sent Del Greco to third. With the game tied 3–3 in the bottom of the ninth, fans anticipated seeing one of the few Pirates victories that season. Gus Bell stepped to the plate and hit a line drive to center that landed safely, scoring Del Greco. Metkovich started celebrating immediately, jumping up and down between first and second base, before joining his teammates in the dugout for handshakes and pats on the back. In the meantime, Duke Snider, the Dodgers' center fielder, threw the ball in to shortstop Pee Wee Reese. Reese stepped on the bag at second and Metkovich was called out, since he had never completed the play and touched the bag. With a force out, the run didn't count, and the Pirates were called back onto the field to play extra innings. The Dodgers scored twice in the top of the tenth and won the game, 5–3. In a season of poor performance, it seemed as if the Pirates were constantly finding new ways to lose.[5]

With virtually no protection in the lineup, which included 12 rookies, Kiner had a rough start to the season. By the All-Star break, his average had dipped to .240. More importantly, he had hit only 13 home runs and driven in a mere 31 runs. He must have looked forward to attending the All-Star Game at Shibe Park in Philadelphia. It was the fifth straight year he had been selected to the team and would be the first time this season when he actually had other Major League talent around him. Hank Sauer, Stan Musial, and Enos Slaughter were the starting outfield for the National League squad in a closely contested game that was called after five innings, due to rain, the only All-Star Game called for inclement weather. Jackie Robinson started the scoring with a one-out solo home run in the bottom of the first inning. The American League mounted a rally in the top of the fourth, turning a walk and three hits into two runs to take a 2–1 lead. In the bottom of the frame, Hank Sauer stroked a two-run homer to deep left-center off pitcher Bob Lemon, to put his team back on top. Neither side scored in the fifth inning, and when the heavens opened following that frame, the umpires called the contest and awarded the victory to the National League. Kiner did not have an opportunity to play in the game, as the only National League reserve player who made it off the bench was Pee Wee Reese, who pinch-hit for the pitcher in the bottom of the third. Even so, it was a win for the National League and a rare meaningful victory for Kiner that year.

Kiner got his home run stroke back in the second half of the season, swatting 24 between the All-Star break and the end of the campaign. He also greatly improved on his runs batted in, with 56 in the second half, to finish at 87, despite a .244 batting average, the lowest of his career thus far. Once more, he led the league in walks, with 110, as opposing pitchers threw around him to challenge one of the many lesser threats in the Pittsburgh lineup. His home run surge in the second half meant that he finished the year with 37 round-trippers, good enough to tie with Hank Sauer for the National League home run crown. It was Kiner's seventh consecutive home run title, a Major League record. Babe Ruth's six consecutive titles had been thought by most to be as unapproachable as his single-season record or his career total. Kiner became the most prodigious home run hitter of his era. In fact, he still holds the record for consecutive home run titles.

Kiner's 1952 campaign is amazing when one looks at the difficulties he had to overcome to break Ruth's record. To begin with, there was the terrible team on which he played. The two Pittsburgh youngsters, Tony Bartirome and Bobby Del Greco, failed to hit over .220 that year. This would be Bartirome's only season in the majors as a player. The light-hitting infielder would have one noteworthy statistic during his single season with Pittsburgh: in 335 at-bats, he never hit into a double play. Bartirome explained, "I simply never hit the ball hard enough to allow the opposition to complete a short-to-second-to-first double killing."[6] He would return to the Pirates in 1967 as their trainer. Bartirome served in this capacity in outstanding fashion through the 1985 season.[7] Seven other players on the team with more than 40 at-bats hit under .200.[8]

One of the bright spots to emerge from the youngsters Rickey had signed was Dick Groat, an All-American basketball and baseball player from Duke. Groat played in 95 games that season, batting .284 to lead the team in average. Joe Garagiola, who caught 118 games, had the next-best batting average with a .273 mark. Kiner's .244, while the lowest of his career, was actually better than the .231 team average. To be sure, Kiner suffered from a lack of support or protection during the 1952 campaign, as attested to by the 110 walks he received. The next closest Pirate in that category was Garagiola with 50, less than half of the total Kiner had. In fact, the other seven starting position players averaged just 30 walks. This was nothing new for Kiner. It was the fifth straight year in which he was issued more than 100 walks, and the third time in the past four seasons when he led the National League. His 1947 campaign, even with Hank Greenberg in the lineup, had resulted in 98 free passes, placing him among the league leaders. The fact was that opposing pitchers didn't need to pitch to him when the game was on the line, and they didn't. With the ability of pitchers to bypass his spot in the batting order, it is truly a wonder that Kiner was able to compile the statistics he did and remain a star of the game while playing on such a bad team.

The second difficulty Ralph had to overcome in order to break Ruth's record involved Branch Rickey and the Pirates' ownership. As the greatest slugger in the game, Kiner felt that he was deserving of a salary commensurate with his accomplishments. The problem was that Rickey was in a serious rebuilding mode. He had already spent close to half a million dollars to acquire contracts of prospects, most of whom would never pan out at the Major League level, and the Pirates' coffers had run dry. They had run more than dry. Pittsburgh was operating in the red, and John Galbreath had been forced to dip into his personal finances to keep things afloat. To Rickey, who already wanted to deal the hefty salary of $65,000 Kiner was currently making to another team, an increase was out of the question. Kiner knew that Rickey was set on getting rid of him, and he resented his general manager's attitude because "I was the reason we drew tremendous crowds." What bothered him the most was the way Rickey took his campaign to eliminate Kiner to the press, spreading numerous slights and slanders about his star. "So he fed the papers a lot of lies," Kiner said. "The Pirates fans would read 'Ralph Kiner demanded that the fences be shortened and insisted that he didn't have to travel with the other players.' But I kept copies of my wires and there were no demands at all on my part. I sent them to John Galbreath because I wanted him to know the truth."[9]

Often discussed by the press, Kiner's contract difficulties seemed to substantiate a statement sports reporters loved to print. Kiner had once stated that "Cadillacs are down at the end of the bat."[10] The statement was oft repeated, usually with an added flourish or twist. One of the most repeated

Branch Rickey was considered throughout the baseball world to be one of the smartest administrators in the game. He had led both the St. Louis Cardinals and the Brooklyn Dodgers to becoming powerhouses of the National League. His time in Pittsburgh would not be so fruitful, as the Pirates became yearly cellar-dwellers. Some of the pieces he put in place would eventually pay dividends for the club, but not until after Rickey's tenure as general manager was over.

versions was "Singles hitters drive Fords, home run hitters drive Cadillacs." Kiner insisted that he never issued a slight against singles hitters, as had been quoted, but he did make the rest of the statement. Whatever the statement might have been, it was certainly true that Kiner was making one of the top salaries in the league because of his home runs.

Kiner found it impossible to negotiate a new contract with Rickey. Indeed, it was difficult for any player to negotiate a contract in those days.

> No matter who you were, you were told no one could negotiate your contract but you. My mother couldn't come in and say, "My son deserves a raise." When you went in to discuss your contract with a manager, general manager, or owner, you had to do it alone, without an agent, an attorney, or a parent. Players kept figures to themselves, but they told other players how they were treated during negotiations. At one time or another, every player confided that the owner or general manager told them, "If you don't want to accept our offer, we'll send you to the minors." Those were the words that would get every player to sign in a hurry. A team like the Dodgers had about 500 players under contract, so major leaguers understood there was a huge supply of players who could be brought up to take their places.
>
> They could shorten or end your career. They could bench you, deal you, or demote you to the minor leagues, and make sure you were never heard from again—in fact, there were many buried or banished players in the minors who had major league talent but never got to show it. The reserve clause was a lifetime contract, unless they decided to release you or trade your contract to another owner with the same powers. The deck was stacked against you.[11]

Kiner began the 1952 season without a contract. Negotiations with Rickey were contentious and unfruitful. The general manager didn't even want him on the team, much less give him a salary increase. Kiner was eventually granted permission to deal directly with John Galbreath, the team's majority owner. Galbreath and Kiner came to terms on a contract that would pay Kiner $90,000 for 1952, making him the highest paid player in the National League. Usually, player salaries were kept confidential, and few if any other players knew what their teammates were making. Kiner was a superstar, however, and as such he attracted a great deal of media attention. When his contract was finalized, reporters lost little time in publishing the details, especially his newly acquired status as the National League's top paid player. "When he read about it, "Stan Musial went to Cardinals owner, Augie Busch and said, 'I'm a better player than Kiner, so I want $91,000.' Busch did better than that and gave him $100,000, and he became the highest paid player. That's why owners didn't want their players to know anybody else's salary."[12]

The contract dispute definitely weighed on Kiner in the early portion of the season, as he fought against management to receive what he felt to be proper compensation for his services. It's never easy to concentrate on one's performance on the field when matters of salary and career are hanging in the balance. Furthermore, having to contend with Rickey's constant barbs and outright lies must have been a source of distraction for the star slugger. He had to challenge himself to play at a high level, despite the fact that the team on which he played was filled with talent unsuited for Major League competition, and he had to do so knowing that he was, in effect, playing for a team that did not want him—more to the point, a general manager who wanted to see him gone. It took a great deal of personal fortitude for Kiner not to become bitter and frustrated by the whole situation, and it is positively amazing that he was able to break Ruth's consecutive season home run record while battling against such external disturbances.

Then again, there were other situations of austerity that affected the Pirates in 1952 that while not impacting Kiner directly, nevertheless took a toll on the team as a whole. Rickey decided to save money by reducing the number of players the team took on road trips. In a cost-cutting maneuver, Rickey allowed the team to travel with only 21 players, as opposed to the 25 members of the full roster.[13] The cost cutting had become necessary because the Pirates had hit rough times, due to Rickey's spending and a lack of revenue from fan attendance. Gate receipts were more than 30 percent below the budgeted amount, as only 686,673 fans came through the turnstiles at Forbes Field that year, down nearly 300,000 from the previous season. The bottom line was that the Pirates finished the 1952 season with a loss to the franchise of some $800,000.[14] With financial difficulty all around him, it is probable that Kiner also pressed a bit to prove that he was worth the hefty salary he was receiving, as well as to provide some reason for fans to come out to the park to watch the team.

Then there was the quite serious matter of Kiner receiving death threats that would rattle anyone's concentration and focus. He received two such threats that season, one of them from a man who tried a hand at extortion by demanding that Kiner place $6,200 under the seat of a cab and have that cab drive to a location in Ambridge, Pennsylvania, a town in Beaver County, where the extortionist would then collect the funds. Kiner refused to comply and instead contacted the authorities, who launched an investigation. The perpetrator was never discovered, but, for Kiner's safety, a guard was assigned to him for a period of time.[15] The threats were in themselves unsettling, but the constant reminder of them in the person of a police guard must have caused Kiner to wonder about the fringe element of society that was jealous of his fame, financial status, or popularity.

Kiner described how unsettling the incident was, not just to him, but to all of his teammates. "We played the game during which I was supposed to get shot. It was on or around the Fourth of July, and people kept setting off firecrackers that made everybody jump. Nobody would sit next to me on the bench. The game ended, and, fortunately, nothing happened. As I came off the field, George [Metkovich], who had played next to me in center field, said, 'Boy, I'm glad that game is over.' I said, 'Gee, George, it was nice of you to worry about me.'" Metkovich quickly informed Kiner that he had not been worried about him. He asked Kiner what number he wore, to which Kiner responded, "4." Metkovich then reminded Kiner that he wore 44. "What if the guy had double vision?" Metkovich asked, implying that he was fearing for his own life if an assailant with poor vision attempted to carry out the threat that had been made on Kiner's life.[16] Regardless of whatever internal conflicts the incidents may have caused, Kiner continued to be the affable, approachable player he had always been, and he refused to allow them to dissuade him from treating people with the kindness and regard he had always shown.

Lastly, there was the matter of Kiner's health. At 29 years old, he should have been in the prime of his life and entering what should have been the most productive years of his career. That was not the case. He was already beginning to experience nagging back pain that would affect not only his swing, but also his play in the field. It was ironic that Kiner should be subjected to a chronic pain such as this. He had been far ahead of his time with his off-season routine of exercise and conditioning, and he maintained himself in top physical condition at all times. This was out of the norm for most players of the era, who left themselves susceptible to just the sort of situation Kiner now found himself in, a strain to his back. Kiner was faced with the prospect of playing through the pain and gritting it out on the field and in the batter's box.

Health issues that may have sidelined other players did not keep Kiner out of the lineup, as he played in 149 games that season. The pain would become so severe that he had to get injections in his back prior to games, but he worked through it with a competitive spirit born of his love for the game. What's more, he never used his condition as an excuse for performance. He didn't even think of making statements about how his aching back was affecting his game, he just went out onto the diamond every day and performed to the best of his ability. His best in 1952 was good enough to earn him his seventh straight home run title and set a record that might never be broken. Babe Ruth's single season and career home run marks have fallen by the wayside, eclipsed by Roger Maris and Hank Aaron. Their records, in turn, have been broken by other players. Barry Bonds now holds both records, though he is considered a usurper of the crown by many, due to allegations of the usage of performance enhancing drugs. Maris's single season home run record has been broken several times, mostly by players associated with performance enhancing drugs. But Kiner had surpassed Ruth with a record that remains unchallenged. Mike Schmidt claimed the title three straight times, from 1974–1976, and Mark McGwire hoisted the crown four consecutive years, from 1996–1999, but no one has yet offered a serious challenge to the seven straight seasons in which Ralph Kiner reigned as the premier slugger in the game.

There was no other way to describe the Pirates' 1952 season than as a disaster. Their dismal record of 42–112 has been the brunt of numerous jokes, a great many of them coming from the Pirates themselves. Joe Garagiola later recounted that "When we had a rain-out we had a victory dance." Of course, there were also members of the team who had a hard time finding anything of humor in the antics performed on the field. Manager Billy Meyer was one of these, but even a tirade he delivered in the locker room assumed a ludicrous aspect. Screaming at his players over their lackluster performance, Meyer yelled, "You clowns can go on *What's My Line* in full uniforms and stump the panel." Branch Rickey's terse commentary on the 1952 season probably sums it up best: "We finished last—on merit."[17]

9: Best Player on Bad Teams

The year had been hard on everybody associated with the Pirates. Honus Wagner, looked around in spring training and saw all of the youngsters Rickey had signed to the team. It was obvious to the greatest Pirate of them all that the squad would not be able to compete. When Rickey brought Clyde Sukeforth into the fold, Wagner started to have doubts about his further affiliation with the team. Sukeforth had been a scout for Rickey with the Dodgers. In fact, it was Sukeforth who had scouted Jackie Robinson for Rickey. Wagner felt that the time had come to retire from baseball. In recognition of his many contributions to the team, the Pirates retired Wagner's number and presented him with a lifetime pass to Forbes Field.[18]

Billy Meyer also decided that his connection with the Pirates should conclude after the 1952 campaign. The winner of the 1948 National League "Manager of the Year" award turned in his resignation on September 27, with two games remaining in the season. Meyer stated that he just couldn't stand being around the team any longer. He would have been more than willing to stick around if he could have seen any future promise in the moves Rickey had made, but to him, the Pirates were hopeless and would remain so for some time to come. Meyer was retained by the team as a scout and troubleshooter. In the latter capacity, it was certain that he would have a full work itinerary, for the Pirates definitely had more than their fair share of trouble with which to contend.

Meyer's resignation left Kiner with one less friend in camp. His manager had always been one of his staunchest supporters and had tried to shield him from Rickey's maneuvers. With Meyer gone, Kiner would lose his supportive advocate in all future dealings with Rickey and team ownership. It was just one more problem he would have to contend with as he prepared for his eighth season with the Pirates.

Kiner wasn't the only member of the family vying for a championship in 1952. His wife, Nancy, had won the National Indoor Singles title in 1950 and 1951 and was ranked as the fourth-best female player in the world. She had also been part of the U.S. women's team that won the Wightman Cup from the British in 1951, playing on the doubles team. Along with Patricia Todd, she had reached the finals of the U.S. doubles competition, though the pair was defeated in straight sets by the duo of

Shirley Fry and Doris Hart. In 1952, she was preparing to defend her singles title and possibly win one of the major events at Forest Hills or Wimbledon.

Kiner was involved in Nancy's career and supported her any way he could. "Nancy is the one who has made the real sacrifices in our marriage," he said. "She insists on following me when the team is on the road. As a result she can't take time out to practice, or to play in the number of tournaments she needs to keep her fine competitive edge. But maybe next season will be different. I think I'd like to give her at least one more full season to tennis. Maybe then she'll win that big one." For her part, Nancy seemed more concerned with his career than with her own. "I just want Ralph to hit home runs. One champion in the family is enough for me."[19] Nancy successfully defended her indoor singles title in 1952, but failed to win any of the major events as she and Ralph had hoped. She effectively retired from the pro circuit following that season to devote herself to domestic life and starting a family. In 1952, the Kiners boasted a three-time singles champion and a seven-time home run champ. Children's pictures with which to adorn the walls were still in the future. For the time being, what the pair needed most was a large shelf to display all of the trophies and awards they had won.

CHAPTER 10

Traded to the Cubs

Branch Rickey continued to make moves in the off-season after the disastrous 1952 campaign. One of the most newsworthy was when he signed two young infielders. Neither player had any Major League experience, but that is not what made their signing noteworthy. They were Johnny and Eddie O'Brien, twin brothers from South Amboy, New Jersey, who had both played for Seattle University. Rickey planned to have the pair anchor his infield, with Johnny at second base and Eddie at short. One of the many problems with Rickey's plan was that the brothers were signed on March 19, after the team had already reported to spring training. When the twins reported to Havana, Cuba, the site of that year's pre-season training, they were already behind the rest of the players in camp and had an abbreviated period of time in which to prepare for the upcoming season. Nevertheless, the pair were part of Rickey's latest attempt to catch lightning in a bottle, and he was committed to making them an integral part of the team. Johnny led the brothers with a .247 batting average, while Eddie batted .238, with both of them appearing in 89 games in 1953. All things considered, it wasn't a bad start for young players with no minor league experience. Where their stats really fell off was in run production. The pair scored a combined 49 times, and batted in only 36 runs. They also hit only two home runs, both by Johnny. It was not the sort of protection Kiner needed in a lineup to keep opposing pitchers honest and throwing him strikes.

Kiner had to go through another contract negotiation for the 1953 season, and this time he was at the mercy of Rickey. The general manager had to admit that Kiner was still the reigning home run king of the league, but the drop-off in his other statistics the previous season could be used against him. Rickey felt that he held all the cards when he offered

Kiner a contract calling for a significant reduction of his 1952 salary. "Why do I get a cut?" the usually mild-mannered Kiner demanded. "I led the league last year in home runs." Rickey looked Kiner in the eye and asked, "Where did we finish last year?" Kiner was on the defensive. "In last place, Mr. Rickey," he answered. "Hmmmmm," Rickey pondered, "well, let me tell you something, son, we could have finished last without you."[1] Facts were facts. Kiner's 37 home runs had done nothing to elevate the play of a team as bad as the Pirates. Without him, they might have lost a few more games, but with a 42–112 record, what difference would that make? Kiner had little choice; it was either sign for a lower salary or find himself out of baseball. He eventually signed for $75,000, significantly less than he had made the year before, but still one of the top salaries in the league. It was not the sort of money a star of his magnitude might have commanded if he were playing for another team, but this was the Pirates, a team in deep financial trouble, and he was dealing with a general manager who wanted to get rid of him. Kiner would be easier to trade if his salary was a bit less cumbersome.

Chuck Connors, the former Chicago Cub turned Hollywood actor, made an observation about Branch Rickey: "It's easy to figure out Mr. Rickey's thinking about contracts. He had both players and money—and just didn't like to see the two of them mix"[2]

The Pirates' new manager for the 1953 campaign was Fred Haney, who came over from the minor leagues. Haney did have Major League managerial experience, having served as the skipper of the St. Louis Browns from 1939 through part of the 1941 season. His first year with the Browns had been nearly as catastrophic as the season Pittsburgh had just concluded, as the team finished with a record of 43–111, just one game better than the Pirates. A 67–87 finish in 1940 was a marked improvement, but only good enough for a 6th-place finish. The Browns were 15–29 in 1941 when a change was made, and Haney was replaced as manager. From there, he went to the minors. He piloted the Hollywood Stars to a pennant in 1949, winning for himself the "Minor League Manager of the Year" Award and earning the sobriquet among the press as "Frederick the Great."[3] In an ironic way, Haney was a perfect fit for the Pirates. He had a history of losing baseball in the majors, and he was used to working with young, minor league players. Taking over as manager of the Pirates would give him the opportunity to continue doing both.

There were plenty of youngsters on the Pirates' roster for Haney to work with. The most tender of years was Nick Koback, a 17-year-old catcher and the latest of Rickey's potential stars. Koback would play in only 16 games for the Pirates. In 33 at-bats, he managed only four hits for a .121 average. His one claim to fame was catching a complete game shutout thrown by Murry Dickson. Another youngster was Vic Janowicz, a catcher and third baseman the Pirates signed straight out of Ohio State University. Janowicz had been an All-American halfback while in college and had won the prestigious Heisman Trophy in 1950. Football was his best sport, but things being as they were in 1953, he could make more money by signing a baseball contract. Janowicz played 42 games in 1953 and hit .252, not too bad for a player who had gone straight from college to the majors. Things took a turn for the worse the following year. In 1954, he played in 41 games, hitting only .151. That was it. Janowicz was out of baseball. Another of Rickey's experiments had ended in failure. For Janowicz, it was not the end of a professional sports career. He signed with the Washington Redskins late in the 1954 season and became their starting halfback in 1955. Tragically, he was involved in an automobile accident in 1956 that left him partially paralyzed.[4]

Kiner would not have a great deal of time to become familiar with these rookies, or with any of the other new faces on the Pirates' roster. Rickey was working in the background trying to make a deal to trade his only star player. With Dick Groat away in the army, Kiner was one of the few legitimate Major League players on the team. He started the season slowly. By the end of April, he had hit only two home runs, and was batting .250. By the end of May, he had raised his average to .271 and had added five more home runs to his total. Little did he know it, but his time with the Pirates was coming to a close. On June 4, Pirates public-address announcer Art McKennan shocked the 3,182 fans at Forbes Field with the pre-game news that Kiner had been traded to the Chicago Cubs, the team Pittsburgh was about to play. McKennan informed the sparse crowd that Kiner, along with Joe Garagiola, Howie Pollet, and George Metkovich, had been traded for Toby Atwell, Bob Schultz, Preston Ward, George Freese, Bob Addis, and Gene Hermanski, plus $150,000 to help defray the expenses of the team. Pirates fans refused to believe that Pittsburgh would trade their hard-hitting hero, and it was not until Kiner stepped out of the visitors' dugout wearing a Cubs uniform that the reality of the situation finally sank in. After so many award-winning seasons in Pittsburgh, Kiner had been sent packing. He would leave town with 301 home runs to his credit, by far the most in franchise history. The most prolific home run-hitting Pirate to date would be shifting his home base from Forbes Field to Wrigley Field. The day after Kiner's trade was announced, the Pirates tried to tear down the shortened left field fence that had become affectionately known as Kiner's Korner. National League officials prohibited them from doing so, ordering the wall to remain through the end of the season.[5]

Rickey had finally gotten his wish. He had unloaded Kiner and his hefty salary, and could sail ahead full steam on his rebuilding plan for the Pirates. The team compiled another miserable record in 1953, ending the season at 50–104, firmly in last place, and 55 games behind the front-running Brooklyn Dodgers. The team finished in last place in each of the next two seasons. Rickey retired in 1955 due to health problems. His five-year plan to turn around the Pirates had been a resounding failure. But he had planted the seeds that would eventually flower into a championship team. Players he signed, like Dick Groat, Bob Friend, and Vernon Law, would play a prominent role in the resurgence of the Pirates, as would another young player put under contract during Rickey's tenure: Roberto Clemente. Rickey's estimate of Pittsburgh's revitalization would be off by five years. The Pirates would indeed become a World Series championship team, just as he had predicted, but it would take until the 1960 campaign.

For Kiner, the change of venue meant that he would be playing alongside a home run champion from the previous year for the second time in his career. In 1947, he had been teammates with Hank Greenberg, the 1946 American League champ. This time around, he would patrol the outfield with Hank Sauer, with whom he had tied for the National League home run crown in 1952. The Cubs, who had finished fifth in the league in 1952, hoped that Kiner's long-ball swing might complement Sauer and help place the team in contention for a pennant.

Kiner traded in the fictitious spirits from the *Angels in the Outfield*

10: Traded to the Cubs

Kiner with Hank Sauer (right) after he had been traded to the Chicago Cubs. Management had hoped that the two sluggers would be able to propel the Cubs into contention in 1953, but both players dealt with injuries during their time together, and the anticipated power production did not materialize.

movie that had been filmed at Forbes Field for the oft-reported real ghosts that haunted Wrigley Field in Chicago. Fly balls hit into the ivy-covered walls of Wrigley's outfield, never to be recovered again, were already part of the Cubs' legend when Kiner joined the team. So was Charlie Grimm, a former manager of the team in the 1930s and 1940s, whose spirit was said to haunt the stadium, whispering names, turning on lights, and ringing the bullpen phone.[6] Among the Cubs' ghosts and ghost hunters, there would be no Janet Leigh to capture Kiner's attention. There would be only baseball and the need to acclimate to a new team and new surroundings.

The 1953 Chicago Cubs could definitely use Kiner's bat. Manager Phil Cavarretta's squad was only slightly better than the Pirates, and though

Kiner's home run swing would not make them contenders, it would help to keep them out of the cellar. The players having the best year that season included first baseman Dee Fondy, whose .309 batting average paced the team. He had the best season of his eight-year career in 1953, swatting 18 home runs and driving in 78 runs. Frank Baumholtz, who played outfield with Kiner and Sauer, also had his best year with the Cubs, batting just below Fondy at a .306 pace. The remainder of the position players were adequate or better at the plate, with shortstop Roy Smalley having the lowest batting average at .249. Hank Sauer was having an off-year, hitting .263 and belting just 19 home runs, about half the total he amassed in 1952, and far less than the 41 he would hit in 1954. Sauer dealt with nagging injuries that year and played only 108 games. Third baseman Randy Jackson provided some additional punch in the Chicago lineup, hitting 19 home runs and batting a solid .285. Overall, it wasn't a bad team at the plate. That was not where the Cubs needed major help. Their deficiency was in the pitching department, where they ranked just above the lowly Pirates. The only two pitchers on the Cubs' staff with winning records were Turk Lown and Jim Willis, and their combined record was 10–8. The rest of the staff posted a 55–81 mark. The team's 4.79 earned run average was next to worst in the National League.

Kiner had a solid season in Chicago, hitting .283 while slugging 28 home runs and driving in 87 runs. Combined with his totals in Pittsburgh, he hit 35 home runs in 1953, his lowest total since his rookie season. Though it was just two short of the number he hit in 1952, it was not good enough to earn him another home run crown. For the first time since 1946, the National League would have a new long-ball champion. Eddie Mathews of the Milwaukee Braves won the crown with 47 homers. Kiner finished fifth in the league, behind Duke Snider's 42, Roy Campanella's 41, and Ted Kluszewski's 40, but he was still in seventh place among all Major League hitters. Though Kiner's back was giving him ever-increasing pain and discomfort, he played in all 117 games after being traded to the Cubs. A deep-rooted work ethic, along with an intense love of the game, kept him in the lineup when other players might have opted to take it easy and try to regain some of their strength and agility. For Kiner, his place was on the field, doing whatever he could to help the team win.

10: Traded to the Cubs

The acquisition of Kiner did little to help the Cubs' outfield performance. Sauer was not particularly fleet-footed as a fielder, and Kiner was not known for his speed or fielding acumen. Manager Cavarretta moved Sauer to right field to open a position in left for Kiner, and Frank Baumholtz was slotted to patrol center. Sauer protested that his arm was not strong enough to play right, but Cavarretta told him it was still stronger than Kiner's. This meant that Baumholtz got plenty of work, covering a great deal of the outfield between the lines. Opposing hitters took liberties running the bases against the outfielders' less-than-average arms and limited range. Chicago fans began making comparisons of Baumholtz to Willie Mays, not because of his speed or fielding abilities, but because he was forced to cover so much ground in the outfield. Though the lack of speed and throwing ability was a big concern to the Cubs, fans and sportswriters soon pounced on the deficit with exaggerated comments and claims. The quips and jibes concerning their lack of out-fielding prowess led some to say that they were "so slow they were known as the Quicksand Kids."[7]

One of the highlights of the year for both Ralph Kiner and Nancy was the birth of their first child: Ralph Michael Kiner, who became commonly known as Mike. The boy followed in his father's footsteps, playing baseball as an outfielder and catcher. After attending UCLA, he got a brief tryout with the Wausau Mets, a farm team of the New York Mets. The young Kiner played in only 25 games in the 1975 season, batting .275. Unlike his famous father, Mike never made it to the Major Leagues. In fact, his 1975 season with the Wausau Mets was his only year in professional baseball.

The couple's second child, Scott McPherran Kiner, was born a couple of years later. Scott would not become a professional baseball player. Tennis was his game, just like his mother. He turned professional for a while but wasn't quite tour material. Though not a baseball player, he would still follow in his father's footsteps in another way. Scott went into the broadcasting field, becoming a sports reporter in the 1970s, and later provided color commentary for ESPN. After running a nationally syndicated radio company, he founded Kiner Communications, an advertising and marketing firm based in Palm Desert, California.

The third child born to Ralph and Nancy Kiner was a daughter,

Kathryn Chaffee Kiner, who was affectionately nicknamed K. C. Ralph remembered that K. C. "may have been the best athlete of all, but her interest in sports never equaled her talent. When I joined the Mets Casey Stengel thought we named her after him and I never told him the truth. Every year, when she was young, we took a picture of her with Stengel. He would make a face and she would give a gap-toothed grin. Those pictures are family treasures now that she's no longer a little girl."[8]

In 1954, Kiner reported to Cubs spring training at Rendezvous Park in Mesa, Arizona, his first spring training with Chicago. He hoped to start the new season off right by bonding with his teammates during the more relaxed and jovial spring workouts. As always, there were some new faces in camp, but one of them stood out above the rest. He was a power-hitting shortstop the club had signed as an amateur free agent the previous year, Ernie Banks. Banks had gotten a brief call-up in 1953, playing in ten games and getting 35 at-bats. He had made the most of this opportunity, batting .314 and clubbing two home runs. The team liked his talent and thought he had the potential to become a mainstay in their infield, so he was slated to start the season as their regular shortstop. Banks would more than justify the assessment team management had made of him, playing for the Cubs for 19 seasons in a Hall of Fame career that saw him hit 512 home runs.

Stan Hack was the new manager of the Cubs, replacing Phil Cavarretta, whose three seasons at the helm for Chicago had yielded no better than a fifth-place finish. Hack was a well-liked and respected figure in Chicago. He broke in the with the Cubs in 1932 and for the next 16 years played third base in an All-Star career. Hack quickly assumed the mantle from Pie Traynor as the premier third baseman in the league. He hit .301 for his career and appeared in four World Series for the Cubs. A smart and experienced player, Hack's debut as a manager came in 1954. Fans hoped that he could infuse the team with the same sort of competitive spirit he had shown when he was on the diamond.

Hack would have a good nucleus to work with, at least so far as the position players were concerned. Dee Fondy played first, Gene Baker was on second, Randy Jackson was the third baseman, and Ernie Banks rounded out the infield. Kiner, Hank Sauer, and Frank Baumholtz would again patrol the outfield, and Joe Garagiola and Walker Cooper did the

10: Traded to the Cubs

majority of the catching. These players combined for a .283 batting average in 1954 with potent power, swatting 139 home runs, paced by Sauer's 41 yard-clearing drives. Banks had a breakout season, hitting .275 with 19 home runs. Randy Jackson hit .273 and turned in 19 home runs himself. Kiner's batting average increased dramatically from the previous season, and he finished with a .285 mark. His home run production was reduced, due to the increasing pain in his back, but he still managed to clout 22 round-trippers, the lowest of his career. His 73 runs batted in were also a low mark in his nine-year career, but it was good enough for third-best on the team.

Indeed, Hack's lineup presented a fearsome challenge to opposing pitching staffs, but offense was not the problem. Pitching was once more the deficient area for the Cubs. The Chicago staff turned in another subpar year in 1954, finishing near the bottom in all pitching stats. Jim Davis was the most effective pitcher on the staff with a record on 11–7, the only winning record on the team. (Brosnan did have a 1–0 record on the mound, so Davis, in strict fact, didn't have the only winning record, but the only one among regular pitchers.) Paul Minner was next with an 11–11 record. The rest of the staff combined for a dismal 42–72 record. The end result was a 64–90 record and another seventh-place finish for Hack's squad, 33 games behind the first-place New York Giants. Pittsburgh occupied the cellar in the league once more, 11 games behind the Cubs. The Cubs were a bad team, and Chicago was lucky that the Pirates were horrible enough to prevent them from being the cellar dwellers of the National League. Kiner had improved his status slightly by being traded from the Pirates to the Cubs, but the difference amounted to going from one last-place team to another.

Then again, maybe the season the Cubs had could not be attributed to the team or its manager. Maybe there really was something to the curse that had been heaped upon the hapless heads of the franchise and its members. Back in 1945, William Sianis, better known as "Billy Goat" Sianis, attended a game of the World Series with his pet goat and mascot, Murphy. Sianis owned the Billy Goat Tavern, and Murphy was his constant companion, even when it came to seeing his beloved Cubs compete against the Detroit Tigers in the fall classic. Sianis brought Murphy to Wrigley Field on a leash and paid for two tickets to gain admittance to the game. At some point, he and Murphy even made an appearance on the field, where the goat was paraded back and forth wearing a blanket that proclaimed "We Got Detroit's Goat." The fans loved it, and Murphy was an instant sensation. Sianis and his pet were applauded wildly. Cubs owner P. K. Wrigley was not nearly as amused by Sianis and his goat as were the rest of the fans in the stands. He ordered security to expel the goat from the stadium when it started to rain, saying "The goat stinks." Sianis vowed retribution and placed a curse on the Cubs, saying the team would never win another world championship. When Chicago fell to Detroit in the Series, he sent a note to Wrigley that simply said, "Who stinks now?" Come to think of it, maybe there really is something to that curse. The Cubs are without a World Series crown to this day, and it's been 70 years since Sianis placed the hex upon them.

Descendants of both Sianis and Murphy have attempted to lift the curse, but to no avail.[9]

For the second year in a row, Kiner was omitted from selection to the 1954 All-Star Game. During this period, players selected to the mid-Summer classic were rated on the merits of the current season they were having, not on their overall career body of work, as has become the case in recent decades. The truth was that Kiner's season was not superior to many of the other outfielders in the National League in 1954. At 31 years of age, he was already past his prime because of his chronic back injury, and at the time when most players are still at their peak of performance, his was in a state of decline. Bob Talbot, the Cubs player who split time in center field with Frank Baumholtz in 1954, remembered, "I knew he was hurting, but Ralph never made excuses. Actually, he was a good teammate and nothing like the image a lot of folks had about him. I found him a very generous man who wanted to win like the rest of us. Maybe a little more, since he was the highest paid player on the Cubs. I think that fact embarrassed him. He once told me, 'If I had it to do over again, I'd work more on my defense and base running.' But home runs were his game. He had the perfect home-run swing. It was a work of art."[10] But that "work of art" was now hampered by a back that would not allow him to swing freely, without agonizing pain, which became so intense that he was forced to get regular shots of painkiller in his back before games. In an era far removed from growth hormones or perform-

10: Traded to the Cubs

ance enhancement drugs, he got injections not to improve his play, but to allow him to play at all. His personal pride and competitive spirit could only take him so far. He now needed the temporary relief of the injections in order to take the field. Surgery was an option, but it was one that he wanted to forestall as long as possible. Medical science and techniques in the 1950s were not what they are today, and back surgery was a serious and tricky enterprise with no guarantee of positive results. Should Kiner elect to have the operation, doctors told him that he had only a 50 percent chance that his back could be restored to its previous strength. Chances were just as good that the surgery would produce no positive benefits, and it could actually worsen his condition. He faced some monumental decisions at the conclusion of the 1954 season. The Cubs faced some decisions of their own at the end of the season, and one of them would involve Kiner.

The one-two punch that Cubs management had dreamed of when they made the trade to bring Kiner to Chicago never materialized. Sauer was hampered and sidelined with a broken finger in 1953 that seriously reduced his output. When Sauer returned to form in 1954 and belted 41 home runs, Kiner could no longer post the lofty totals that had so defined his career to date. The Cubs would have to look to another player to provide the additional pop they desired in their lineup. Luckily for them, that player was already wearing a Cubs uniform. In 1955, Ernie Banks would emerge as the next great Cubs power hitter, swatting 44 home runs to finish third for the MVP Award.

The esteem with which Kiner had been held by other players in the National League, as well as his reputation for being an upstanding, responsible man, had led to his selection as the National League's player representative in negotiations with the owners. Allie Reynolds, the star pitcher for the Yankees, had been selected as his counterpart by American League players. Kiner didn't recall being elected to the position. "We were the player reps for our teams, but I don't know how either of us got the jobs as chief negotiators. We didn't step forward, but all the other reps stepped back and we got left out there. One reason they wanted us is that we didn't worry that we were putting our careers in jeopardy when doing battle with the owners. Also, because we were stars, the media was more inclined to write about us and bring attention to our fight. *The Sporting News* made us their cover boys for one issue."[11]

Kiner and Reynolds hired John Norman Lewis, an attorney, to provide legal advice for the players. The main issue was the players' pension plan, which was about to expire. It was up to Kiner and Reynolds to get an extension for the plan and, if possible, to enhance it. They also sought to increase the minimum player salary, which at that time was $5,000 a year.

The owners had selected an executive committee to deal with the players, headed by Walter O'Malley, the majority owner of the Brooklyn Dodgers. Also on the committee were Hank Greenberg and John Galbreath, both well-known and friendly to Kiner. They also had retained the services of an attorney to counsel them in the negotiations. Kiner remembered, "We had packed our suits and ties for our four or five days in Georgia," which is where the talks were being held,

> "But we were such bad business men that we didn't even carry briefcases for show. It was obvious that we needed legal help in the negotiations, so Allie contacted the attorney J. Norman Lewis in New York and told me that Lewis wanted to represent us. I told him it was OK with me. We walked in with Lewis and O'Malley said we couldn't have him. We said, 'You have attorneys representing you, why can't we?' And he said, 'It isn't going to be that way.' So we walked out, which was the closest we got to being militant. There was something un-American about not being allowed to have our lawyer there while a lawyer sat with the owners. We were angry and felt our competitive juices flowing. So now we were at an impasse and were afraid of losing the pension plan entirely. That was a real possibility. We were helped by the media; they played both sides as they always do, and of course there were some writers who accused us of being greedy. But the fact that the players were so underpaid pushed several influential newspapers toward our side, as did O'Malley's refusal to let us have a lawyer. The wave of bad publicity and rumblings among players convinced O'Malley that he had to have good-faith negotiations with us and our lawyer. For our part, Allie had to argue that the hiring of Lewis was not the first step in the formation of a union. He also made sure the owners didn't feel they had lost control or they wouldn't have accepted changes."[12]

The objectives for Kiner and Reynolds were to attain a continuation of the pension plan and to get the amounts being paid increased. Currently, players with five years served in the majors were receiving a $50-a-month pension. Ten-year veterans were getting $100 a month. The players reps sought to increase that to $100 for five year vets and $150 for those who had played ten years or more. Reynolds was also passionate about getting a raise in the minimum salary from $5,000 to $8,000

10: Traded to the Cubs

a year. He argued that most players were forced to maintain two households, one of them in the city where they played, where housing costs were very high. They also pressed for 66 percent of the revenues from television broadcasts of games, including the World Series and All-Star Game. That was the amount the players were then receiving from radio broadcasts.

> When Greenberg and Galbreath took back our requests to the owners, they had to put up a fight. They did it successfully because Hank convinced them that our terms were reasonable. The raise in the amount of monthly checks to retired players was increased to the numbers we wanted. However, there were compromises on the other major issues. The raise in the minimum from $5,000 to $8,000 was rejected, but if a player stayed with his team for a month he'd get $6,000. We got 60 percent of the revenue for TV and radio broadcasts.

Kiner thought that it "was a big concession from owners who wanted to give us nothing and probably could have gotten away with it."[13] In their dealings with the owners, Reynolds had made some of his best pitches, and Kiner had hit a long bomb, on behalf of the other players they represented. More years passed before the Major League Baseball Players' Association was formed, as a formal union to represent the players, but Kiner and Reynolds had taken great steps toward gaining more equitable compensation for their peers.

Chapter 11

Last Stand with the Indians

The Cleveland Indians won the American League pennant in 1954, beating out the Yankees for the top spot by eight games. The Tribe set an American League record for wins that year, compiling a mark of 111–43. For the first time in six years, someone other than the Yankees would represent the American League in the fall classic. They were a great team, boasting star players like Bobby Avila, Al Rosen, Larry Doby, Jim Hegan, and Vic Wertz. With a team batting average of .262 and 156 home runs, they presented an imposing lineup for opposing pitchers. Avila paced the team with a .341 batting average, best in the league. Doby provided much of the power punch for the Indians, stroking 32 home runs and driving in 126 runs, both league highs. It was the most productive season Doby had turned in during his eight years with the club. Doby held the distinction of being the first black player in the American League, following Jackie Robinson into the majors less than three months after Robinson debuted with the Dodgers. Though Robinson got most of the headlines, Doby dealt with the same prejudice and hardships in breaking the color barrier. Al Rosen, Doby's teammate from 1947–1955, thought he had it even tougher than Robinson.

> This is not to denigrate Jackie Robinson, but Jackie was a college educated man who had been an officer in the service and who played at the Triple-A level. Jackie was brought in by Branch Rickey specifically to be the first black player in major league baseball. Larry Doby came up as a second baseman who didn't have time to get his full college education, and who was forced to play a different position in his first major league season. I think, because of those circumstances, he had a more difficult time than Jackie Robinson. I don't think he has gotten the credit he deserves. I saw Larry get knocked down on four straight pitches by Dizzy Trout [of the Detroit Tigers], but Larry just got up, brushed himself off and walked to first base. I've always admired him.[1]

The year 1954 marked Doby's 6th straight season being selected as an All-Star, and he finished second behind Yogi Berra for the American

League MVP honors. Bobby Avila, his teammate, finished third in the voting.

The Indians' pitching staff was it's strongest unit, however. Boasting future Hall of Fame members Bob Feller, Early Wynn, Bob Lemon, and Hal Newhauser, it also got strong performances from Mike Garcia, Don Mossi and Art Houtteman. Cleveland starters amassed a record of 93–36. The staff boasted a league best 2.78 earned run average, as well as leading in complete games, innings pitched, fewest hits, fewest runs, and fewest walks allowed. It was an outstanding unit, led by Bob Lemon, whose 23 wins tied Wynn for tops in the league, earning him 5th place in the MVP voting.

This powerhouse lineup had breezed through the American League in 1954 and seemed destined to bring a World Series crown back to Cleveland. But the New York Giants had other plans. The Giants, led by manager Leo Durocher, had a couple of stars of their own, including Monte Irvin, Don Mueller, Al Dark, Hoyt Wilhelm and a power-hitting speedster in center field named Willie Mays. The Giants' pitching staff had a pretty good season themselves in 1954. Their staff earned run average of 3.09 led the National League. Starters Johnny Antonelli and Ruben Gomez posted ERAs of 2.30 and 2.88, respectively. One of the strengths of the Giants' pitching staff, however, was their bullpen. Hoyt Wilhelm had a superb year, posting an ERA of 2.10, and Marv Grissom was right behind him with an average of 2.35.

The Giants shocked the Indians by sweeping the Tribe in four straight games. The much-vaunted Cleveland pitching did not hold up against the New York bats, while the Giants' pitchers looked like they, and not Cleveland, had been the best pitching staff in the majors. In short, the Giants were hot and the Indians went into a slump at precisely the wrong time. Game One, at the Polo Grounds in New York, was an absolute thriller, pitting Bob Lemon against Sal Maglie. The game was tied 2–2 after nine innings, and the Giants won it with three runs in the bottom of the tenth.

The most notable thing about the game was not the pitching, but an unbelievable catch that was made in deep center field. In the top of the eighth inning, with the score tied, the first two Indians reached base on a walk and an infield single. Vic Wertz strode to the plate. He had already accounted for three of Cleveland's hits and had whacked the ball hard in every at-bat. Leo Durocher decided it was time to make a change on the mound, so he brought in southpaw Don Liddle to face Wertz. Liddle quickly got ahead in the count, and with one ball and two strikes on Wertz, he threw a fastball that stayed out over the plate. Wertz connected and drove a hard line drive just to the right of second base that was carrying to the deepest part of the Polo Grounds. The baserunners started to run but Larry Doby, who was on second, decided to go back and tag up, just in case a miracle catch was made. Doby felt that even if the center fielder caught the ball, the distance, combined with his momentum running full-tilt away from the infield, would be enough that he would still be able to score from second. But the center fielder was Willie Mays. Jack Brickhouse, who was announcing the game for NBC, said: "There's a long drive … way back at center field … way back, way back, it is a—Oh, my! Caught by Willie Mays! Willie Mays just brought this crowd to its feet with a catch which must have been an optical illusion to a lot of people. Boy!" Mays had made one of the most thrilling catches in the history of the game, but he wasn't done yet. As baseball writer Arnold Hano described it, Mays whirled and threw "like some olden statue of a Greek javelin hurler, his hat twisted away to the left as his right arm swept out and around." Hano noted it was "the throw of a giant, the throw of a howitzer made human, arriving at second base … just as Doby was pulling into third and as Rosen was scampering back to first."[2]

The Giants managed to get out of the inning without surrendering a run and won the game in the tenth. That set the tone for the rest of the Series. Game Two was a close contest, with the Giants eventually winning, 3–1. In Games Three and Four, played in front of the Cleveland fans, the Giants took early leads and easily held off any Indians rallies to sweep the Series in the Indians' home park.

Indians ownership and management were shattered by the outcome of the Series. After finishing as also-rans to the Yankees for several years, they had finally bested the Bronx Bombers and earned their ticket to the World Series. The Yankees were the defending champions of the last five World Series, and it stood to reason with the Cleveland brass that if their team had finally topped the best team in baseball, they would be a sure bet to win the Series. The Giants' victory convinced Indians management that they still had some work to do in adjusting their roster if they wanted to bring a title to Cleveland.

Hank Greenberg was serving as general manager of the Indians, and one of the things he looked to improve on the team was its power potential. He didn't have to look any further than his old protégé, Ralph Kiner. Post-season talks with the Cubs revealed that they were open to dealing Kiner, and Greenberg began negotiating in earnest to make a deal. The Cubs agreed to sell his contract for a sum variously reported between $60,000 and $150,000, and received Cleveland pitcher Sam Jones and minor league prospect Gale Wade, to sweeten the deal. Kiner would once more be on the same team with his pal, Greenberg, even if he would be on the field and Greenberg in the front office.

Kiner's contract with the Cubs had only gone through the 1954 season, so he would have to negotiate a new one with the Indians. He had been embarrassed by his performance in 1954. He wanted to earn his money, not merely get paid for what he had done in the past or for his name recognition. In his talks with Greenberg, Kiner offered to take a 25 percent cut from the salary he had received in Chicago, the maximum allowed under the rules of Major League Baseball. That would mean that he would still be receiving $50,000 to play for the Indians in 1955. It would be the least he had made since the 1949 season in Pittsburgh, but he thought the reduction was fair. To get big money in Cleveland, he would earn it, the same way he had in Pittsburgh. Even with the salary reduction, he was one of the top paid players in the league, a fact that didn't sit well with one of his teammates, Al Rosen. Having been selected as the American League's Most Valuable Player in 1954, after a stellar season in which he missed out on winning the Triple Crown by only one hit, Rosen was himself negotiating a new contract. Rosen had been asking for a $55,000 deal, but Greenberg offered only $37,500, and Rosen was forced to accept.[3] Rosen, still in the prime of his production, was being underpaid, while Kiner, in the throes of decline, was being overpaid.

While Rosen may have held animosity toward the team and Hank Greenberg for what he felt to be their cheap treatment on his part, he held no ill feelings toward Kiner. He understood the fact that Kiner brought more to the team than just his batting average or home run totals. Kiner brought proven leadership and baseball savvy that could only help the Indians in their quest to repeat as champions in the American League, plus other intangibles that would elevate the team, both on the field and in the clubhouse. Rosen remembered that Kiner was "a great gentleman in every sense of the word. I remember when he joined our club, he brought a new level of dress. He was very urbane, very suave, well-dressed and many of us tried to do that to no avail. He would just fit in everyplace. And being around him, you felt better."[4]

Kiner reported to spring training at Hi Corbett Field, in Tucson, Arizona, to prepare for the 1955 season. The team was little changed from the pennant-winning squad of the previous season. The only big difference Herb Score joined Wynn, Bob Lemon, and Mike Garcia in the starting rotation. Score, a 22-year-old, rookie left-hander, would prove that management had been correct in slotting him among the starters in baseball's best pitching staff. In his rookie campaign, he posted a record of 16–10, with a 2.85 earned run average, and his 245 strikeouts led the American League. Wynn contributed 17 victories against 11 losses, and his 2.82 earned run average paced the starters. So far as the pitching staff was concerned, the changes made for the 1955 campaign seemed to be good ones. The only other difference between the 1954 and 1955 squads was that Ralph Kiner was slotted in left field. Kiner, it was hoped, would elevate the power potential of the team and provide some big hits at key moments that would win a few extra games. But this Ralph Kiner was not the same player that Hank Greenberg had mentored back at Forbes Field in Pittsburgh. Plagued by almost constant back pain, Kiner was able to play in only 113 games that year for Cleveland and had only 390 at-bats. His once artful swing was hampered due to his chronic condition, resulting in fewer hits and majestic drives. By season's end, his batting average stood at .243, he had hit only 18 home runs and driven in 56 runs, all lows for his career. Though he fought his way through the pain to play, it was obvious that his injury had reduced him from one of the top stars of the game to an average player.

Despite the lack of lofty play that they had expected from Kiner, the Indians seemed to be fulfilling their expectation of repeating as American League champions. For most of the season, it was a four-team

11: Last Stand with the Indians

race between the Indians, Boston Red Sox, Chicago White Sox, and New York Yankees. On August 9, all four teams were within one and a half games of one another, and it looked like the final two months of the season would be a dog fight. The Red Sox went into a slump and faded from contention by Labor Day, and the White Sox dropped from contention in the first two weeks of September. Kiner remembered a September 11 doubleheader against the Yankees at Yankee Stadium. The Indians earned a split in the twin bill when Whitey Ford uncharacteristically bounced a wild pitch with Kiner at the plate that allowed the winning run to score. Ralph remembered, "that night Bob Feller and I celebrated our first-place status at the Stork Club."[5]

With the end of the campaign in sight, the Indians seemed to be in full control of their destiny, holding a two-game lead over the Yankees with only eight games left. Then the bottom came out of the bucket for the Tribe. After losing at Washington, they hosted Detroit to open a three-game set on September 16. Billy Hoeft took the mound for the Tigers against Early Wynn. Wynn pitched a spectacular game, giving up only one earned run in eight innings. But Hoeft and reliever Steve Gromek pitched better, stifling the Indians' bats and pitching a shutout on only four hits. The result was a 3–0 victory for Detroit. The Indians looked to get even the following day, when they sent their ace, Bob Lemon, to the mound. He was opposed by Frank Lary, a Detroit starter whose record was 13–14, even though he had a very respectable 3.17 earned run average. For the second straight day, Cleveland batters were stifled. Though the Tribe pounded out ten hits, Lary was constantly able to work out of trouble, stranding ten runners on base. The final result was a 3–1 victory for Detroit. The final game of the set matched up Mike Garcia of the Indians against Bob Miller of the Tigers. Detroit struck first, plating a run in the top of the first. They exploded for six more tallies in the top of the sixth to take firm control of the game. Cleveland managed to eke out two runs in their half of the seventh and add another tally in the eighth in a 10–3 rout for a disappointing sweep at home. Kiner did not play in the series against Detroit. His only appearance came when he pinch-hit for Bob Lemon in the bottom of the eighth inning, in game two. He managed to get a hit, but was stranded on base when the team failed to rally.

On September 20, the Indians opened a series against the White Sox in Chicago. Early Wynn won a closely contested 3–2 victory to snap the Tribe's losing streak and keep them in contention for the pennant. The White Sox evened the series the following day, giving Bob Lemon his second straight loss in a 7–2 victory. Kiner did not appear in either game in Chicago. At a crucial time, when the Indians most needed his big bat in the lineup, Kiner was unable to answer the bell. The slugger who had provided so many clutch hits in his career could not even make his way to the batter's box because of the pain in his back.

From Chicago, the Indians traveled to Detroit to open a crucial three-game set with the Tigers, the same team that had swept them six days before. Herb Score led off a double-header, going the distance for an 8–2 victory. Al Lopez decided to shake things up a bit in the next— Cleveland was out of the race, so there was nothing to lose—by sending Hank Aguirre to the mound for a spot start. Lopez's hunch proved to be the right move. Aguirre pitched a masterful game, going the distance and shutting the Tigers out on only three hits. The Indian bats erupted for 13 hits and seven runs for the 7–0 victory. Winners of two in a row, it looked as if Cleveland had righted the ship, even if there was no hope of repeating as American League champs. On September 25, Al Lopez decided to repeat his move of the previous day. Knowing that his starting pitchers were tired, Lopez chose to send another spot starter to the mound for the Indians, handing the ball to Bud Daley. Aguirre had performed brilliantly in the same role the day before. The move seemed to work, at least initially. Daley gave up a run in the bottom of the first, then bore down in the following innings. After three frames, the score was knotted, 1–1. But the Cleveland pitcher got into trouble in the fourth, surrendering a run, and gave up three more in the fifth. The Indians tried to mount a rally in the top of the seventh. Joe Altobelli hit a one-out home run to make the score 5–2. Kenny Kuhn then swatted a single to right. Hank Foiles followed with a popup to the shortstop. With two outs and a runner on, Lopez told Kiner to grab a bat and pinch-hit for Daley. Kiner struck out looking to end the inning, and the rally was snuffed out. The Tigers went on to a 6–2 victory. The Indians had gone 3–6 in the last nine games of the season. In the meantime, the Yankees had won eight straight to surge past Cleveland and claim their fifth pen-

11: Last Stand with the Indians

nant in the last six years. At what could have been a clutch point of the season for his team, Kiner was able to manage only two pinch-hit appearances in the nine-game stretch that left them as also-rans to the Yankees for another year.

Kiner's at-bat against the Tigers in the last game of the season would also be his last at-bat in the majors. He did not go out with a mighty, memorable blast, giving the fans a final punctuation point to remember him by. Instead, as he remembered it, "like Casey of Mudville, I, too struck out."[6]

One can only speculate as to how much a healthy Ralph Kiner could have contributed to the Indians in 1955, but with major contributions earlier in the season, the Tribe could have built up an insurmountable lead that the Yankees couldn't surpass in the last furious stretch. The truth is that Kiner could have done little to alter the outcome of the final nine games. Other than the brilliant performance turned in by Score, the vaunted Indians' pitching staff, regarded as the best in baseball, simply failed to seal the deal in the closing games of the season. Outscored by a margin of 32–10 in the six losses, a home run by Kiner here and there would have done little to alter the final outcome. The aces of the staff, Lemon and Wynn, took three hard losses during this stretch, and Al Lopez felt that his pitching staff was so used up that he opted to switch to spot starters for the final two games of the year. Yes, a healthy Ralph Kiner most probably could have elevated the team to its second consecutive American League pennant, but his absence from the lineup in the final nine games of the year was not the reason for the team's collapse.

The Yankees went on to yet another World Series appearance, where, for the second year in a row, the favored American League representative fell to the National League squad in the fall classic. This time, it was the Brooklyn Dodgers who claimed the crown. It was the first World Series win for the Dodgers, who prevailed in a tough, seven-game Series.

Kiner did not receive a large amount of the blame for Cleveland's failure to repeat and claim the pennant. That was mostly reserved for Hank Greenberg. As late as September 15, the team was in first place, and Greenberg was certain of their chance to repeat. Even then, there were rumblings from fans and the press. In Cleveland, sports reporters constantly printed items concerning Greenberg's lack of security in keeping his post as general manager. One story even had him being traded to the Pittsburgh Pirates, to take over for Branch Rickey. Indians president Mike Wilson quashed all such speculation when he renewed Greenberg's contract before the season ended. Wilson stated, "This also is our vote of confidence for the splendid job which Greenberg has done for us."[7]

So Greenberg would be back for another year with the team. Kiner would not. Following the end of the 1955 season, he once more consulted with doctors about the degenerating condition of his back. With a risky surgery as the only viable option, he decided to hang up his glove and call it quits. In some ways, it was easier for Kiner to walk away from the game than it might have been for other players. While he was still only 32 years old, he had saved a good portion of the money he had made during his peak years in the game. He had also made some very good investments that were providing appreciable returns. In short, he was not financially strapped, as many players were, and did not need to keep playing in pain to keep a roof over his head or pay the monthly bills.

So Kiner retired after only ten years in the majors. He had been one of the most feared hitters of his era, the man who had been anointed as the slugger who could break Babe Ruth's single-season home run record. That he had failed to do, but his seven consecutive home run crowns set a record that has not been broken to this day. With 369 home runs to his credit, Ralph Kiner retired from his abbreviated career in sixth place all-time for home runs. It is certain that he could have added to that total, at albeit a reduced rate, if he had continued to play, but, having seen his skills diminish over his last two seasons with the Cubs and the Indians, he decided to walk away before he became the sort of player fans talked about in the past tense. Though he was not on top at the time of his retirement, he was also not a pitiable shell of his former self, and he wanted to walk away before that happened. For the first time since his boyhood years, he faced the prospect of a life that didn't include suiting up and taking the field on a baseball diamond. His great passion for the game would have to be filled in some other manner, but for the present, he had no idea what that would be.

CHAPTER 12

Out of the Game

Baseball was nearly all that Ralph Kiner had known since his days shagging flies at the Bodkin house, back in Alhambra. From that time onward, it had been his passion, his obsession, and the source of his fame and fortune. The coming of spring had always signified the start of a new season, complete with the smell of the grass, the feel of a bat making solid contact with a ball, the chatter of enthusiastic teammates, and the roar of the crowd when a towering fly ball went over the fences. Now, at the age of 32, Kiner would have to find a new career. One thing was certain. He would never stray too far from his passion when selecting a new vocation. It was also assured that his large circle of friends and associates would weigh heavily in helping him find a new job. The amiable and dignified manner with which he had conducted his life would surely pay dividends.

Kiner would not be out of baseball long. With Hank Greenberg serving as the general manager of the Cleveland Indians, he had a good friend in a position of power who could quickly help him land a position that would keep him in the game, if not on the field. The Indians had a working arrangement with the San Diego Padres of the Pacific Coast League, and Kiner was named as general manager of the team.

The Padres were well known to Kiner. For a period of time, the team was called the Hollywood Stars and played at Wrigley Field in Los Angeles, where he had seen some games. He had even played some games at Wrigley. Originally formed in 1903 as the Sacramento Solons, the team had spent time in Tacoma, San Francisco, Salt Lake City, and Los Angeles before moving to San Diego in 1936. The Padres played their games at Lane Field, a waterfront stadium built on the site of a U.S. Navy athletic field. As an affiliate of the Boston Red Sox, the Padres

After his playing days were through, Hank Greenberg (right) became an executive for several baseball franchises. He never forgot his old friend and helped Kiner to land jobs in management and broadcasting after his retirement from the Indians.

played their first game at Lane Field on March 31, 1936. In their inaugural season, the club finished in second place in the Pacific Coast League. In 1937, the team won the PCL pennant, led by a budding star who made his debut that year, Ted Williams. From 1949 to 1951, and again from 1957 to 1959, the team had been the Triple A affiliate of the Cleveland Indians. In the years between 1951 and 1957, the Padres had a working agreement with the Indians, while not serving as a direct affiliate. It was during the mid–1950s that the Pacific Coast League was trying to establish itself as a Major League operation, the equal of the National and American Leagues. During this time, most of the teams in the league operated under an open classification, having no formal affiliation with a Major League club. Instead, they maintained working arrangements, like the Indians had with the Padres, allowing minor league prospects from that franchise to play for them.

12: Out of the Game

The manager of the Padres was Bob Elliott, a man well-known to Kiner. Elliott had been the third baseman for the Pirates during Kiner's rookie season with Pittsburgh in 1946. He had been traded to the Boston Braves prior to the 1947 season and played for them through 1951, before ending his career as a journeyman with the New York Giants, St. Louis Browns, and Chicago White Sox. After the 1953 campaign, he was signed to a minor league contract by the Padres. In 1955, he took over as manager of the club, replacing Lefty O'Doul, a former two-time batting champ with the Philadelphia Phillies and Brooklyn Dodgers. In Elliott's first season at the helm, the club finished 92–80, down slightly from their 102–67 finish the previous year.

The team that Kiner took over as general manager was filled with players who would eventually make it to the Major Leagues, but only one would attain star status during their careers. That notable exception was Rocky Colavito, a power-hitting outfielder who would play 14 seasons in the majors, swatting 374 career home runs and winning the home run title as an Indian in 1959. Colavito had been up with the Indians for five games during the 1955 season, and though the Cleveland brass was high on his potential, it was thought that he still needed some seasoning before being ready to take a full-time roster spot with the Indians. Accordingly, he was assigned to San Diego for the start of the 1956 season.

Kiner got into a bit of trouble with Hank Greenberg concerning his management of Colavito. Kiner knew that Colavito had a tremendous throwing arm and he tried to use that fact to increase gate revenue for the team.

> When I was the GM for the San Diego Padres in 1956, Hank Greenberg, the Indians' GM, sent Rocky Colavito down to our team for some seasoning (we had a working agreement with Cleveland). I was trying to get people in the stands, so between games of a doubleheader, I had Rocky compete in a throwing contest with a few jai alai players. They used a cesta to hurl a pelota, a hard rubber ball that is half the size of a baseball and is harder than a golf ball. Rocky didn't beat them, but he threw a baseball over the center-field fence, which was 421 feet away. Greenberg gave me hell because he thought I was jeopardizing Colavito's throwing arm, but I did get a sellout crowd that day.[1]

Greenberg's apprehension was ill-founded. Colavito's arm was not put at risk, and he went on to a successful career in the bigs with six different teams, including two stints with the Indians.

The Padres had a miserable year in 1956, finishing with a record of 72–96, a dramatic decline from 1955. As with so many clubs with which Kiner had been associated, pitching was the main problem with San Diego. Pete Mesa led the squad with 13 victories, but he also tallied 12 losses. Arnie Atkins was the only other starter to have a winning record, at 12–6, and had to be considered the ace of the staff. Eddie Erautt posted the worst record at 9–19, despite having an earned run average that placed him in the middle of the pack on the staff. Kiner must have wondered if he was ever destined to be associated with a winning team.

During the off-season, Kiner spent time with his family and engaged in golf when time permitted. Though he had left the Pirates several years before, he had remained close with Bing Crosby, and the two often got together on the golf course when they were both in Palm Springs. Kiner also played in the Bing Crosby National Pro-Amateur Tournament whenever possible. In 1956, he was paired with a man who had previously been a member of the Stanford University golf team, a Walker Cup contender, and the California state amateur champion. At the end of the round, the man asked for Kiner's autograph for his son, who was a budding Little League player that the father boasted had the stuff to make it to the Major Leagues. The boy was a right-handed pitcher who had been a fan of Kiner's. In his usual gracious manner, Kiner signed the autograph that was requested by Charlie Seaver for his son, Tom. Little did Kiner know at the time that the boy would grow up to indeed play in the majors, or that he and Tom Seaver would one day find themselves together in the Baseball Hall of Fame.[2]

The 1957 season saw the Padres improve over their 1956 performance with a winning record of 89–79. Bob Elliott was replaced during the season by George Metkovich as manager. Metkovich was another player well-known to Kiner, having played with him as both a Pirate and a Cub. The Padres were a good hitting team that season with an overall batting average of .270. Outfielder Dave Pope was one of the stars, batting .313 and swatting 18 home runs. Pope would have a brief four-year career in the majors. Rudy Regalado was another standout, batting .306. Regalado had already spent parts of three seasons in the majors and had been sent to San Diego for more seasoning. Regrettably, he never made it back to the bigs and finished out his pro career in the minors.

12: Out of the Game

The Padres' pitching staff showed marked improvement in 1957 over the previous year. The greatest reason for that was the acquisition of a right-handed flamethrower named James "Mudcat" Grant. He led the staff with a record of 18–7 and an earned run average of 2.32, earning his promotion to the Indians the following season. In a 14-year career in the majors, Grant was a two-time All-Star and led the American League in wins with 21 in 1965. He finished his time in the bigs with a record of 145–119. Another notable starter was Dick Brodowski, who posted a 13–6 record with a 2.93 earned run average. Brodowski had already played parts of three seasons with the Boston Red Sox and Washington Senators. He would be called up for parts of the 1958 and 1959 seasons with the Indians, but would never establish a place for himself on the Major League roster.

For the most part, Kiner spent time trying to figure out how to get more fans into the seats at Lane Field. Budgets for minor league teams were small, and there was little cash to work with. Kiner sought to increase revenue by getting more fans through the gates. Following the breaking of the color barrier by Jackie Robinson in 1947, Major League teams had sought talent in a number of previously untapped markets, primarily the Latin American countries. During the 1950s, before Fidel Castro came to power, Cuba had been a favorite destination for baseball scouts. Minnie Miñoso, the star outfielder known as the "Cuban Comet," had been signed by the Indians, playing briefly for the team before being traded to the White Sox, where he enjoyed an All-Star career.

Kiner's old team, the Pirates, were also heavily involved in acquiring talent from Latin American countries. One of their scouts, Howie Haak, spoke fluent Spanish and regularly scoured foreign lands in search of promising prospects. One such prospect was Roberto Clemente, from Puerto Rico. A number of teams were interested in Clemente, however, including the Dodgers and Giants. Brooklyn feared the prospect of Clemente and Willie Mays in the same Giants outfield, so they outbid their cross-town rivals and signed Clemente for a $10,000 bonus in February of 1954. The Dodgers assigned Clemente to their Montreal minor league team for the 1954 season, despite the fact that they might lose him by doing so. According to the bonus rule, any player receiving more than $4,000 who was not on the team's 25-man roster was subjected to being drafted by another club, with the first choice going to the club that finished last the previous season. The Pirates had definitely been interested in Clemente before he had signed with the Dodgers, so they took full advantage of their last-place finish the previous year and eagerly paid the $4,000 purchase price to acquire him. As Howie Haak said, "If we didn't, any of fourteen other clubs would have."[3]

Kiner sought to cash in on this current trend of signing Latin American players by setting his sights across the border to Mexico. He reasoned that the signing of Mexican players would "draw fans from the border towns of Mexico. We did sign one Mexican star, and I had visions of the entire Mexican population coming through our turnstiles. I wondered where I could seat them all. But he never did anything and no Mexican fans showed up at all."[4]

The Padres ran frequent promotions in an effort to get more fans in the seats, but without a consistent way to keep them coming through the gates, Kiner was faced with the need to cut expenses in order to meet payroll and operate within the budget. One cost-cutting move he made had a long-lasting impact on his own career. In an effort to raise more revenue, he had sold a package of ten Saturday afternoon games to a local television station. "I couldn't afford to pay a broadcaster, so I did them myself. That was the first broadcasting I ever did," he later recalled. It was indeed the first time he had ever broadcast baseball games, but it was far from the first time he had ever been before a microphone. Though he had never thought of becoming a baseball announcer, he acknowledged that he had put together a lot of "good credentials" during his playing career, when he had made "numerous guest appearances on a variety of television and radio shows, pitched products, done studio work, and even had my own shows." Kiner said that he "didn't get into any analysis at all. Nobody did back then. It was simple 'Ground ball ... one out.' No verbs needed. It was a new experience, and I enjoyed it. I thought we did a pretty good job although we were on a shoestring budget. We wanted to get exposure and it worked. People would watch the Saturday game on television and come out Sunday for a doubleheader."[5] Kiner had learned a great deal about hitting from Hank Greenberg. He had also emulated his mentor when it came to adopting his style and living standards. As the general manager of the Padres, he was

12: Out of the Game

proving himself to be an innovative and efficient administrator, once more following in the footsteps of his friend and benefactor.

George Metkovich was back to manage the Padres for the 1958 season, hoping to improve on the previous year's campaign. They would have a new stadium to play in this year, as Padres owner C. Arnholt Smith spent $1 million to replace the deteriorating Lane Field. Westgate Park was constructed to hold 8,268 fans but could be expanded to accommodate 40,000, should Major League baseball ever come to San Diego. The Padres played their first games there on April 28, 1958, in a day-night doubleheader against the Phoenix Giants. Though neither game witnessed a capacity crowd, the nightcap did draw 7,129 fans.

The new stadium was a needed improvement to the aging Lane Field, but there was another reason why the Padres sought to improve their position in San Diego: Major League baseball was coming to southern California. Brooklyn Dodgers owner Walter O'Malley had made plans to move the team to the West Coast following the 1957 season. O'Malley had purchased the rights to the Los Angeles area from Cubs owner Phil Wrigley. The Cubs owned a minor league team playing in L.A., and O'Malley acquired the franchise rights for the city by trading Wrigley a team the Dodgers owned in Fort Worth, playing in the Texas League. O'Malley did not plan to make his West Coast venture a solitary experiment. He knew that he would need at least one more team in California to make it more economical for other members of the National League to make road trips there. He contacted Horace Stoneham, owner of the Giants, to feel him out on the subject. Stoneham said that he had intentions of moving the Giants out of New York and was leaning toward Minneapolis, since they already had a minor league team there. O'Malley suggested, "Why don't we both go to the Far West together?" After some discussion, Stoneham "told him that I liked the San Francisco area, that I had worked there when I was a young fellow. I didn't even know he was intending to move. But when he saw I was, he saw we could make a rivalry on the Pacific Coast."[6] Major League baseball had never existed west of St. Louis, and Smith knew that the arrival of the Dodgers and Giants in California would create a stir of excitement that would cut deeply into his ability to draw fans to see the Padres. He hoped that the new stadium would help keep the San Diego faithful coming through the gates.

Just as in his first two seasons with the club, Kiner had a roster filled with prospects, many of whom would make their way to the Major Leagues. He had one star attraction with name recognition who would help bring fans into the new stadium. Bob Lemon, the seven-time All-Star and ace pitcher for the Indians since 1946, would play part of the season for the Padres. At the age of 36, Lemon had experienced a bad season in 1957, posting a record of 6–11, his first losing mark since 1946, when he broke in with Cleveland. His 4.60 earned run average was by far the worst of his career, and the first time he had topped 4.00. His trouble continued the following season, when he went 0–1 with a 5.33 earned run average in just 25 innings. Lemon pitched in 12 games for the Padres in 1958, starting eight of them. Though past his prime, he was a big name whose career would later make him a Hall of Fame inductee, and San Diego fans got to see a real star of the game when he was on the mound. Kiner and Lemon had broken into the majors together back in 1946. Kiner had been forced to retire after the 1955 season. Lemon still seemed to be in top form and was a 20-game winner in 1956. Then the wheels came off the cart, and the once proud ace struggled to get opposing batters out. 1958 would be his last year in the game before he hung up his cap and glove.

The addition of Lemon did little to assist the Padres in adding to the win column in 1958, as the aging star posted a record of 2–5. Overall, the team lost a little ground from the previous year, ending with a mark of 84–69 for a second-place finish in the Pacific Coast League behind the Phoenix Giants. Still, they had finished two places higher than in 1957, even though they had won five fewer games.

The 1959 season would be Kiner's last as general manager of the Padres. Though the team posted a record of 78–75, the third consecutive winning season with Kiner at the helm, and finished third in the league, the franchise was struggling to survive. Monetary issues became steadily worse, caused by the presence of two Major League teams in the state, and Kiner saw the writing on the wall. "When the Dodgers and Giants moved to the West Coast, that was the death knell for the PCL. Thanks to some insensitive number-crunching by Walter O'Malley's puppet, Major League Commissioner Ford Frick, we received peanuts for compensation for their infringement on our territory. Four PCL teams had to relocate, and the others struggled badly. Seeing that the league's days were numbered, I resigned as GM of the Padres in 1960."[7]

When the Pittsburgh Pirates made it to the World Series in 1960, team announcer Bob Prince called Kiner with an offer. Prince had been selected to announce the games on television with Mel Allen. He asked if Kiner would be interested in doing a post-game interview show with him for the games in Pittsburgh. Kiner readily accepted. The shows were sponsored by Mellon Bank, one of the largest banks in the world.

> The Series opened with two games in Pittsburgh and came back for the final two, including the fantastic seventh game in which Bill Mazeroski won the Series with a home run. I couldn't get Mazeroski or any of the other players on the air because we were in a studio, so we looked around for people who were indirectly involved with the Series. When Russ Hodges walked by, for instance, we shanghaied him and had him on the show. Curt Gowdy, the Red Sox announcer, was in town, so we pulled him into the studio. We always found someone.[8]

Kiner was still a big celebrity and fan favorite in Pittsburgh, and he had a blast doing the post-game shows. It also served as another feather in his cap and gave him more experience in front of the microphone and camera. He was once more out of the game, but he already had an option in the offing that would get him back into it in a major way. Hank Greenberg would yet again play a significant role in influencing Kiner's decision about this latest career move. Greenberg had ended his affiliation with the Indians in 1958, when his shares in the team were bought out by Bill Daley. Bill Veeck approached Greenberg in 1959 with a proposal that the two purchase the White Sox. Grace and Chuck Comiskey were the sole owners of the team, but Grace was the majority owner, having been left 54 percent of the team shares in her father's will. Grace was interested in selling her shares, and Veeck was looking to buy, if he could put together a partnership he was agreeable to. Having previously worked with Greenberg with the Cubs, Veeck thought him to be the perfect partner, and he knew that Greenberg had the cash, having just been bought out by the Indians. A third partner, Arthur Allyn, Jr., was brought into the fold, and the deal was made. Veeck became the club president, with Greenberg serving as vice president and treasurer. The White Sox won the American League pennant in 1959, their first in 40 years, but they lost to the Los Angeles Dodgers, 4–2, in the World Series.

Chicago finished third in 1960 while setting a league record for attendance, with 1,644,460 fans coming through the turnstiles.[9]

Following the 1960 season, the American League announced plans to establish two expansion franchises, one of them to be located in Los Angeles. The league wanted Greenberg to head up the new club, and he quickly put together a partnership. C. Arnholt Smith, the owner of the Padres, was quickly brought into the fold, as was Kiner, whom Greenberg called as soon as he got the news that the league wanted him for the Los Angeles team, yelling "I got it!" Kiner recalled that he was to have a front office position with the new team. "We had signed a TV contract with KMPC, which Gene Autry owned, so we were ready to go. But then Frick flew out to L.A. to meet with O'Malley, and they changed the ground rules for owning an L.A. franchise." The partnership was told "they would have to pay damages to the Dodgers and be a tenant to Dodgers Stadium. O'Malley wanted L.A. all to himself, and Frick tried to help him." O'Malley also had objections to Smith being one of the partners in the venture. It seems that Smith's brother had tried to prevent O'Malley from purchasing the land at Chavez Ravine, where Dodger Stadium was built, and O'Malley used the incident to open a family feud with the Smiths. In the end, Greenberg was forced to cancel plans to acquire an American League team in Los Angeles in November of 1960. The following month, Gene Autry put together a partnership that was agreeable to O'Malley, and the league awarded the franchise to him.[10]

The deal had been quashed, but Greenberg didn't forget about his friend, who was now out of a job. Kiner had received a good deal of notice from the post-game shows he had done with the Pirates during the World Series, and offers began to come in. He was offered a job doing sports on a television news show in Pittsburgh. The Cincinnati Reds' general manager, Gabe Paul, offered him a job broadcasting games on television with Frank McCormick. Kiner was giving serious consideration to Paul's offer when he was contacted by Greenberg, who wanted him to become the radio play-by-play announcer and commentator for the White Sox. The television broadcasting spot with the Reds might have been more prestigious, but Kiner couldn't pass up the opportunity to work with his old friend again, so he accepted the job with Chicago.

12: Out of the Game

> My job description at WCFL in Chicago was pretty weird. The station had air time to fill up in the afternoons, so I'd do two games each day, unless I was on the road with the Sox. When the Sox were at home in Chicago, I'd go to the radio station and do re-created games by myself between two other major league teams, and then I'd go to the ballpark and do a Sox game live with Bob Elson. When there were no games, I'd have to do a radio disc jockey show, playing music and talking sports.

Kiner did well with the baseball broadcasts, but admitted he was lousy at the disc jockey segments and that he "hosted perhaps the worst radio show of all time." Naturally, he recognized the music of Bing Crosby and Glenn Miller, "but otherwise I was lost. It wasn't rock 'n' roll, but I didn't know who I was playing. WCFL was a major fifty-thousand watt station that went all over the country, so everyone heard me."[11]

After Kiner's first year broadcasting for the White Sox, Greenberg and Veeck sold their interest in the team. Kiner decided to stay on. He signed a contract with the new Chicago general manager and continued to do the radio broadcasts for another season.

He enjoyed his time spent broadcasting games with Chicago. He felt that the re-created ones were particularly helpful in developing his skills as an announcer. His time with Bob Elson was another matter. Though he got along with Elson, as was his nature, Kiner felt him to be pompous and demanding and not much help in his development, and noted that his nickname was "Commander." Elson was also a bit of a name-dropper, especially when it came to getting free things around town. He had a not-too-subtle habit of announcing the names of businesses that were not sponsors of the team on broadcasts, in return for free meals, drinks, or whatever else he might be able to get by doing so. Kiner himself was a person who traveled with a celebrity crowd, but they were friends, and he viewed what Elson did with disdain.[12] Even so, the experience was a good one for Kiner, and it improved on the broadcasting experience he had been attaining over the last several years. He was putting together a nice little portfolio of work in the field of media, one that would serve him well as a stepping-stone to bigger and better opportunities. Little did he know it, but that bigger and better opportunity was just around the corner.

CHAPTER 13

Kiner's Korner Moves to New York

Ralph Kiner had not only participated in Bing Crosby's annual golf tournament as a player for years, he had also served as one of the broadcasters. In 1961, he was set to work in this capacity when he received an offer to become part of a new television and radio broadcast team that was being put together to work in New York City. The Major Leagues were completing a four-team expansion that year. The American League had, the previous year, put teams in Los Angeles and in Washington, the latter to fill the place of the Senators, who moved to Minnesota. In 1961 the National League planned to establish a presence in New York once more, since the Dodgers and Giants had relocated to the West Coast. They also planned to put a franchise in Houston, Texas. There had been a sense of urgency at the commissioner's office to get this done, due to Branch Rickey's plans to open a rival Continental League to compete with the Major Leagues. Ford Frick had been forced to purchase Rickey's options in these cities at an exorbitant price, in order to prevent him from placing franchises there. Rickey got rich because of the transaction, which many people believe was his real intention, not actually creating a new league.

The New York team was to be called the Mets. This was in remembrance of the Metropolitans, a team that had played in New York during the 19th Century. William Shea had been instrumental in getting the Mets franchise for New York. A prominent lawyer in the city, he had been solicited by New York mayor Robert Wagner to chair a committee to get a National League team to come there after the Giants and Dodgers departed. Shea tried to convince the Reds, Phillies and Pirates to move to New York, but was unsuccessful in his overtures. He then dreamed up the idea of starting a new league, the Continental League, and convinced Branch Rickey to come out of retirement to help him create it. They announced their intentions in 1959 and set 1961 as the year their teams would start playing. This threat of competition spurred Commissioner Ford Frick and the baseball executives into action and resulted in the expansion of the league described above.

The team would be owned by a group led by Joan Payson, who held a majority share. Payson had previously been a minority owner of the Giants and had opposed their move to California. After the majority owners voted to relocate the team, she sold her shares and immediately set about trying to get another team in New York. Payson convinced M. Donald Grant, the only other Giants' minority owner who had opposed the move, to join her as a partner. When the National League awarded the franchise to Payson's group, she became the first woman majority owner of a major North American sports team to purchase a team, and not inherit it.[1]

Casey Stengel was hired to be the first manager of the Mets. It was hoped that he could bring with him from the Yankees some of the magic that had led to seven World Series titles while he was in charge. The coaching staff was filled with experience. It included former greats Rogers Hornsby and Red Ruffing, as well as Red Kress, Solly Hemus, and Cookie Lavagetto. The colorful and quotable Stengel quickly became the face of the franchise, a position he seemed to enjoy. Though considered to be a brilliant manager, Stengel had been fired by the Yankees following the 1960 season for "getting old." When he took the job as the Mets skipper, he alluded to his age (71), and to a Civil War era New York team by saying "It's a great honor to be joining the Knickerbockers."[2]

Then again, Casey Stengel had always seemed to be old. Back in 1923, when he played with the New York Giants, he almost lost a bride because he was known as good "old" Stengel. He had planned to be married immediately following the World Series that year and invited his bride-to-be and her parents to watch him play. His future in-laws had never seen him in a game, and he hoped to impress them. Stengel hit winning home runs in the first and third games of the Series and was trumpeted as a hero in the New York newspapers, but his accomplishments did little to increase his standing with his potential in-laws. In fact, the press he received almost led to the cancellation of the wedding.

In all of the stories, he was referred to as "old" Stengel, or "good old" Stengel, leading the girl's parents to believe that he was far too advanced in age to marry their daughter. Stengel was 33 at the time, which was old for a ballplayer, but not for a man. It took a great deal of convincing to win the approval of the girl's parents and to explain to them that "old" had a different connotation when it came to baseball.[3]

The Mets and the Houston Colt 45s (later renamed the Astros) would be part of baseball's second expansion draft. According to the rules of the draft, each existing team in the National League was required to select 15 players, seven of them from their 25-man roster, to be available to be drafted by Houston and New York. The expansion teams were required to take two players from each existing team, at a cost of $75,000 each. They could also select a third player at a cost of $50,000. Following this draft, the existing teams would make two more players from its 25-man roster available, that they had previously protected. In this "premium draft," the expansion teams could select a total of four players at $125,000 each. The draft was held on October 10, 1961. The Houston team picked first, and chose Eddie Bressoud, an infielder with the San Francisco Giants. The first player drafted by the Mets was catcher Hobie Landrith, also from San Francisco.

The Mets were able to get a few good names through the draft, including outfielder Gus Bell, first baseman Gil Hodges, and outfielder Frank Thomas. They would later purchase the contract of Richie Ashburn from the Cubs. All of these players were at or nearing the end of their careers, however, and there was not a great deal of talent among the crop of younger players. Ed Kranepool would be signed by the team as an amateur free agent midway through the inaugural season and made his debut with the team that September. Kranepool became a legitimate star with New York, but it would be some time before his star was in full ascendancy.

The team's Opening Day lineup was Hodges on first, Charlie Neal at second, Felix Mantilla at shortstop, Don Zimmer on third, Landrith as catcher, Thomas in left, Ashburn in center, and Bell in right. Of these, Ashburn led the pack in batting average at .306. Most of the position players batted under .250 for the year. Frank Thomas had a good season, batting .266 and clouting 34 home runs.

13: Kiner's Korner Moves to New York

The primary starting pitchers were Roger Craig, Al Jackson, Jay Hook, and Bob Miller. This quartet combined for only 27 wins, while amassing a staggering total of 75 losses. The overall earned run average for the staff was 5.04, last in the National League. They also finished last in hits, runs, and home runs allowed, and recorded the fewest strikeouts. The only thing the staff would finish first in was losses, and in that they would excel. With a record of 40–120, the Mets set a record for futility not equaled by any Major League team in the rest of the 20th Century.

But all of the losing and frustration was still in the future when Kiner was contacted by George Weiss, the former Yankees executive hired by Payson to be the Mets' first president and de facto general manager, regarding the broadcasting offer. Kiner was informed that he was to be the third member of a team that already included Lindsey Nelson and Bob Murphy. Nelson was already a nationally renowned announcer who had been doing games for NBC since 1957. He also did play-by-play for college football and was the regular announcer for many bowl games. Already a sportscasting celebrity on a national level, his acquisition by the Mets was considered a major coup. Nelson was known to Kiner. They had met a year before, and Kiner remembered that he "liked him instantly." As luck would have it, Nelson was also one of the announcers for Crosby's golf tournament when Kiner received the Mets' offer. Kiner immediately sought out Nelson to ask his advice on the matter. Nelson said "Take the job," stating that New York was a great place to be a broadcaster. He also pointed out that since the Mets were a new team, the three of them would be able to establish a new tradition and would not be replacing established broadcasters who were already familiar to the fans.[4]

Bob Murphy had broken into broadcasting with the Boston Red Sox in 1954, working alongside Curt Gowdy. In 1960, he took a contract with the Baltimore Orioles, replacing Ernie Harwell. When Roger Maris hit his record-tying 60th home run off Baltimore pitcher Jack Fisher in September of 1961, Murphy was in the booth. His call of that momentous occasion became an audition tape for the Mets job and landed him the position. He and Nelson would one day be honored in Cooperstown as winners of the Ford C. Frick Award, for broadcasters making major contributions to the game.

When Kiner contacted George Weiss to accept his offer, he was told that there was a particular hurdle he would have to overcome before a contract could be given. Rheingold beer had signed on as the Mets' principle sponsor and had agreed to pay $6 million for five years of commercial time on WOR-TV, the station that would broadcast Mets games. This amount was more than Joan Payson had paid for the team and its players. With so much invested, the executives of Rheingold beer naturally wanted to exercise a level of control over the broadcasters selected to call the games. Kiner would have to be approved by Norm Varney, the account executive for the firm that was handling Rheingold's sponsorship deal. Weiss informed Kiner that Varney would watch Crosby's golf tournament in order to evaluate Kiner's ability.

The following day, Kiner was doing interviews on the 18th green. He was interviewing Gay Brewer, who was leading the tournament, when the producer pushed Phil Harris in front of the camera. Harris had been a friend of Kiner's for some time, and his quick wit and searing sense of humor were well known. Kiner tried to take a safe course by asking, "Phil, you know Gay Brewer, don't you?" Harris immediately responded, "Yeah, he's a fag wine maker from Modesto." Kiner was in shock. Knowing that his performance was being evaluated by Varney, he was sure that Harris' retort had probably cost him the job. "I would have no recollection of what I said afterward, but somehow I got out of the interview in a hurry." When the cameras stopped rolling, Kiner asked Harris, "Why the hell did you say something like that?" Harris answered, "Well, we were only on a short time, so I had to get their attention." Fortunately for Kiner, the gaffe did not work against him. In fact, he believed that it might have helped his case. After all, if he could handle a situation like that on national television without coming unglued, then he should be able to handle interviewing baseball players with no problems.[5]

The Mets played their home games at the Polo Grounds, the former home of the Giants, when they opened the 1962 season. The team had already broken ground for a new stadium in Queens, to be named in honor of William Shea, whose efforts were largely responsible for bringing National League baseball back to New York. Completion of Shea Stadium was still a couple of years off, however, so the Mets made a deal to occupy the Polo Grounds temporarily as their home. The surroundings would be familiar to many of New York's baseball faithful, as well as to Kiner, who had played many games there. Team colors were selected to appeal to a sense of nostalgia among former Dodgers and Giants fans. Blue from the Dodgers was combined with orange from the Giants to create the Mets' distinctive look. When the team reported to spring training at St. Petersburg, Florida, it was met with a buzz of excitement from the nation's sports journalists. Stengel toyed with the press by trotting out his two worst rookies and introducing them as the future face of the franchise. The reporters took the bait, and the following day their names appeared in all seven of New York's newspapers. The rookies were soon cut, however, and were never heard from again.[6]

The Mets opened the 1962 season on the road with a series against the St. Louis Cardinals. Kiner was in the booth on April 11 when the Mets took the field for their first regular season game. The teams had been rained out the previous night, and as he put it, "Their luck, however, was not to last. The rain abated before they could get out of town." Roger Craig took the mound for New York and promptly surrendered two runs in the bottom of the first inning. The floodgates opened from there, and the Cardinals went on to an 11–4 trouncing of the Mets, despite home runs by Gil Hodges and Charlie Neal.[7]

The Mets returned home to New York on April 12 to a ticker-tape parade up Broadway and were met by Mayor Robert Wagner. The following day, Friday the 13th, they opened their first home stand against the Pittsburgh Pirates, Kiner's old team. The game resulted in a 4–3 loss for the Mets and was the first of three losses to the Pirates. Houston then came to town for a single game and exerted its dominance as the better expansion team by beating New York. After two more losses to the Cardinals, the Mets were ready to embark on their second road trip, to Pittsburgh. *Sports Illustrated* had assigned a reporter to follow the Mets to chronicle their first victory. The reporter had recently been married, and Casey Stengel, commenting on the play of his team thus far, told him, "There's a chance you may not see your bride until October." New York dropped a two-game set to the first-place Pirates and found themselves in an unusual position. After losing their first nine games, the Mets were 9.5 games behind Pittsburgh, who had won all ten of their games.[8] Kiner must have shaken his head in disbelief and wondered about the irony of the whole thing. When he was with the Pirates, they were playing with the same ineptitude New York now displayed. Now that he was gone, they were playing like world beaters and setting the league on fire. He must surely have wondered if he would ever be associated with a winner. Casey Stengel openly admitted that he was afraid his new team would wind up 0–162 for the season.[9]

The first victory for the Mets came on April 23, during their second visit to Pittsburgh. Jay Hook, a right-handed journeyman the Mets had acquired from the Cincinnati Reds, threw a five-hitter against the Pirates and helped his own cause by scoring two runs and driving in two runs. The end result was a 9–1 victory for the Mets, their first in franchise history. Casey Stengel quipped after the game that he might pitch Hook every night. The team seemed to have righted the ship and played over .500 ball in the next 22 games. After sweeping a doubleheader on May 20, their record was 12–19. The team lost its next 17 games, going into June. In July, they went on an 11-game losing streak, and they lost 13 consecutive games in August. Their longest winning streak of the year was three games.

They won their next-to-last game of the season on September 29, with a 2–1 victory over the Cubs, and hoped to finish the season on a high note with another win the following day. But Chicago had other ideas. The Cubs were having a pretty miserable season themselves and had already lost 103 games. Normally that would have been good enough to assure Chicago a firm grasp on last place. Not this year. A 5–1 victory over the Mets left the Cubs with a 59–103 record, 18 games above New York. The Mets' 40–120 record, and their .250 winning percentage, set modern standards for futility in Major League baseball. Despite this pitiful beginning, New Yorkers faithfully supported the team, and nearly one million of them came through the gates at the Polo Grounds to watch the Mets play.

Kiner, Nelson, and Murphy, on the other hand, had a good year in the booth. Though the games were often almost unwatchable, the trio did their best to make the broadcasts enjoyable. Kiner constantly told stories, connecting the present with the past, as he talked about players he had faced and those he had idolized as a boy. He also benefited from the vast number of acquaintances he had made in the celebrity circle, and many notable figures stopped by the booth to say hello when Kiner was broadcasting a game. Inevitably, he would put them on the air, and a short but lively interview would follow. Over the years, the practice of stopping in to see Kiner would become an almost never-ending parade of who's who. This was especially true when the team made a West Coast trip to play in California. "When we were in Los Angeles, it was nothing for George Carlin to come into the booth and say hi to Ralph. Or Chuck Connors. They were friends of Ralph. He had many friends in Southern California because he was from there and lived in Palm Springs."[10] The truth was that everyone liked Kiner, and everyone seemed to want to be near him. With so many transplanted New Yorkers across the country, he became the face of the Mets to a generation of fans and served as an ambassador for the game he loved.

In 1963, the Mets seemed to pick up right where they left off the previous year. There were a number of changes in personnel this year. Rogers Hornsby died in January of 1963, and Red Ruffing retired following the 1962 season, so the Mets had two new coaches when they reported to spring training: Ernie White and Clyde McCullough. There were also numerous changes in the player roster. Most notably, Richie Ashburn retired following the end of the 1962 season. Knowing he was at the end of his career, Ashburn couldn't deal with the prospect that as bad as the Mets were, he might not be a starter if he returned for another season. "He sat on the bench for a while with another team once and it bothered him badly. And he said that if he ever had to be a benchwarmer for the New York Mets he'd commit suicide."[11] The Mets replaced Ashburn with another aging superstar who was well known to New York fans, Duke Snider. The Duke of Flatbush had been a regular fixture in the Dodgers' outfield since 1947 and had played his first 11 seasons in Brooklyn before the team departed for California. The Mets purchased the contract of the seven-time All-Star and two-time World Series champion. A sentimental favorite to New York fans who had rooted for the Dodgers, Snider's acquisition by Mets management proved a stroke of genius in gaining support for the team. Snider did not fill Ashburn's shoes in the lineup, however, despite the fact that he was the Mets' representative to the All-Star Game that year. Hitting just .243 for the season, Snider still had one of the higher batting averages for the Mets. Five starting position players had averages lower than .230, and two of them batted under .200.

Kiner must have felt a great deal of sympathy for Snider, a fellow power hitter, as he knew all too well what it was like to bat in a lineup where there was no protection for a slugger. Another big change was the departure of Gil Hodges. Shortly after the start of the season, the team traded him to the Washington Senators for Jimmy Piersall. The trade was a disaster for the Mets. Piersall played in 40 games for New York and batted only .194 before being released on July 27. Maybe it was just a Mets thing, though, because Piersall was signed by the Los Angeles Angels and hit .308 for them through the rest of the year. He had an even better campaign with the Angels the following season, hitting .314.

The Mets' pitching staff was every bit as anemic as it had been the year before. As a group, they finished last in the National League in almost every pitching category. The only exceptions were complete games (8th) and base on balls (9th). Roger Craig once more led the league in losses, with 22. In two seasons with the Mets, the hard-working Craig had compiled a record of 15–46, and his 5–22 record in 1963 resulted in a .185 winning percentage, the lowest in the majors that year. The only pitcher on the team with a winning record was Ken MacKenzie, a reliever who appeared in 34 games and finished with a record of 3–1.

Casey Stengel's boys finished the 1963 season with a slight improvement over their first year, with a record of 51-111, but they were still firmly in control of last place in the National League, 15 games behind 9th-place Houston and 48 games behind the first-place Dodgers.

One of the most memorable things about the 1963 season took place in the broadcast booth, and not on the playing field. On April 30, New York fans were introduced to something that would become a mainstay of Mets broadcasts for decades to come when Ralph Kiner hosted his first "Kiner's Korner" post-game interview show, named for the famed Kiner's Korner in left field in Forbes Field. His first guests were comedian Buddy Hackett and actor Phil Foster. Foster had acted in several comedy shorts for Universal Studio and had been a writer for Joey Bishop. He would later be known for his role as Frank DeFazio on the television show "Laverne & Shirley." Over the next several decades, Kiner would interview hundreds and hundreds of celebrities and baseball players on

13: Kiner's Korner Moves to New York

"Kiner's Korner." He connected with all of them, regardless of their profession or walk of life, due to his easygoing style and knowledge of so many things and people, in and out of baseball. The interviews were more akin to something seen on the "Tonight Show" than to normal post-game wrap ups, and their entertainment value was quickly recognized by the fans and network executives alike. Kiner had found a niche beyond the usual duties of a broadcaster, and it was one that fit his talents and personality to perfection. Generations of Mets fans and baseball enthusiasts would become Kiner fans as they watched the affable host interact seamlessly with a wide array of guests.

A young college intern, Gary Myers, who worked for Kiner in the 1970s, described the experience of being part of "Kiner's Korner."

> I have to admit, I had the coolest summer job in 1974 and 1975 after my sophomore and junior years at Syracuse. I was a production assistant for WOR-TV on the home game telecasts of Mets games. I was a Mets fan from their first game in 1962 and I still love them today.... Ralph Kiner was a real prince and I learned a lot from him—mainly how to treat people. He was a Hall of Famer, an icon, but treated everybody with respect, including a 20-year-old kid, making me feel like an important part of the show. He may not have been the smoothest broadcaster, but his knowledge of the game and his insights—tossed in with malapropos—made him extremely entertaining and a New York legend.... By far the best part of the job was standing outside the Mets clubhouse if they won or the visitors' clubhouse if the Mets lost and rounding up guests for Ralph. In the two years I had the job, not one player ever said no and it had nothing to do with the $50 they received for appearing on the show, which, by the way, I thought was a fortune compared to the $25 per game I was getting paid. Not only did players from all around the National League know Ralph, they loved and respected him. Rose, Morgan, Mike Schmidt, Henry Aaron, Willie Stargell, Willie McCovey, Joe Torre—all I had to do was tell them Ralph wanted them and they would hustle to the studio. I would escort them down the hallway, sometimes they were still in their cleats, from the visitors' locker room behind the third base dugout to the "Kiner's Korner" studio behind the first base dugout. If the Mets won, it was about a 10-second walk. Either way, "Kiner's Korner" started not long after the game ended and it was my job to make sure the players were there on time. I never let Ralph down. The players considered it an honor when Ralph wanted them on "Kiner's Korner." Besides the $50, which in those days was enough to buy dinner, it was great exposure for them in the New York market. Kiner would discuss the key plays of the game with his guests, they would leave and he would narrate the highlights.

Myers would remember, "Kiner was a Klassic and, thanks to a man that helped me get my career started, Kiner's Korner is still the Koolest job I ever had."[12]

One of the most memorable episodes of "Kiner's Korner" involved his old team, the Pittsburgh Pirates. The Bucs had beaten the Mets in a 1963 game at the Polo Grounds, and Kiner requested two of their players for the post-game interview. Jim Pagliaroni and Don Schwall were selected. Instead of appearing in their baseball uniforms, Pagliaroni and Schwall created impromptu togas out of bed sheets, combed their hair down over their foreheads, and grabbed bunches of grapes from the visitors' locker room. Kiner was stunned when the pair appeared in the studio booth, but he nevertheless tried to conduct the interview. Pagliaroni and Schwall responded to all his questions with an array of slapstick antics, without giving a serious response to any of them. The interview was cut short, and Pirates general manager Joe L. Brown was furious that his players would act in such an irresponsible manner. Pagliaroni, Schwall, and all the viewers who watched the program thought it was hilarious, and it quickly became one of the favorite episodes in the early days of "Kiner's Korner." When asked about his impression concerning the zany antics, Kiner responded, "No comment."[13] The interviews had not gone as anticipated, but they added to his already growing fame as a Mets broadcaster and helped to ensure that New York fans didn't turn off the television at the end of the game. Everyone wanted to see what would happen next on "Kiner's Korner."

CHAPTER 14

A World Series and a Trip to the Hall

The 1964 version of the Mets entered spring training knowing that they would have at least one thing to look forward to when the regular season began. Though they were considered contenders for nothing more than another season at the bottom of the National League, they would be playing in a new stadium when they went north, and they could kiss goodbye forever the antiquated surroundings of the Polo Grounds. Shea Stadium opened it doors on April 17. The stadium was originally to be called Flushing Meadows Stadium, but the name had been changed due to a movement to honor William Shea, the man responsible for bringing National League baseball back to the city. There were many changes to the 1964 roster, but most things remained the same for the team. The Mets lost their home opener to the Pittsburgh Pirates by a score of 4–3 before a crowd of 50,312. It was but the first of many losses the Mets suffered in their new stadium. The team finished last for its third consecutive season, with a record of 53–109. Casey Stengel's numerous shiftings of lineups could not prevent the team from losing more than 100 games for its third straight year.

There were some memorable events to mark the inaugural season of Shea Stadium, however. On Father's Day that year, the Mets hosted the Philadelphia Phillies, who sent their ace, Jim Bunning to the mound. Bunning got off to a hot start, setting the Mets batters down in order through the first few innings. By the middle of the game, fans and players alike realized that Bunning was on course to accomplish something spectacular in the annals of the game. He continued to deny New York batters any hits or walks, and excitement built in the later frames. By the time Bunning reached the bottom of the ninth, the Mets fans were firmly behind him. Knowing that they were watching history in the making, the New Yorkers cheered for their opponent for one of the few times in Mets history. The roar of the crowd increased with every pitch, as Bunning got the first two batters out. When he struck out John Stephenson to end the game, the crowd went wild. Bunning had successfully notched a perfect game, the first in the National League since 1880. Their team had lost, but Mets fans had been treated to a great moment in baseball history.[1]

Another milestone for the fans came when the All-Star Game was staged at Shea. New Yorkers were proud to show off their new stadium to the world, and they were anxious to actually see some good baseball played there. The game was a thriller. The National League squad was trailing, 4–3, entering the bottom of the ninth, and it looked like it was just going to be another heartbreaking loss for all the Mets fans in attendance. But the host team started a rally. After scratching out a run to tie the score, the senior circuit got two men aboard and Johnny Callison, the right fielder for the Philadelphia Phillies, stepped to the plate. Callison launched a three-run homer off of Red Sox pitcher Dick Radatz to take the walk-off, 7–4 victory and send the Mets fans home happy. It was the high point of the season for the New York fans. The second half of the season brought nothing but an ever-increasing number of losses for the hapless Mets, and left their fans hoping for a better year in 1965.

The Mets continued a practice that was fast becoming a team mantra during the off-season: signing big-name players who were at the end of their careers and could do little or nothing to help put the club on the path to winning. Warren Spahn's contract was purchased from the Milwaukee Braves, and Yogi Berra was signed as a free agent. Both were brought into the fold as part-time players and part-time coaches, and it was hoped that their veteran experience would aid the younger players, while their name recognition would help fill the seats at Shea. Spahn, a future Hall of Famer considered by many to be the best left-handed pitcher ever to play the game, had a miserable year, going 4–12 with an earned run average of 4.36. On July 17, the team released him. The San Francisco Giants picked him up for the remainder of the season, but poor performances there convinced Spahn to retire at the end of the campaign. Yogi Berra didn't even make it that long. By May 17, the Mets decided

14: A World Series and a Trip to the Hall

that the once powerful slugger had come to the end of the line. He had only two hits in nine at-bats before the team decided to cut him loose.

The season proved to be pretty much a carbon copy of the three preceding ones, as the Mets finished last once more with a record of 50–112. Little did Mets fans realize, but pieces were starting to come into place that would end their misery and give them something to cheer about. A 20-year-old first baseman named Ed Kranepool had taken over the starting position for the team, joined by 21-year-old left fielder Ron Swoboda. These two youngsters would figure prominently in the coming years, as the Mets clawed to climb out of the National League basement. Whatever success they were to achieve, it would be under a new manager. Casey Stengel announced his retirement from the Mets on August 30, 1965. The 75-year-old skipper had broken his hip the previous month and decided it was finally time to walk away from the game that had been so much a part of his life for 53 years.

Catcher Jerry Grote and outfielder Cleon Jones were added to the regular lineup for the 1966 season in an effort to bolster the team's offensive output. Pitching was also addressed, with long-time Pirates ace Bob Friend added to the rotation. Like so many big-name acquisitions before him, Friend was at the end of his career, and he would play his final season in a Mets uniform. His 5–8 record in New York was typical of the sub-standard performance the Mets had received from the aging stars they had signed over their first four years. The team did have some success in gathering together pieces that would eventually solve their pitching puzzle in 1966. Tug McGraw was one of the starting pitchers who would play a large role in the team's run for a championship. More importantly, the Mets had signed a young, can't-miss prospect who would become the face of the franchise. Ralph Kiner must have been pleasantly surprised to find that the young pitcher was Tom Seaver, the son of Charlie Seaver, his golf partner at the Crosby Pro-Am a decade earlier who had asked Kiner for an autograph while declaring that his boy would one day pitch in the majors. For the first time in their history, the Mets managed to lose fewer than 100 games in 1966, finishing with a record of 66–95 under new manager Wes Westrum. They also managed to climb out of the basement in the National League, finishing ninth, 7.5 games ahead of the Chicago Cubs.

In 1967, Mets fans got their first look at their new star and fan favorite when Tom Seaver made his debut. The rookie, who would quickly become known as "Tom Terrific," gave the New York faithful something to cheer about that season, as he went 16–13, posting a 2.76 earned run average and recording 170 strikeouts. Midway through the year, he was named to the All-Star team as the only Mets representative, where he added to his already growing legend among Mets fans. For the longest time, it looked as if Seaver would not play in the game, but the summer classic went into extra innings and turned into a marathon. When the National League took the lead in the top of the 15th inning, Seaver was brought in to close out the bottom of the frame and secure the win. He pitched a scoreless inning, much to the delight of Mets fans. Seaver would conclude the 1967 season by walking away with "Rookie of the Year" honors. The Mets had finally found their ace.

Another future ace would come to the team through rather odd circumstances. Jerry Koosman was discovered when the son of an usher at Shea Stadium wrote his father about a pitcher he had caught in the army at Fort Bliss, Texas. The team sent scouts to take a look at the hurler, and he was offered a contract after his discharge. But the Mets weren't yet sure that Koosman could cut it in the majors, and they were going to cut him in 1966. An assistant farm director advised that the team hold onto him until after his first payday, as the Mets had advanced him money when his car broke down on the way to spring training, and the debt had yet to be repaid.[2] Koosman would end up repaying the loan with dividends. He led all pitchers in strikeouts in the International League in 1966 and got called up to the Mets for a brief stint toward the end of the season. Though his record was 0–2 in nine appearances with the big team, the Mets had found their one-two punch in the starting rotation. For the moment, however, the Mets' additions merely held promise of better days to come. They had changed little in the fortunes of the fumbling franchise, as New York booted its way to a 61–101 record and eased back into the familiar surroundings of last place.

The 1968 season would see a number of changes for the Mets. For starters, Gil Hodges was back with the team, not as a player, but as their manager, replacing Wes Westrum. Yogi Berra had also returned as a full-time coach. Seaver had another good season, going 16–12, but Koos-

14: A World Series and a Trip to the Hall

man emerged as the star that year, posting a 19–12 record and a fantastic 2.08 earned run average. The pair was joined in the rotation by another hard-throwing right-hander who had initially been signed by the team in 1965, Nolan Ryan. He had been called up briefly in 1966 and had missed the 1967 season due to illness, an arm injury, and service with the Army Reserve. The Mets, usually the worst pitching team in the game, turned a corner that season when Ryan had the highest earned run average among all the starters with a more than respectable 3.09. All the other starters turned in earned run averages under 3.00. The performance of the pitchers allowed the Mets to have their best campaign to date, but it was not enough to propel them into any sort of contention. The team finished with a record of 73–79, good enough for only ninth place. It was a significant improvement in wins over the previous year, and the second time they had finished out of the basement, but how long would it be before all the parts came together and the Mets had their first winning season? Not long. A miracle was about to happen.

For Ralph Kiner, the seven years of struggling and misery with the Mets must have mirrored the seven years he had played in Pittsburgh. To be sure, there were many similarities between the two teams, including their last-place finishes and lack of pitching. In his whole Major League baseball career, no team that Kiner had been associated with had finished higher than second place, and that was the Indians in his final year. Before that, a fourth-place finish with the Pirates had been the high point. Everything would change in 1969. To begin with, there would be two more teams in the league: the San Diego Padres and the Montreal Expos. With baseball experiencing its second round of expansion in less than a decade, everyone was sure that the Mets would surely finish well above last place.

Things would come around full circle for the Mets, or the "Miracle Mets," as they came to be called in 1969. Instead of losing 100 games, they had their first 100 game-winning season in franchise history and clinched their first spot in the playoffs. Tom Seaver was on fire that year with a record of 25–7 and an earned run average of 2.21. Seaver would do more than his part to get the team to the post-season en route to winning the Cy Young Award. Jerry Koosman did his part as well, contributing a 17–9 record to the cause, and Gary Gentry added 13 wins to the total. With all these wins, one might think that New York coasted to the first-ever National League East title. Such was not the case. Eighteen games into the season, the Mets were 7–11 and tied for last place with the fledgling Expos and the Cardinals. By May 21, they ran off a sting of victories to pull even at 18–18, but they lost the next five games to post a record identical to where they had been after 41 games in the 1968 season.

But these were a new set of Mets. They didn't fold when adversity came their way. Instead, they rose up to challenge it. Winning the next five games, they were once more playing .500 ball on June 2. They didn't stop there, winning six more games before suffering another loss. In the middle of June, the front office made a move that seemed to be the final piece that might put the team over the top, a trade with the Expos to acquire power-hitting Don Clendenon. For the first time in their existence, the Mets found themselves in second place, three games behind the front-running Chicago Cubs. They were 3.5 games behind the Cubs in July, when the whole world stopped to bear witness to one of the greatest achievements in human history: the landing of men on the moon. On July 20, millions of eyes were glued to television sets as two American astronauts climbed down out of their lunar lander to walk on the surface of the moon. It was a very fitting event. Many people had predicted that there would be a man on the moon before the Mets ever won a pennant, and the first of those conditions had now been met. It was now up to New York to hold up its part of the bargain.[3]

On August 13, the team fell to third place, 9.5 games behind the Cubs, but they won 14 of their remaining 17 games that month to get right back into the thick of the race. When the Cubs came to New York to open a two-game series on September 8, the Mets trailed by only 2.5 games. A sweep of Chicago left the Cubs limping out of town with a narrow half-game lead. On September 10, the Mets swept a doubleheader against the Expos, and the clubhouse went wild when word was received that the Cubs had been beaten by the Phillies, meaning that New York now was in first place. As the Cubs began to fade, the Mets kept pouring it on. They kept their momentum going and pulled away from Chicago, building up a comfortable lead. On September 24 against the St. Louis

14: A World Series and a Trip to the Hall

Cardinals, Gary Gentry got the decision in a 6–0 victory that clinched the National League East Division title. The fans went wild, charging the field to tear out chunks of sod as mementoes of the event. The team would finish out the year with a record of 100–62, eight games ahead of the Cubs.

Ralph Kiner enjoyed the celebration every bit as much as the Mets players. "I never played for a championship team, so my experience at such affairs was as limited as that of the players. Perhaps, because of my age, however, I was more inclined to drink champagne than to pour it over someone else's head." That didn't keep him from having champagne poured over his head. While Kiner stood on a platform, interviewing Gil Hodges for WOR-TV, Tom Seaver led the first rush to drench Kiner in the bubbly. M. Donald Grant, Chairman of the Board for the Mets, was the next to give Kiner a good soaking as he shouted, "Our team finally caught up with out fans. Our fans were winners long ago." Kiner remembered the elation he shared with millions of Mets fans that night. "I found myself, like millions of New Yorkers, swept up in the emotion. In 10 years of playing major-league baseball, I had no pennant to celebrate. So this would be it for me, too. I wouldn't have missed it for the world."[4]

But the Mets weren't quite done with their miracle run. Next up was an appearance in the first-ever National League Championship Series against the Atlanta Braves. Tom Seaver took the mound to oppose Phil Niekro in the first game of the best-of-five series on October 4. Seaver didn't have his best stuff, but the Mets brought their bats and pounded out a 9–5 win with five runs in the top of the eighth. The Mets' vaunted pitching was again absent in the second game of the series, but they powered past the Braves with home runs by Tommie Agee, Ken Boswell, and Cleon Jones on their way to an 11–6 pounding. Game Three was played before the home fans at Shea Stadium, with Gary Gentry taking the hill for New York. For the third straight game, Mets pitching got roughed up, and Gentry was chased in the third inning. Nolan Ryan came in to hold the fort and try to keep the Mets in the game. Ryan did just that, and the Mets came roaring back. Tommie Agee and Ken Boswell each hit his second home runs of the series, and Wayne Garrett added another long shot to propel the team to a 7–4 victory and a sweep of the series. In the World Series the Mets would face the Baltimore Orioles, considered by most to be the best team in baseball.

Game One was played at Memorial Stadium in Baltimore on October 11, with Mike Cuellar toeing the rubber for the home team, opposed by Tom Seaver. The Orioles got to Seaver early, scoring a run in the bottom of the first inning, and it was pretty much over after a three-run fourth. New York was able to eke out only a single run, and Baltimore captured a 4–1 win and an early lead in the Series. Through the first four games of post-season play, the Mets' pitching staff had failed to display the dominance that had been such a large factor in winning the National League East. That was about to change. Jerry Koosman took the ball for the Mets in Game Two, facing Dave McNally. Both pitchers were brilliant, but Koosman was the better of the two. Allowing only two Baltimore hits, he earned a 2–1 win in the closely contested game. New York's pitching had arrived. It would make its presence known for the remainder of the Series.

Game Three was played in New York before a capacity crowd at Shea Stadium. Gary Gentry opposed Jim Palmer, and Gentry got the better of the Baltimore ace by shutting out the Orioles on three hits over 6 2/3 innings. The Mets collected only six hits themselves, but two of them were home runs, and New York walked away with a 5–0 victory. Tom Seaver took the mound for his second start of the Series on October 15, facing Mike Cuellar. In a classic pitchers' duel, the score was 1–0 New York going into the top of the ninth. Frank Robinson scored the tying run on a sacrifice fly, and when the Mets failed to score in the bottom of the frame, the game went into extra innings. New York manufactured a run in the bottom of the tenth for a 2–1 win. Mets fans could smell blood. Their team was only one game away from making the miracle complete. Jerry Koosman was the Mets' starter in Game Five, versus Dave McNally. The game was a very close affair, and the Orioles led 3–2 after six innings. Al Weis homered in the bottom of the seventh to tie things up, and the Mets pushed across two more runs in the bottom of the eighth to take a 5–3 lead. Koosman came on in the top of the ninth, and after giving up a leadoff walk, got the next three batters to slam the lid down tight. New York fans went wild, charging the field to celebrate with the team. The Miracle Mets had done the impossible. In one of the

14: A World Series and a Trip to the Hall

greatest upsets in sports history, they had brushed aside the mighty Baltimore Orioles to win bragging rights as the best team in baseball.

Kiner had been drinking it all in.

> The series was a big thrill for me. I was chosen to broadcast the games in Baltimore over the radio for the National Broadcasting Company while Lindsey Nelson did the telecasts from New York with Curt Gowdy. I can remember sitting in the booth with NBC's Jim Simpson prior to the start of the first game and being visited by Joe Garagiola. "I just wanted to remind you," my old teammate said, "that over 80 million people will be listening to this game on radio." Thanks for the reminder, Joe. I got through the Series somehow, and so did the Mets.... Yes, it was a helluva season.[5]

Twenty-three years after walking onto the field at Forbes Field, Kiner was finally associated with a winner. He had only been announcing the games, not playing in them, but he had enjoyed the experience immensely.

The Mets expected to repeat in the 1970 season, and though they made things interesting, the team ended up third in the East that year. Third-place finishes also crowned their efforts in 1971 and 1972. In 1973, the Mets once again won the National League East. They faced the Cincinnati Reds in the Championship Series and beat the Big Red Machine three games to two. In the World Series, they faced the Oakland Athletics, losing the highly competitive Series in seven games. In 1974, the team suffered its first losing season since 1968, finishing next to last in the division. 1975 saw the Mets rise above .500 again with a record of 82–80, but that was not the big story that year for Ralph Kiner or for his faithful fans in Pittsburgh or New York.

In Kiner's 15th and final year on the ballot, the baseball writers voted him into the Hall of Fame, the only player that year to receive the necessary votes for induction. He got 273 of the 362 votes available, for a percentage of 75.4, just squeaking by the 75 percent required for induction. He would be joined by three players voted in by the Veterans Committee: Billy Herman, his old manager, Earl Averill and Bucky Harris. The last member of the class would be Judy Johnson, elected by members of the Negro Leagues Committee.

Kiner had eagerly watched the results of the Hall of Fame voting for the last several years.

> I had come close to receiving the required 75 percent of the vote on several occasions, but now I was down to the final ballot. If I didn't get the necessary number

of votes in January 1975, I would have to wait a minimum of five more years for consideration by the Veterans Committee. God I wanted it. I'd been knocking on the door for so long. In my mind, I had earned it. It wasn't an ego thing. I started to think of it as a degree, a doctorate. I had excelled in what I did. Yet, I steeled myself for the worst on the day the votes were tabulated. I was in St. Petersburg at the time, and I didn't dare to pack for the trip to New York, where the official announcement would be made. Jack Lang, the secretary of the BBWAA, was to call with the results between 3:30 and 5 P.M. Five o'clock came and went. At about 5:25, I figured, well, that's it, Jack doesn't want to give me the bad news. Then the phone rang. I let it ring four times. Four was my uniform number. I'm not generally superstitious, but in this case I couldn't help myself. It was Jack's voice, all right, and he said, "Ralph. How does it feel to be a member of the Hall of Fame?" I said "You're kidding!" And he said he wasn't kidding. Then I said something clever, like "Wow!" The reason for the delay, it developed, was that of the 362 votes cast, I needed 272. I received 273. That was all right with me. I would gladly have settled for 272. I flew to New York that night and appeared at a press conference in the Americana Hotel the following morning. Hank Greenberg joined me there, making the day complete.[6]

Induction Day at the Hall of Fame was held on Monday, August 18. Kiner broadcast the Mets game on Sunday and then left in a chartered plane for Cooperstown. His daughter K.C. traveled with him. The rest of the family went by car and had already departed. The weather was terrible, and the plane couldn't make a landing at Cooperstown. After considering several other options, the pilot finally set the plane down in Albany, where Kiner rented a car for the rest of the trip. He and K.C. started out and drove for a few hours before they saw a sign for Montreal and discovered they had

Kiner being presented with his Hall of Fame plaque by Commissioner Bowie Kuhn. Elected on his final year of eligibility, he attained just over the minimum 75 percent of the votes from the baseball writers that was required for election. Kiner would attend the induction ceremonies yearly after his induction, to welcome new members to the Hall and to reminisce with other greats of the game.

14: A World Series and a Trip to the Hall

been traveling in the wrong direction. After getting their bearings, he pointed the car in the direction of Cooperstown, and the pair arrived in the town well after midnight. He joined the rest of his family, including his wife, Barbara, and prepared for the ceremony. Barbara was Ralph's second wife. He and Nancy had divorced in 1968, and he had married Barbara in 1969.

The induction ceremony was held outdoors, in a grove of trees next to the National Baseball Library. The inductees were presented in alphabetical order by Bowie Kuhn, the Commissioner of Baseball, which meant Kiner would go last, after Judy Johnson.

> This was one time I didn't mind being dropped from the cleanup position. As calm as I was speaking to millions on radio and television, the thought of an acceptance speech in a small village named for James Fenimore Cooper left me shaking. Still, I struggled through it, recounting some of the standout moments in my life. These included the backyard burial of the magazines in Alhambra, the embarrassing date with Liz Taylor, and memories of Pittsburgh, where the laughs certainly outnumbered the victories.

Nerves aside, Kiner remembered that "the ceremony went well. I was rewarded with a Hall of Fame plaque that reads:

> RALPH MCPHERRAN KINER
> PITTSBURGH, N.L. CHICAGO, N.L.
> CLEVELAND, A.L. 1946–1955
> HIT 369 HOME RUNS AND AVERAGED BETTER
> THAN 100 RUNS BATTED IN PER SEASON IN
> HIS TEN-YEAR CAREER. ONLY PLAYER TO LEAD HIS
> LEAGUE OR SHARE LEAD IN HOMERS SEVEN
> YEARS IN A ROW, 1946–1952. TWICE HAD
> MORE THAN 50 IN SEASON. SET N.L. MARK
> OF 101 FOUR-BAGGERS IN TWO SUCCESSIVE
> YEARS WITH 54 IN 1949 AND 47 IN 1950.
> LED N.L. IN SLUGGING PCT. THREE TIMES."[7]

Kiner was rightfully proud of his induction into the Baseball Hall of Fame. He had earned the honor on the field of play, and for his many fans, the recognition was long overdue. He made it a point to attend all of the induction ceremonies that followed, to welcome the incoming members into the Hall and to commune with the other greats of the game. He also served on the Veterans Committee, responsible for selecting players for inclusion in the Hall who were beyond the 15-year window of eligibility to be voted in by the baseball writers.

CHAPTER 15

Mr. Met

Kiner's induction into the Baseball Hall of Fame only increased his stature among the players and fans in New York, and made it all the more desirable to be a guest on his "Kiner's Korner" segment. It didn't alter the manner in which he dealt with people, however. Still the same gracious and affable character, his standing as one of the select greats of the game only served to exemplify the fact that he had never allowed fame or success to alter the caring and kind way he interacted with others. He was, in all respects, a gentleman, the sort of well-mannered and dignified patriarch that has so often been depicted as Southern chivalry in the movies. It was no wonder everyone liked him and wanted to be near him. What was there that was not to like?

The Mets continued to be a force in the National League East for a couple of years following Kiner's induction into the Hall of Fame. In 1977, Tom Seaver was traded to the Cincinnati Reds for Pat Zachary, Doug Flynn, Steve Henderson, and Dan Norman. Dave Kingman was traded to the San Diego Padres for Bobby Valentine and Paul Siebert, and Mike Phillips was sent to the St. Louis Cardinals for Joel Youngblood. In New York, it was known as the "Midnight Massacre."[1] Without Seaver, the heart and soul seemed to go out of the team, and the Mets fell into last place in the division for the next several years. They rose to prominence again in the mid 1980s, with new stars like Darryl Strawberry, Dwight Gooden, Keith Hernandez, and Gary Carter.

In 1986, Kiner and the Mets went to their second World Series. The team finished the season with a franchise-best record of 108–54, easily capturing the division title. In their 25th year of existence, it was fitting that the Mets were to face the Houston Astros, also celebrating their 25th year in existence, in the best-of-seven National League Champi-

15: Mr. Met

onship Series. The series opened at the Astrodome in Houston on October 8, with New York ace Dwight Gooden facing Mike Scott. In one of the best pitching duels in post-season history, the Astros defeated the Mets, 1–0. Bob Ojeda faced former Met Nolan Ryan the following day. There was a great deal more offense in this contest, and the Mets got the better of it with a 5–1 victory.

Game Three was at Shea Stadium in New York, and featured Ron Darling on the hill for New York facing Bob Knepper for the Astros. The game was closely contested, and the Mets were trailing 5–4 in the bottom of the ninth inning with a runner on and one out when Lenny Dykstra came to the plate. Dykstra got hold of a Dave Smith pitch, sending a long fly ball down the right field line that ended up in the bleachers for a walk-off, two-run homer. The Mets were up in the Series, 2–1. Game four pitted Sid Fernandez against Mike Scott, who was making his second start of the Series for Houston. The Astros got to Fernandez for two runs in the top of the second inning, and that was all they would need. Scott allowed only three Mets hits on the way to a 3–1 victory.

Game Five, the last to be played at Shea Stadium, saw Dwight Gooden and Nolan Ryan both make their second starts. In a nail-biter that lasted 12 innings, Gooden scattered nine hits while allowing only a single run in ten innings. The Mets managed only four hits of their own, but clustered two of them, with a walk sandwiched in between, in the bottom of the 12th, to escape with the 2–1 win.

The Series returned to Houston on October 15, with Bob Ojeda facing Bob Knepper. At the end of nine innings, the score was tied 3–3, and the teams again went into extra frames. The Mets scratched out a run in the top of the 14th, but the Astros answered with a solo home run in their half to continue the contest. The Mets clustered three hits and a walk in the top of the 16th to plate three runs and take a 7–4 lead. But the Astros would not go quietly. They collected three hits and a walk of their own in the bottom of the frame, but could push only two runs across the plate. The final was 7–6 Mets, and New York was headed to the World Series for the second time. Their opponent would be the Boston Red Sox.

It was fitting that Kiner and the Mets were going to the World Series together again. After all, he was celebrating his 25th anniversary with the team, as one of the original Mets, and what could have been a better anniversary gift? Kiner and Bob Murphy were the remaining members of the trio that had been brought together to broadcast the Mets games back in 1962. Lindsey Nelson had left following the 1978 season for the San Francisco Giants. His departure ended a 17-year partnership, the longest for a trio of broadcasters in baseball history. Kiner had thought about leaving himself after the 1978 campaign. He remembered that this was a "depressing period" as it "was clear to all of us that the organization was collapsing. The team was in the cellar, the farm system had dried up, and the Mets weren't participating in the free-agent draft. Worst of all, there was no professional baseball man at the top. At least in 1962, there was George Weiss." The Dodgers made an inquiry about Kiner's availability to fill in for Vin Scully while he did the "Game of the Week" telecasts for the network, but no offer was made. "I don't know whether or not I would have gone," Kiner said, "but it wouldn't have occurred to me if the Mets weren't in such dire straights."[2]

Perhaps Kiner felt that with the Mets in a state of decline, he couldn't bear to go through another extended period of losing, hopeless seasons. There had been enough of that thus far in his career, both with Pittsburgh and New York. It would be a difficult decision. After 25 years with the team, New York was home and the Mets were family. Still, the prospect of watching that family struggle as a punching bag for the rest of the league must have been agonizing. Family won out, and he decided to stay for the long haul. In 1983, he and Murphy were joined in the booth by Tim McCarver, the All-Star catcher who had played 22 years in the majors. McCarver had already established himself as a first-rate broadcaster with the Philadelphia Phillies from 1980–1982, and had done work for ABC, including calling the World Series in 1985. It would be the beginning of another long partnership, with McCarver staying in the Mets booth for 16 years.

The World Series also served as something of a distraction for Kiner. On September 4, 1986, he received word that his longtime friend and mentor, Hank Greenberg, had died. Kiner had known for some time that his friend was sick, but Greenberg had concealed the fact that he was suffering from terminal kidney cancer. The news hit Kiner hard. Greenberg had been a tremendous influence in his life. As a boy, Ham-

15: Mr. Met

mering Hank had been his idol, his favorite player in the game he loved. When they played together with the Pirates, Greenberg became his teacher, mentor and friend. He took a fatherly interest in the boy's life and career that continued as long as both of them lived. He had been instrumental in getting Kiner as a player with the Indians, and had helped him to get jobs as general manager with the San Diego Padres and announcer with the Chicago White Sox. True, Kiner owed a great deal to Greenberg, but it was more than that, much more. Greenberg and Kiner were the same sort: gentlemen of the highest order, with Greenberg serving in the role of the doting older brother. They admired, respected and loved one another, and the bond they had formed was as strong as it was compassionate. The elation Kiner felt about going to another World Series would be tempered by the great sense of loss he felt for the passing for the man who had held the most important place in his life.

The 1986 World Series has gone down in history as one of the best and most bizarre ever played. The Red Sox sought to capture their first title since 1918 and erase the "curse of the Bambino," a superstition held among Boston fans that the selling of Babe Ruth, back in 1919, had jinxed the Red Sox from that time forward. It would be a Series filled with heroes and goats, with desperation and clutch performances that turned hopelessness into unbounded elation. Fans of the teams and baseball aficionados alike were treated to a classic, and they tuned in to watch in such numbers as to make the 1986 Series the highest rated to that date.

The Series started at Shea Stadium on October 18, and featured Ron Darling for the Mets against Bruce Hurst for the Red Sox. Darling was spectacular, allowing only three hits in seven innings of work. The Red Sox got an unearned run in the top of the seventh, and it was all the scoring that Mets pitching would give up. But that was enough. Hurst matched Darling pitch for pitch, scattering just four hits himself in eight innings and keeping the Mets off the scoreboard. Calvin Schiraldi took over for Hurst to close out the ninth, and Boston walked away with the 1–0 win. The following day saw both teams send their aces to the mound, with Roger Clemens opposing Dwight Gooden. The game promised to be a pitching classic but did not turn out that way. Both Clemens and

Gooden got into trouble early, and both were gone by the sixth inning. Boston jumped out to the lead with three runs in the top of the third, and they never looked back. Adding runs in four of the next six innings, the Red Sox cruised to the 9–3 victory, taking a commanding 2–0 lead in the Series.

With the next three games to be played at Fenway Park in Boston, it looked as if the Mets were all but out of the Series. Bob Ojeda was tapped to start Game Three in Boston and hopefully stop the bleeding. Oil Can Boyd got the start for the Red Sox. The Mets set the pace for the game when Lenny Dykstra led off the top of the first inning with a home run to right. New York tacked on three more runs before the inning was over and took a commanding 4–0 lead. That was all the support Ojeda would need. Scattering five hits over seven innings, Ojeda allowed only one run. Roger McDowell threw shutout ball for the final two frames as the Mets bounced back with a 7–1 victory. They were down, but not out. Game Four pitted Ron Darling against Al Nipper with a chance for New York to even the Series and make it a best-of-three. Gary Carter got the scoring started with a two-run homer in the top of the fourth inning. The Mets added another run and held a 3–0 lead going into the seventh frame. Lenny Dykstra added a two-run shot of his own in the seventh, and Carter launched another solo shot in the eighth as the Mets flexed their muscles and used the long ball for a 6–2 win.

Game Five featured a showdown between Dwight Gooden and Bruce Hurst. Gooden struggled again, surrendering four runs in only four-plus innings of work. Hurst made the lead stand up, turning in another stellar performance, and Boston took the 4–2 victory, placing them one win away from clinching the Series.

Game Six went back to New York. The Mets had their backs against the wall. Anything less than a sweep of the next two games would result in a loss of the Series. New York sent Bob Ojeda to the mound, hoping he could repeat his performance in Game Three and give the Mets a chance to pull even for a winner-take-all seventh game. Roger Clemens got the nod for Boston. Ojeda turned in a solid performance, going six innings and allowing only two runs. Clemens matched him, going seven innings and giving up two runs, one of them unearned. The Red Sox

15: Mr. Met

scratched out a run in the top of the seventh to take a 3–2 lead, and the fans at Shea started to despair, but the game was far from over. The Mets came back, scoring the tying run on a sacrifice fly in the bottom of the eighth to knot the game at 3–3. After a scoreless ninth, the game went into extra innings. Boston plated two runs in the top of the tenth when Dave Henderson led off with a home run to deep left and Marty Barrett singled home Wade Boggs. The Mets came up in the bottom of the inning and quickly made two fly ball outs. Fans and players alike thought the game was over. But Gary Carter got things started with a single to left. Kevin Mitchell followed with a single to center. When Ray Knight hit a liner to center that fell safely, Carter scampered home to score and Mitchell advanced to third. The tying run was now just 90 feet away. Boston brought in Bob Stanley to try to get the final out. Mookie Wilson stepped to the plate for the Mets, and Stanley threw a wild pitch, allowing Mitchell to score from third and Knight to move to second. Wilson then hit a ground ball to first that should have ended the inning. Bill Buckner was the Red Sox first baseman, and he slid over to field the ball, but it took a last-second bounce, squirting through his legs and just beneath his glove out into right field. Knight was rounding third as the ball made its way to the outfield grass. Turning it on, he raced for home to give the Mets an unbelievable 6–5 comeback win.

The seventh and deciding game of the Series was played at Shea Stadium on October 27. Bruce Hurst got his third start for the Red Sox and was opposed by Ron Darling. Hurst had been virtually untouchable for the Mets in his two previous outings, and he looked to be continuing the hot stretch on this day. Boston struck for three runs in the top of the second inning, and Hurst kept the Mets scoreless through five. Then, in the bottom of the sixth, the Mets' bats finally got to him, parlaying three hits and a walk into three runs. Calvin Schiraldi replaced Hurst in the bottom of the seventh, and New York jumped on him quickly. Ray Knight led off with a homer, and by the time the rally ended, the Mets had put three runs on the board. The Red Sox plated two runs in the top of the eighth, but New York answered with two of their own in the bottom of the frame, started with a leadoff home run by Darryl Strawberry. Jesse Orosco came in to pitch a scoreless top of the ninth, and the Mets had done it. The 8–5 win gave them their second World

Series championship in front of the home-town crowd. The Mets' return to prominence was complete.

Kiner would stay on, through the good times and the bad. The original Met would become the everlasting Met, as he continued to broadcast through the 1980s, the 1990s, the 2000s, and into the next decade. Faces came and went, but one remained constant: Ralph Kiner. The Mets returned to the post-season as division champs in 1988, but were eliminated in the National League Championship Series. The team then went on a ten-year decline, not resurging into prominence until the 1997 campaign, when they challenged for a wild card spot. In 1998, they once more fell just short of the playoffs, losing a spot in the post-season by one game. In 1999, they made it to the National League Championship Series, where they fell to the team of the decade, the Atlanta Braves. The Mets finally put it all together again in 2000, getting into the post-season as a wild card team and capturing the National League title. In what came to be referred to as the Subway Series, they faced the cross-town New York Yankees, but were easily defeated in five games. The Mets were up and down in the new millennium, mostly down, except for the 2006 season, when they made it to the National League Championship Series, but lost to the St Louis Cardinals in seven games.

The 2008 season was the last campaign that the Mets called Shea Stadium home. A new ballpark was built in Flushing Meadows, adjacent to Shea, and was named Citi Field. The Mets played their first game there on March 29, 2009, and it has been their home ever since. Shea Stadium was torn down, but a large part of that place moved to Citi Field when Kiner accompanied the team to its new park. The Mets have yet to bring any more titles home since departing Shea, but each new season brings with it the hope of spring, when baseball fans across the country are filled with the enthusiasm that this will be the year for the team they love. There have, to date, been no miracles at Citi Field, but sitting as it does, right next to the site where Shea Stadium once was, one must imagine that there is still a little magic left on that ground and that the Mets will find it, sooner rather than later.

Kiner continued to be a mainstay of the Mets' broadcasting team well into the first decade of the new century, even after Bob Murphy retired in 2003. His familiar figure was seen around the ballpark frequently, well into his 80s, despite a bout of Bell's Palsy that caused him to have slightly slurred speech, and he continued to appear on the air, though less often, right up until the time of his passing.

In his personal life, Kiner divorced Barbara in 1980. It was apparently an unhappy union, as he described the marriage as "an experience I did not enjoy." He stated that it was his broadcast partner, Bob Murphy, who had introduced them, and he used to kid Murphy frequently about it. "Hell, I just introduced you to her. I didn't say you had to marry her," was Murphy's pat response.[3] Whether it was true or not, Kiner blamed Barbara for taking a number of his baseball memorabilia items when the two parted. In 1982, he married DiAnn Shugart, a businesswoman from the Palm Springs area. The pair seemed to be happy together, though DiAnn knew little about sports, and he said that he had to explain a lot of things about baseball, including his accomplishments, to her. Something tells me that he really didn't mind recounting all the stories of his past glory to the loving ears of his new spouse. And what the heck, he could always embellish the stories a little if he wanted to, since she was a novice and couldn't call him on it. Then again, his accomplishments were such that he didn't need to embellish, and knowing the man, it probably never entered his mind to do so. DiAnn passed away in 2004 of cancer.

Kiner was never what you would call a smooth and polished announcer, but he was definitely real and human, and he was a font of baseball information. He might not have been as good as he was if he had been polished and suave. It was the human factor that made him so beloved by Mets fans, and by baseball enthusiasts around the world. He was constantly spewing out malapropos, or Kinerisms, as they came to be known, which was a huge part of his mystique. Everyone had their favorites, including long-time broadcast partner Tim McCarver. On one occasion, Kiner mistakenly called McCarver Tim MacArthur. McCarver corrected him on it and stated that he was probably thinking about the general. The pair then discussed Douglas MacArthur for a few minutes during the broadcast. Later, when the Mets were being blown out of the game, McCarver said that one of General MacArthur's favorite lines was "Chance favors the prepared man, and obviously the Mets weren't prepared tonight." Kiner then turned toward the camera and quipped,

"MacArthur also said, 'I shall return,' and we'll be right back after this," as he broke away for commercials.[4] Calling McCarver the wrong name was nothing. Kiner even did it to himself, when he stated his name as Ralph Korner.[5]

Among his other great Kinerisms were:

"On Father's Day, we again wish you all Happy Birthday."
"All of his saves have come in relief appearances."
"Two-thirds of the Earth is covered by water. The other third is covered by Gary Maddox." [talking about a great fielding play]
"If Casey Stengel was alive today, he'd be spinning in his grave."
"Hello everybody. Welcome to Kiner's Korner. This is … uh. I'm … uh."
"The Mets have gotten their leadoff batter on only once this inning."
"There's a lot of heredity in that family."
"It's [Phil Niekro's knuckleball] like watching Mario Andretti park a car."
"[Don Sutton] lost thirteen games in a row without winning a ballgame."
"Now up to bat for the Mets is Gary Cooper." [referring to Gary Carter]
"All of the Mets' road wins against the Dodgers this year occurred at Dodger Stadium."
"Solo homers usually come with no one on base."
"We'll be back after this word from Manufacturer's Hangover."
"Darryl Strawberry has been voted to the Hall of Fame five years in a row."

These, and hundreds more, only added to the charm and humanity that was Ralph Kiner. They were pearls that were to be savored almost as much as the baseball wisdom and knowledge he regularly dispensed. In a world of the here and now, Kiner was more of a here and then sort of man. While current and informed on everything that was going on in the present, he also connected viewers to the past in a way that allowed his fans to experience the vast panorama that is the history of professional baseball, and he did it in an enjoyable and entertaining way that made him more of a friend than an icon.

Ralph McPherran Kiner passed

A long-time broadcast partner of Kiner's, Tim McCarver always remembered him for his gentlemanly bearing and for his kindness to all he came in contact with.

15: Mr. Met

away of natural causes on Thursday, February 6, 2014, at his home in Rancho Mirage, at the age of 91. Upon learning of his death, Mets CEO Fred Wilpon said, "Ralph Kiner was one of the most beloved people in Mets history—an original Met and extraordinary gentleman. After a Hall of Fame playing career, Ralph became a treasured broadcasting icon for more than half a century. His knowledge of the game, wit, and charm entertained generations of Mets fans. Like his stories he was one of a kind. We send out deepest condolences to Ralph's five children and 12 grandchildren. Our sport and society today lost one of the all-time greats." Jeff Idelson, the president of the Hall of Fame, echoed those sentiments. "As one of baseball's most prolific power hitters for a decade, Ralph struck fear into the hearts of the best pitchers of baseball's Golden Era despite his easy-going nature, disarming humility and movie-star smile. His engaging personality and profound knowledge of the game turned him into a living room companion for millions of New York Mets fans who adored his game broadcasts and later 'Kiner's Korner' for more than half a century. He was as comfortable hanging out in Palm Springs with his friend Bob Hope as he was hitting in front of Hank Greenberg at Forbes Field." His old partner, Tim McCaver, simply stated, "His universal love was something to behold, and with Ralph's passing, baseball has lost its best generational connection."[6]

One thing is certain, Ralph Kiner was a giant of a man, both as a player and as a broadcaster. Then again, he was a giant of a man simply as a human being, and that is probably the single greatest feature that made his success not only possible, but assured. There's an old saying that a man never stands taller than when he stoops to help a child. Ralph Kiner had that sort of quality. Always caring, always compassionate, always ready to give of his time and knowledge to others, he was the sort of man that every mother hopes her son will grow up to be. Beatrice Kiner had done herself proud in rearing her boy into the sort of man Ralph Kiner became. But I'm sure she knew that.

Epilogue

It is a wonderful thing indeed when a person gets to spend his life doing something he is good at and has passion for. Most people, regrettably, never get to experience that thrill. Ralph Kiner was a baseball player. That is what he was intended to be from the time he was born. His father's love of the game was already instilled in him before he ever shagged his first fly ball at the Bodkin household back in Alhambra, California. His love for the game grew throughout his boyhood years, and, along with his talent, made his life's work an obvious choice. His path to the Major Leagues became almost assured when he was signed to a contract by the Pittsburgh Pirates. More than two years in the service of his country during World War II may have interrupted his baseball career, but it also turned the boy into a man, and when he returned to the game, it was as a fully developed man—physically, intellectually, and emotionally.

In 1946, he broke in with the Pittsburgh Pirates, as baseball helped to bring about a sense of normalcy to a country that had just experienced the hardships and sacrifices of war. Kiner's rookie season was both a glimpse of promise and a foreshadowing of things to come. Kiner thrilled Pirates fans by blasting 23 home runs and bringing the National League home run championship to Pittsburgh. While Pirates fans had become used to having star players on their teams over the years, a power hitter who could regularly launch balls over the outfield fences was a novelty. Kiner became the greatest power hitter in Pirates history by the time his seven-plus years in Pittsburgh had come to a close. He had won outright, or tied, for the National League home run title in all seven seasons, breaking Babe Ruth's record for consecutive titles and setting a mark that has not been broken. He was also the first National League player

Epilogue

to hit 50 or more home runs twice in his career, and he averaged over 100 runs batted in for the duration of his ten-year career.

His accomplishments are all the more amazing when one considers the fact that almost all of his playing time was on inferior teams, particularly in Pittsburgh, where the team finished no higher than fourth place. The rest of the years, the Bucs were either last or next to last, and the 1952 squad was one of the worst teams of the 20th Century. Kiner accomplished his feats largely alone, bereft of protection in the lineup for most of his career. Opposing pitchers often would throw around him during critical situations, as attested to by the numerous times he led the league in walks. But he never sulked or complained. He merely went about doing his job in the best way he knew how, and his best was pretty darned good.

He didn't even bemoan his ill fortune when a chronic back condition forced him to walk away from the game he loved at an age when many superstars often experienced some of their best production. He simply took it in stride and moved on to the next chapter of his life, with grace and confidence. His personality, intellect, and love of the game made his success as a broadcaster almost a foregone conclusion, even before he began his second career. The affable and approachable star found a perfect way to stay connected to the game he loved, and to connect new generations of baseball fans to the heroes of the past. He became such an iconic figure as a Mets broadcaster that younger fans often had to be educated about the fact that he had been a star of even greater magnitude as a player.

Baseball writers debated Kiner's qualifications for election to the Baseball Hall of Fame for more than a decade before he finally received the required number of votes to gain his admittance. His right to be in that hallowed hall continues to be debated even to this day by those who point to his home run total and compare it to those of later players. All those who question Kiner's qualifications are missing one all-important point. The Hall of Fame was created to recognize players who displayed superiority and dominance during their careers. For seven years, Ralph Kiner was the most feared home run hitter in the game. The fact is that Kiner's numbers, when compared to some other members of the Hall, were reduced by the limited number of years he got to play, but during

Epilogue

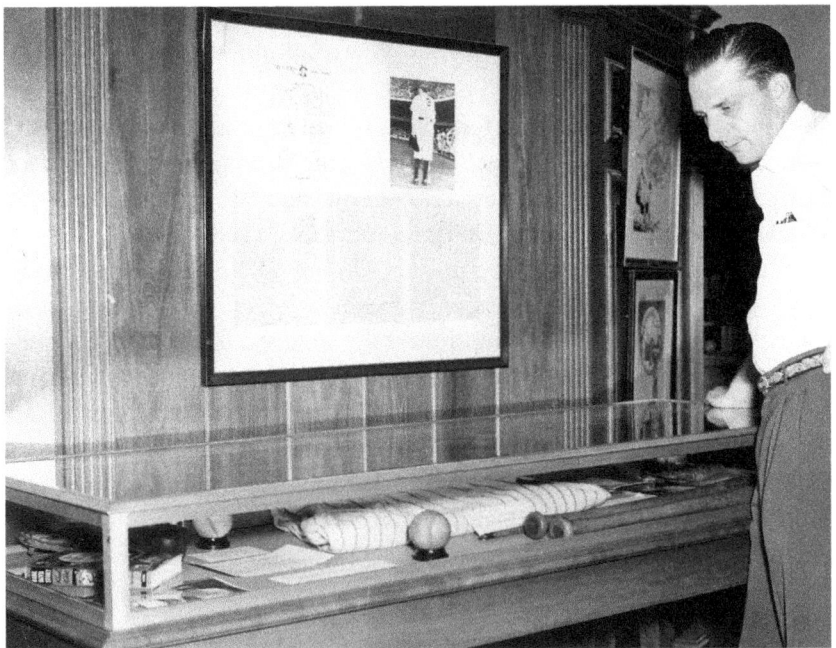

Kiner looking at some of the memorabilia collected during his playing days. His memories were not kept under glass, but rather shared with Mets audiences who listened to his broadcasts for more than 50 years. Kiner's ability to connect the present with the past was one of his most endearing qualities, giving listeners a link to the great players of other eras of the game.

those ten years, he was absolutely among the very best in the game. That's saying something when one considers that Kiner played during a time that many consider to be the Golden Age of baseball. A quick perusal of the American and National League All-Star Game rosters of which Kiner was a part reveals a veritable who's who of the greats of the game. Does Ralph Kiner belong in the Hall of Fame? Absolutely!

Though I was born too late to see him play, I have talked to numerous people over the years who were fortunate enough to watch Kiner and to follow his career. Invariably, their eyes will light up and their lips will curl into a smile when asked about him. They recount their favorite Kiner stories with the same enthusiasm and reverence reserved for greats like Mantle, Mays, and DiMaggio. In some ways, there seems to be an even greater connection for Kiner's fans. Most of us root for our team's star players as part of rooting for the team itself. From what I have been able to conclude from the responses to my many questions, Kiner was more than just a player to his fans, he was more like a part of the family, even if he was an adopted part. He was one of their own, the perfect example of the hometown boy made good, and his success somehow made those who rooted for him feel good about themselves.

In the end, the best that can be said about Ralph Kiner is that he was a good man. That somehow transcended even his greatness as a player or broadcaster. He was universally beloved because of his personality and character, and he could make a room better just by walking into it. People loved to be in his company, loved to bask in his grace and charm. Regardless of their station in life, can anyone hope for more than to be universally loved and respected? Tim McCarver captured the essence of the man when he said, "What Ralph learned was how to treat people, and he evidently learned that at an early age because he was across the board nice to everybody."[1]

APPENDIX ONE

Career Stats and Comparison to Other Hall of Fame Members

Ralph Kiner's seven consecutive years as home run champion of the National League is still a record in the Major Leagues. His 175 home runs at Forbes Field were the most hit by any player at that park. Second place in that category is held by another Pirates great, Roberto Clemente, who hit 86 home runs at Forbes. At the time of his retirement, Kiner stood sixth on the all-time home run list. That placement has dropped significantly over the past several decades, dropping him to 78th on the all-time list at the time of this writing. When one considers that he still ranks fifth in home run percentage, with a rate of 7.09, it is evident that his abbreviated career totals belie the fearsome impact he had at the plate. He was the first National League player to hit 50 or more home runs in two seasons, though he has been joined in that department by several other players over the years. In fact, Sammy Sosa performed the feat four times.

Kiner's career .279 batting average represented solid performance over his time in the majors, but it is on the low end of the spectrum for Hall of Fame members. He and Rickey Henderson tie for the lowest batting average among left fielders inducted into the Hall. His on-base percentage, aided by the 110 walks he averaged each season, was .398, placing him in sixth place in the same group. The only left fielders with a better on-base percentage were: Rickey Henderson (.401), Joe Kelley (.402), Ed Delahanty (.411), Jesse Burkett (.415), and Ted Williams (.482). Considering that Delahanty, Burkett, and Kelley were all players from the late 1800s, Kiner's on-base percentage places him in select company among his peers.

He was sixth among all Major League players in home runs at the

Appendix One: Stats and Comparison to Other HoF Members

time of his retirement, but 369 places him sixth among left fielders currently in the Hall of Fame. Above him are: Jim Rice (382), Billy Williams (426), Carl Yastrzemski (452), Willie Stargell (475), and Ted Williams (521). Still, he rates higher than the other 13 left fielders to be inducted. Kiner excelled at slugging percentage, with a career .548 average, placing him in second place, behind Ted Williams' astounding .634 average. In fact, Kiner's slugging percentage is better than all four left fielders who led him in home runs: Willie Stargell (.529), Jim Rice (.502), Billy Williams (.492), and Carl Yastrzemski (.462).

Kiner's 1,015 runs batted in place him near the bottom of the list, tied with Fred Clarke for fifth from the bottom. The only left fielders with fewer runs batted in are Jim O'Rourke (1,010), Jesse Burkett (952), Lou Brock (900) and Chick Hafey (833). This stat can be deceiving because Kiner played so many fewer seasons than most of his peers in the Hall. His value to his teams can better be seen when one looks at his season average of runs batted in, which was 101.5. Of all left fielders in the Hall of Fame, he holds the highest average. Behind him are Joe Medwick (98.79), Ted Williams (96.79), Ed Delahanty (91.5), and Jim Rice (90.69). All other left fielders averaged fewer than 90 runs batted in per season. In fact, more than half of them averaged fewer than 80 RBI per year.

When it comes to runs scored, Kiner's 971 is next to last, above only the 777 scored by Chick Hafey. It's a far different story when one looks at the season average for these players. Kiner's 97.1 runs scored per season ranks him fourth among all left fielders and second among those playing in the modern era. Above him are: Jesse Burkett (107.5), Lou Brock (100.62) and Ed Delahanty (99.94). The only other left fielders to average more than 90 runs scored per season are: Joe Kelley (94.73), Ted Williams (94.63), and Rickey Henderson (91.8).

For a power hitter, Kiner didn't strike out a great deal. He logged only 749 strikeouts in 6,256 plate appearances in the course of his career. That meant that he went down on strikes once in every 8.32 plate appearances. Considering that he averaged 4.25 plate appearances per game, that meant he struck out only once every two games. That's far above average for a dead pull power hitter.

When it comes to stolen bases, Kiner rates at the bottom of the list,

Appendix One: Stats and Comparison to Other HoF Members

just above Willie Stargell for last place. Kiner managed only 22 swipes during his career, with Stargell stealing only 17. This is a stat not worth making comparisons to when contrasted with the 1,406 steals Rickey Henderson amassed or the 938 swipes by Lou Brock.

All things considered, Kiner rates well among the left fielders who have been elected to the Baseball Hall of Fame. That said, he was elected with the next to lowest percentage of votes from the baseball writers of anyone in his group. He received 273 of 362 votes cast, for 75.41 percent. A player must receive a minimum of 75 percent to be inducted, and he sneaked in in his last year of eligibility in 1975. The only left fielder receiving a lower percentage was Al Simmons, one of the most complete left fielders to ever play the game, at 75.38. The top three are Rickey Henderson (94.81), Carl Yastrzemski (94.63), and Ted Williams (93.38).

Kiner's numbers are all the more impressive when one considers the fact that he accomplished all his Hall of Fame stats on teams that were mostly lousy. In his seven-plus years with the Pirates, the team had a winning record only once, when it finished in fourth place. His two seasons with the Cubs resulted in back-to-back seventh-place finishes, and woefully losing records. Kiner's only chance to play on a good team was with the Cleveland Indians in 1955. That year the Tribe finished with a record of 93–61 and finished second in the American League, three games behind the New York Yankees. He could not take full advantage of his time with the Indians, as his back problems were becoming severe, causing his to miss 45 games, or more than 25 percent of the season. His swing and his running ability were greatly impacted, causing him to have his lowest batting average (.243) and his fewest home runs (18) of his entire career. His diminishing abilities, along with the intense pain he had to endure to play, caused Kiner to retire from the game following his season in Cleveland, so his one chance to play with a team in contention for a pennant went for naught. Indians fans were left to speculate whether a healthy Kiner might have provided enough punch to allow the Indians to top the Yankees and earn a spot in the World Series.

Among his other records, Kiner's 301 homers ranks second among Pittsburgh Pirates, behind the 475 hit by Willie Stargell, and ahead of the 240 hit by Roberto Clemente. His 54 homers in 1949 and 51 in 1947

Appendix One: Stats and Comparison to Other HoF Members

are the top two single-season totals in Pirates history, and he holds five of the team's top seven totals. No other Pirate has ever swatted 50 long balls in a year. He is fifth on the Pirates' all-time list in walks and holds four of the top ten season totals, including the top spot, with 137 base on balls in 1951. He had the second-best season for runs batted in, with 127 in 1947, repeating that total in 1949, and he ranks seventh on the all-time list with 801. He also ranks second in total bases for a season with 361 in 1947 and again in 1949. His on-base and slugging percentages also place him among the Pirates' leaders, both for an individual season and all-time. Not bad for a player who only had 4,732 plate appearances in a Pittsburgh uniform. It is little wonder that the Pirates retired his number "4" uniform number in 1987.

Kiner became the first Major League player to hit home runs in four straight at-bats on two separate occasions. He also hit three home runs in a game four times. Kiner put up triple figures in walks and runs batted in for five of the years he played for last-place Pittsburgh. Not only did Kiner lead the National League in home runs for seven consecutive years (1946–1952), he also led the Major Leagues for six years (1947–1952). His 369 home runs also represent the most hit by any player in the first ten years of his career, which, regrettably, accounted for Kiner's entire career. He also is one of only seven players to have at least four 30 home run and 100 RBI seasons in their first five years. The others on that list are Chuck Klein, Joe DiMaggio, Ted Williams, Mark Teixeira, Albert Pujols, Ryan Howard, and Ryan Braun.

Kiner set records off the field as well. His 53-year broadcasting tenure with the New York Mets was the third-longest for any broadcaster with a single team, just behind Dodgers announcers Vin Scully and Jaime Jarrin. His 17-year partnership with Lindsey Nelson and Bob Murphy also marked the longest period a three-man team stayed together in Major League baseball broadcasting. During his last season with the Mets, in 2013, he became the oldest active announcer in Major League baseball, at the age of 91.

APPENDIX TWO

Major League Players' Career Home Run Totals

Ralph Kiner stood sixth on the all-time home run list at the time of his retirement in 1955. At the time of this writing, he has slipped to 78th place on that same list. The players having 300 or more home runs in their careers are listed in descending order (names listed in italics are for those individuals still playing at the time of this writing).

Players having 700 or more home runs: Barry Bonds (762), Hank Aaron (755), Babe Ruth (714)

Players having 600 or more home runs: *Alex Rodriguez* (686), Willie Mays (660), Ken Griffey, Jr. (630), Jim Thome (612), Sammy Sosa (609)

Players having 500 or more home runs: Frank Robinson (586), Mark McGuire (583), Harmon Killebrew (573), Rafael Palmeiro (569), Reggie Jackson (563), *Albert Pujols* (557), Manny Ramirez (555), Mike Schmidt (548), Mickey Mantle (536), Jimmie Foxx (534), Willie McCovey (521), Frank Thomas (521), Ted Williams (521), Ernie Banks (512), Eddie Mathews (512), Mel Ott (511), Gary Sheffield (509), Eddie Murray (504), *David Ortiz* (502)

Players having 400 or more home runs: Lou Gehrig (493), Fred McGriff (493), Stan Musial (475), Willie Stargell (475), Carlos Delgado (473), Chipper Jones (468), Dave Winfield (465), Jose Canseco (462), Adam Dunn (462), Carl Yastrzemski (452), Jeff Bagwell (449), Vladimir Guerrero (449), Dave Kingman (442), Jason Giambi (440), Paul Konerko (439), Andre Dawson (438), Juan Gonzalez (434), Andruw Jones (434), Cal Ripken, Jr. (431), Mike Piazza (427), Billy Williams (426), Darrell Evans (414), Alfonso Soriano (412), *Adrian Beltre* (411), Duke Snider (407) *Miguel Cabrera* (407)

Appendix Two: Major League Players' Career Home Run Totals

Players having 300 or more home runs: Andres Galarraga (399), Al Kaline (399), Dale Murphy (398), Joe Carter (396), *Mark Teixeira* (394), Jim Edmonds (393), *Carlos Beltran* (391), Craig Nettles (390), Johnny Bench (389), *Aramis Ramirez* (386), Dwight Evans (385), Harold Baines (384), Larry Walker (383), Frank Howard (382), Jim Rice (382), Albert Belle (381), Orlando Cepeda (379), Tony Perez (379), Matt Williams (378), Norm Cash (377), Jeff Kent (377), Carlton Fisk (376), Rocky Colavito (374), Gil Hodges (370), Todd Helton (369), **Ralph Kiner (369)**, Lance Berkman (366), Joe DiMaggio (361), Gary Gaetti (360), Johnny Mize (359), Yogi Berra (358), Carlos Lee (358), *Ryan Howard* (357), Greg Vaughn (355), Luis Gonzalez (354), Lee May (354), *Torii Hunter* (353), Ellis Burks (352), Dick Allen (351), Chili Davis (350), George Foster (348), Ron Santo (342), Jack Clark (340), Tino Martinez (339), Dave Parker (339), Boog Powell (339), Don Baylor (338), Joe Adcock (336), Darryl Strawberry (335), Moises Alou (332), Bobby Bonds (332), Hank Greenberg (331), Derrek Lee (331), Shawn Green (328), Mo Vaughn (328), Jermaine Dye (325), Willie Horton (325), Gary Carter (324), Lance Parrish (324), Ron Gant (321), Vinny Castilla (320), Troy Glaus (320), Cecil Fielder (319), Roy Sievers (318), George Brett (317), Ron Cey (316), Scott Rolen (316), Jeromy Burnitz (315), Reggie Smith (314), Ivan Rodriguez (311), Jay Buhner (310), Prince Fielder (310), Edgar Martinez (309), Greg Luzinski (307), Al Simmons (307), Miguel Tejada (307), Fred Lynn (306), Richie Sexson (306), Ruben Sierra (306), Raul Ibanez (305), David Justice (305), Reggie Sanders (305), Steve Finley (304), Rogers Hornsby (301), Chuck Klein (300).

APPENDIX THREE

Pittsburgh Pirates Hall of Famers

Players Going into the Hall as Pirates

Jake Beckley—First Baseman 1888–1907
Max Carey—Center Fielder 1910–1929
Fred Clarke—Left Fielder 1894–1915
Barney Dreyfuss—Executive
Ralph Kiner—Left Fielder 1946–1955*
Roberto Clemente—Right Fielder 1955–1972
Bill Mazeroski—Second Baseman 1956–1972
Willie Stargell—Left Fielder 1962–1982
Pie Traynor—Third Baseman 1920–1937
Arky Vaughan—Shortstop 1932–1948
Honus Wagner—Shortstop 1897–1917
Lloyd Waner—Center Fielder 1927–1944
Paul Waner—Right Fielder 1926–1945

Hall of Fame Players Who Played or Managed Part of Their Careers as a Pirate, but Entered the Hall Representing Other Teams

Bert Blyleven—Pitcher 1970–1992
Jim Bunning—Pitcher 1955–1969
Jack Chesbro—Pitcher 1899–1909
Joe Cronin—Shortstop 1926–1945
Kiki Cuyler—Right Fielder 1921–1938
Frankie Frisch—Second Baseman 1919–1937

Appendix Three: Pittsburgh Pirates Hall of Famers

Pud Galvin—Pitcher 1875–1892
Goose Gossage—Pitcher 1972–1994
Hank Greenberg—First Baseman 1930–1947
Burleigh Grimes—Pitcher 1916–1934
Ned Hanlon—Manager 1889–1907
Billy Herman—Second Baseman 1931–1947
Waite Hoyt—Pitcher 1918–1938
Joe Kelley—Left Fielder 1891–1906
Chuck Klein—Right Fielder 1928–1944
Freddie Lindstrom—Third Baseman 1927–1936
Al Lopez—Manager
Connie Mack—Manager
Heinie Manush—Left Fielder 1923–1939
Rabbit Maranville—Shortstop 1912–1935
Bill McKechnie—Manager
Hank O'Day—Umpire
Branch Rickey—Manager
Billy Southworth—Manager
Casey Stengel—Manager
Dazzy Vance—Pitcher 1915–1935
Rube Waddell—Pitcher 1897–1910
Deacon White—Catcher 1871–1890
Vic Willis—Pitcher 1898–1910

*One will note that Ralph Kiner had the shortest playing career of any of the Pirates listed in the Hall of Fame. The brevity of Kiner's time in the Major Leagues is a testament to his impact on the game and his stature as a superstar during his career.

Chapter Notes

Introduction

1. *New York Post,* February 7, 2014.

Chapter 1

1. Ralph Kiner and Danny Peary, *Baseball Forever: Reflections on 60 Years in the Game* (Chicago: Triumph Books, 2004), x.
2. *Ibid.,* x–xi; Gregory Lalire, "Baseball in the West," *Wild West Magazine,* March 31, 2011, 26.
3. Kiner and Peary, *Baseball Forever,* xi.
4. *Ibid.*
5. Vincent, Fay, *The Only Game in Town: Baseball Stars of the 1930s and 1940s Talk About the Game They Loved* (New York: Simon & Schuster, 2006), 195; Ralph Kiner with Joe Gergen, *Kiner's Korner: At Bat and On the Air—My 40 Years in Baseball* (New York: Arbor House, 1987), 32.
6. *Milwaukee Journal,* December 5, 1945.
7. Vincent, 195.
8. Kiner and Gergen, *Kiner's Korner,* 34–35.
9. *Ibid.,* 35–36.
10. Kiner and Peary, *Baseball Forever,* xii.
11. *Explorations in Economic History,* 10, No. 1 (Autumn 1972): 53–73.
12. Kiner and Gergen, *Kiner's Korner,* 34.
13. Kiner and Peary, *Baseball Forever,* xii; Kiner and Gergen, *Kiner's Korner,* 62.
14. Vincent, 196.
15. Kiner and Peary, *Baseball Forever,* xii.
16. Kiner and Gergen, *Kiner's Korner,* 60.
17. Vincent, 197.
18. Tom Meany, *Ralph Kiner: The Heir Apparent* (New York: A.S. Barnes, 1951), 10.
19. Kiner and Gergen, *Kiner's Korner,* 61–62.
20. Kiner and Gergen, *Kiner's Korner,* 62; Kiner and Peary, *Baseball Forever,* xii.

Chapter 2

1. Kiner and Gergen, *Kiner's Korner,* 62.
2. *Ibid.*
3. *Ibid.,* 62–63.
4. *Ibid.,* 63.
5. Kiner and Peary, *Baseball Forever,* 65.
6. *Ibid.,* 65–66.
7. *Ibid.,* 66.
8. *Ibid.,* 67.
9. Jackie Robinson and Alfred Duckett, *Breaking Through to the Big League: The Story of Jackie Robinson* (Eau Claire, WI: E.M. Hale, 1965), 6–10.
10. *Ibid.,* 13.
11. Kiner and Gergen, *Kiner's Korner,* 63.
12. *Ibid.*
13. Vincent, 198.
14. Henry C. Herge, *Navy V-12* (Nashville, TN: Turner Publishing, 1996), 22.
15. Kiner and Gergen, *Kiner's Korner,* 64.

Chapter 3

1. Todd Anton and Bill Nowlin, *When Baseball Went to War* (Chicago: Triumph Books, 2008), 7, 14.
2. *Ibid.,* 5–6.

3. Vincent, 199.
4. *Desert Sun*, February 17, 2013.
5. *Ibid.*
6. *ESPN Page 2*, November 9, 2009.
7. *Ibid.*
8. ESPN.
9. Kiner and Gergen, *Kiner's Korner*, 64.
10. *Desert Sun*.
11. Kiner and Peary, *Baseball Forever*, xiii.
12. *Desert Sun*.
13. *Journal of American History*, 53, no. 3 (December 1966): 558–561.
14. *Desert Sun*.

Chapter 4

1. Ed Fitzgerald, *The National League* (New York: Grosset & Dunlap, 1966), 53.
2. John McCollister, *Tales From the Pirates Dugout: A Collection of the Greatest Pirates Stories Ever Told* (New York: Sports Publishing, 2013), 57, hereafter referred to as McCollister, *Pirates Dugout*.
3. Bill Stern, *Bill Stern's Favorite Baseball Stories* (Garden City, NY: Blue Ribbon Books, 1949), 72–73.
4. Fitzgerald, 54.
5. Kiner and Peary, *Baseball Forever*, 2.
6. Kiner and Gergen, *Kiner's Korner*, 64.
7. Anton and Nowlin, 215–228.
8. *Ibid.*, 219.
9. Kiner and Peary, 4–5.
10. Vincent, 200.
11. McCollister, *Pirates Dugout*, 65.
12. Joshua E. Hanft, *Jackie Robinson* (New York: Baronet, 1996), 127.
13. Jackie Robinson and Alfred Duckett, *Breakthrough to the Big League: The Story of Jackie Robinson* (Eau Claire, WI: E. M. Hale, 1965), 55.
14. Hanft, 124–25, 128.
15. Joseph Thomas Moore, *Pride and Prejudice: The Biography of Larry Doby* (New York: Praeger, 1988), 40.
16. Arnold Rampersad, *Jackie Robinson: A Biography* (New York: Alfred A. Knopf, 1997), 129.
17. James W. Loewen, *Lies My Teacher Told Me: Everything Your American History Textbook Got Wrong* (New York: Simon & Schuster, 1995), 163.

Chapter 5

1. Kiner and Gergen, 158.
2. Vincent, 206.
3. Kiner and Peary, 5–6.
4. Kiner and Gergen, 159.
5. *New York Times*, December 1, 2012.
6. Fitzgerald, 74.
7. John McCollister, *The Bucs: The Story of the Pittsburgh Pirates* (Lenexa, KS: Addax Publishing, 1998), 129–130, hereafter referred to as McCollister, *The Bucs*.

Chapter 6

1. John Rosengren, *Hank Greenberg: The Hero of Heroes* (New York: New American Library, 2013), 291.
2. *Ibid.*, 294.
3. *Ibid.*, 296–297.
4. *Ibid.*, 297–299.
5. *Ibid.*, 300.
6. *Ibid.*, 302.
7. *Ibid.*, 303–304.
8. Kiner and Peary, 12.
9. *Life*, March 31, 1947.
10. Kiner and Peary, 12.
11. Kiner and Gergen, 12.
12. Kiner and Peary, 12–13.
13. Vincent, 207–208; Kiner and Gergen, 13.
14. Meany, 21–22.
15. Kiner and Peary, 72, 74.
16. Rosengren, 308–309.

Chapter 7

1. Kiner and Peary, 161.
2. *Ibid.*, 164.
3. *New York Post*, February 7, 2014.
4. Vincent, 214–215.
5. Kiner and Peary, 103.
6. Stern, 29–30.
7. *Ibid.*, 165.
8. *Ibid.*, 166.
9. *Movie Life*, August 1951.
10. Kiner and Peary, 167.
11. Meany, 15–16.
12. *Focus Magazine*, September 1951.
13. Kiner and Gergen, 224.

Chapter Notes

14. *Ibid.*, 226.
15. Rosenberg, 313.
16. McCollister, *Pirates Dugout*, 89.
17. McCollister, *The Bucs*, 136.
18. Tom Meany, *Ralph Kiner: The Heir Apparent* (New York: A. S. Barnes, 1951), 6.
19. *Boys' Life Magazine*, May 1951.
20. Peter Keating, *Dingers: A Short History of the Long Ball* (New York: ESPN Books, 2006), 63.
21. McCollister, *The Bucs*, 137.
22. Bennett Wayne, *Heroes of the Home Run* (Champaign, IL: Garrard Publishing, 1973), 162.
23. Kiner and Gergen, 160.

Chapter 8

1. *Sports Illustrated*, April 1, 1985.
2. Brent P. Kelley, *Baseball's Biggest Blunder: The Bonus Rule of 1953–1957* (Lanham, MD: Scarecrow, 1997), 9–11.
3. *Ibid.*; Dennis Snelling, *The Greatest Minor League: A History of the Pacific Coast League, 1903–1957* (Jefferson, NC: McFarland, 2012), 351.
4. McCollister, *The Bucs*, 138–139.
5. Fitzgerald, 54; McCollister, 139.
6. "Baseball Yearbook," *True, The Man's Magazine*, 1951.
7. Fitzgerald, 54.
8. George Robinson and Charles Salzberg, *On a Clear Day They Could See Seventh Place: Baseball's Worst Teams* (Lincoln, NE: University of Nebraska Press, 2010), 186–187.
9. McCollister, *The Bucs*, 139.
10. Robinson and Salzberg, 186.
11. Mark Alvarez, et al., *The Ol' Ball Game: A Collection of Baseball Characters & Moments Worth Remembering* (New York: Barnes & Noble, 1990), 25–28.
12. McCollister, *The Bucs*, 133–134.

Chapter 9

1. Robinson and Salzberg, 182.
2. Kiner and Gergen, 161.
3. Andrew O'Toole, *Rickey Dinks: Branch Rickey in Pittsburgh* (Jefferson, NC: McFarland, 2000), 77.
4. Andrew Finoli and Bill Ranier, *The Pittsburgh Pirates Encyclopedia* (New York: Sports Publishing, 2003), 114.
5. McCollister, *Pirates Dugout*, 120–121.
6. *Ibid.*, 9.
7. McCollister, *The Bucs*, 141.
8. Finoli and Ranier, 114.
9. Kiner and Peary, 106.
10. Bert Randolph Sugar, *The Book of Sports Quotes* (New York: Quick Fox, 1979), 112.
11. *Ibid.*, 101–102.
12. *Ibid.*, 102.
13. Finoli and Ranier, 114.
14. O'Toole, 77.
15. Finoli and Ranier, 114.
16. Kiner and Peary, 17.
17. McCollister, *The Bucs*, 141.
18. Finoli and Ranier, 113.
19. *Quick Pocket News Weekly*, November 24, 1952.

Chapter 10

1. McCollister, *The Bucs*, 141–142.
2. *Ibid.*, 142.
3. *Los Angeles Times*, January 25, 1950.
4. *New York Times*, February 29, 1996.
5. McCollister, *The Bucs*, 142–143.
6. Lew Freedman, *For the Love of the Chicago Cubs* (Lincolnwood, IL: West Side Publishing, 2009), 270–271.
7. Mike Royko and Studs Terkel, *One More Time: The Best of Mike Royko* (Chicago: University of Chicago Press, 1999), 29–31.
8. Kiner and Gergen, 227.
9. Freedman, 14–15.
10. *Pasadena Star-News*, February 6, 2014.
11. Kiner and Peary, 103–104.
12. *Ibid.*, 104–105.
13. *Ibid.*, 105–106.

Chapter 11

1. Russell Schneider, *Tales From the Tribe Dugout: A Collection of the Greatest Cleveland Indians Stories Ever Told* (Champaign, IL: Sports Publishing, 2002), 43–44.
2. James S. Hirsch, *Willie Mays: The Life, The Legend* (New York: Scribner, 2010), 193–196.

Chapter Notes

3. Rosenberg, 326, 333.
4. *Desert Sun*, February 6, 2014.
5. Kiner and Gergen, 96.
6. *Ibid.*, 162.
7. Rosenberg, 331.

Chapter 12

1. Kiner and Peary, 39–40.
2. Kiner and Gergen, 98.
3. Kal Wagenheim, *Clemente!* (New York: Praeger, 1973), 34–36, 42.
4. Kiner and Peary, 89–90.
5. *Ibid.*, 186–187.
6. Peter Golenbock, *Bums: An Oral History of the Brooklyn Dodgers* (New York: G. P. Putnam's Sons, 1984), 441–442.
7. Kiner and Peary, 187.
8. *Ibid.*
9. Rosengren, 338–339.
10. Kiner and Peary, 187; Rosengren, 339.
11. Kiner and Peary, 188.
12. *Ibid.*, 189.

Chapter 13

1. *New York Sun*, June 13, 2008.
2. *New York Times*, February 19, 2012.
3. Stern, 204–205.
4. Kiner and Peary, 190.
5. *Ibid.*
6. *New York Times*, February 19, 2012.
7. Kiner and Gergen, 37.
8. *Ibid.*, 38.
9. Joe Funk, *So Long Shea: Five Decades of Stadium Memories* (Chicago: Triumph Books, 2008), 6.
10. *New York Post*, February 7, 2014.
11. Jimmy Breslin, *Can't Anybody Here Play This Game?* (New York: Viking, 1963), 54.
12. *New York Daily News*, February 6, 2014.
13. McCollister, *Pirates Dugout*, 130–131.

Chapter 14

1. *New York Times*, June 22, 1964.
2. Jack Lang and Peter Simon, *The New York Mets: Twenty-Five Years of Baseball Magic* (New York: Henry Holt, 1987), 70.
3. Kiner and Gergen, 114–118.
4. *Ibid.*, 125–126.
5. *Ibid.*, 127–128.
6. Kiner and Gergen, 176–177.
7. Kiner and Gergen, 177–178; Kiner and Peary, 231–232.

Chapter 15

1. *New York Times*, June 15, 2012.
2. Kiner and Gergen, 191–192.
3. *Ibid.*, 193.
4. *New York Post*, February 6, 2014.
5. *Sports Illustrated*, May 20, 1985.
6. *New York Post*, February 6, 2014.

Epilogue

1. *New York Post*, February 6, 2014.

Bibliography

Newspapers, Magazines and Periodicals

Baseball Yearbook
Boys' Life
Desert Sun
ESPN Magazine
Explorations in Economic History
Focus
Journal of American History
Life
Los Angeles Times
Milwaukee Journal
Movie Life
New York Daily News
New York Post
New York Sun
New York Times
Pasadena Star-News
Quick
Wild West

Books

Allen, Maury. *Brooklyn Remembered: The 1955 Days of the Dodgers*. New York: Sports Publishing, 2007.
Alvarez, Mark, et al. *The Ol' Ball Game: A Collection of Baseball Characters & Moments Worth Remembering*. New York: Barnes & Noble, 1993.
Anton, Todd, and Bill Nowlin. *When Baseball Went to War*. New York: Triumph Books, 2008.
Breslin, Jimmy. *Can't Anybody Here Play This Game?* New York: Viking, 1963.
Canter, Len. *Babe Ruth*. New York: Baronet Books, 1996.
Feller, Bob, with Burton Rocks. *Bob Feller's Little Blue Book of Baseball*. New York: Triumph Books, 2009.
Finoli, David, and Bill Ranier. *The Pittsburgh Pirates Encyclopedia*. New York: Sports Publishing, 2003.
Fitzgerald, Ed. *The National League*. New York: Grosset & Dunlap, 1966.
Freedman, Lew. *For the Love of the Chicago Cubs*. Lincolnwood, IL: West Side Publishing, 2009.
Funk, Joe. *So Long Shea: Five Decades of Stadium Memories*. Chicago: Triumph Books, 2008.
Golenbock, Peter. *Bums: An Oral History of the Brooklyn Dodgers*. New York: G. P. Putnam's Sons, 1984.
Haberstam, David J. *Sports on New York Radio*. Dallas: Master's Press, 1999.
Hanft, Joshua E. *Jackie Robinson*. New York: Baronet Books, 1996.
Herge, Henry C. *Navy V-12*. Nashville, TN: Turner Publishing, 1996.
Hirsch, James S. *Willie Mays: The Life, The Legend*. New York: Scribner, 2010.
Kahn, Roger. *The Boys of Summer*. New York: Signet, 1973.
Keating, Peter. *Dingers: A Short History of the Long Ball*. New York: EPSN Books, 2006.
Kelley, Brent P. *Baseball's Biggest Blunder: The Bonus Rule of 1953–1957*. Lanham, MD: Scarecrow, 1997.
Kiner, Ralph, with Joe Gergen. *Kiner's Korner: At Bat and On the Air—My 40 Years in Baseball*. New York: Arbor House, 1987.
Kiner, Ralph, with Danny Peary. *Baseball Forever: Reflections on 60 Years*

Bibliography

in the Game. Chicago: Triumph Books, 2004.

Lang, Jack, and Peter Simon. *The New York Mets: Twenty-Five Years of Baseball Magic*. New York: Henry Holt, 1987.

Loewen, James W. *Lies My Teacher Told Me: Everything Your American History Textbook Got Wrong*. New York: Simon & Schuster, 1995.

McCarver, Tim, and Danny Peary. *Tim McCarver's Baseball for Brain Surgeons and Other Fans*. New York: Villard, 1998.

McCollister, John. *Tales From the Pittsburgh Pirates Dugout: A Collection of the Greatest Pirates Stories Ever Told*. New York: Sports Publishing, 2013.

_____. *The Bucs: The Story of the Pittsburgh Pirates*. Lenexa, KS: Addax Publishing, 1998.

Marshall, William R. *Baseball's Pivotal Era*. Lexington: University of Kentucky Press, 1999.

Meany, Tom. *Ralph Kiner: The Heir Apparent*. New York: A. S. Barnes, 1951.

Moore, Joseph Thomas. *Pride and Prejudice: The Biography of Larry Doby*. New York: Praeger, 1988.

Nelson, Don. *Baseball's Home Run Hitters: The Sultans of Swat—The Definitive Work on Home Runs and Home Run Hitters*. New York: Macmillan, 1984.

O'Toole, Andrew. *Rickey Dinks: Branch Rickey in Pittsburgh*. Jefferson, NC: McFarland, 2000.

Rampersad, Arnold. *Jackie Robinson: A Biography*. New York: Alfred A. Knopf, 1997.

Roberts, Russell. *100 Baseball Legends Who Shaped Sports History*. San Mateo, CA: Bluewood Books, 2003.

Robinson, George, and Charles Salzberg, *On a Clear Day They Could See Seventh Place: Baseball's Worst Teams*. Omaha, NE: Bison Books, 2010.

Robinson, Jackie, and Alfred Duckett. *Breakthrough to the Big League: The Story of Jackie Robinson*. Eau Claire, WI: E. M. Hale, 1965.

Rosengren, John. *Hank Greenberg: The Hero of Heroes*. New York: New American Library, 2013.

Royko, Mike, and Studs Terkel. *One More Time: The Best of Mike Royko*. Chicago: University of Chicago Press, 1999.

Schneider, Russell. *Tales from the Tribe Dugout*. Champaign, IL: Sports Publishing, 2002.

Smith, Don, and Ed Croke. *Professional Baseball: The First 100 Years*. New York: Major League Promotion Corporation, 1967.

Smizik, Robert, and Gerald Astor. *The Pittsburgh Pirates: An Illustrated History*. New York: Walker, 1990.

Snelling, Dennis. *The Greatest Minor League: A History of the Pacific Coast League, 1903–1957*. Jefferson, NC: McFarland, 2012.

Starr, Bill. *Clearing the Bases*. New York: Michael Kesend, 1989.

Stern, Bill. *Bill Stern's Favorite Baseball Stories*. Garden City, NY: Blue Ribbon Books, 1949.

Strasberg, Andy. *Baseball Fantography: A Celebration in Snapshots and Stories from the Fans*. New York: Abrams, 2012.

Sugar, Bert Randolph. *The Book of Sports Quotes*. New York: Quick Fox, 1979.

Sullivan, George. *Baseball Backstage*. New York: Holt, Rinehart and Winston, 1986.

Turner, Frederick. *When The Boys Came Back*. New York: Henry Holt, 1996.

Veneziano, John, ed. *National Baseball Hall of Fame and Museum: 2011 Yearbook*. Lynn, MA: H.O. Zimman, 2011.

Vincent, Fay. *The Only Game in Town: Baseball Stars of the 1930s and 1940s Talk About the Game*. New York: Simon & Schuster, 2007.

Wayne, Bennett. *Heroes of the Home Run*. Champaign, IL: Garrard, 1973.

Index

Aaron, Hank 101, 149, 181
Adcock, Joe 182
Agee, Tommie 157
Aguirre, Hank 126
Albany Senators 19, 23, 24, 27, 29
Albosta, Ed 41, 49
Allen, Dick 182
Allyn, Arthur, Jr. 137
Alou, Moises 182
American Baseball Guild 56
Anderson, Alf 41
Antonelli, John 121
Appling, Luke 22
Arnez, Desi 71
Arnez, Luci 71
Ashburn, Richie 76, 90, 142, 147
Atkins, Arnie 132
Autry, Gene 138
Averill, Earl 8, 159
Avila, Bobby 120, 121

Bagwell, Jeff 181
Bahr, Ed 41, 67
Baines, Harold 182
Baker, Bill 41
Baker, Gene 114
Ball, Lucille 4
Banks, Ernie 114, 115, 117, 181
Barber, Red 46
Barnhart, Vic 41
Barrett, Johnny 49
Barrett, Marty 48, 167
Bartirome, Tony 87, 94, 99
Baumholtz, Frank 112, 113, 114, 116

Baylor, Don 182
Beaumont, Ginger 1
Beckley, Jake 183
Bell, Bill 94
Bell, Gus 97, 142
Belle, Albert 182
Beltran, Carlos 182
Beltre, Adrian 181
Bench, Johnny 182
Benny, Jack 71
Benswanger, Ben 39, 40, 57, 58
Berkman, Lance 182
Berra, Yogi 4, 120, 152, 154, 182
Binghamton Triplets 28
Blackwell, Ewell 16, 83
Blyleven, Bert 183
Bodkin, Bob 6, 7, 13, 14
Bodkin, Robert 6, 13
Bodkin, Rose 6, 7, 9, 10, 13
Boggs, Wade 167
Bonds, Barry 104, 181
Bonds, Bobby 182
Borowy, Hank 52
Boston Braves 14, 51, 77
Boswell, Ken 157
Braun, Ryan 180
Brecheen, Harry 51
Brett, George 182
Brewer, Chet 25
Brickhouse, Jack 122
Briggs, Walter 61
Briggs Stadium 90
Brissie, Lou 80
Brock, Lou 178
Brodowski, Dick 133
Brooklyn Dodgers 33, 45, 51, 66, 87, 91, 110, 118, 131

Brookside Park 44
Brown, Jimmy 48
Brown, Joe L. 150
Buhner, Jay 182
Bunning, Jim 151, 152, 183
Burkett, Jesse 177, 178
Burks, Ellis 182
Burnitz, Jeremy 182
Busch, Augie 101

Cabrera, Miguel 181
Callison, Johnny 152
Camelli, Hank 41
Campanella, Roy 112
Canseco, Jose 181
Carey, Max 1, 183
Carlin, George 4, 147
Carson, Johnny 29
Carter, Gary 162, 166, 182
Carter, Joe 182
Casey, John 12
Cash, Norm 182
Castilla, Vinny 182
Cavarretta, Phil 111, 113, 114
Cepeda, Orlando 182
Cey, Ron 182
Chaffee, Nancy 4, 74, 75, 105, 106
Chambers, Cliff 87, 88, 90
Chandler, Happy 56
Chesbro, Jack 183
Chicago Cubs 16, 51, 55, 82, 110, 111, 112, 114, 115, 116, 156
Chicago White Sox 20, 22, 44
Cincinnati Reds 9, 14, 16, 88

Index

Clark, Jack 182
Clarke, Fred 1, 178, 183
Clemens, Roger 165, 166
Clemensen, Bill 41
Clemente, Roberto 110, 133, 134, 177, 179, 183
Clendenon, Don 156
Cobb, Ty 72
Cochrane, Mickey 9
Colavito, Rocky 131, 182
Cole, Dick 87
Collins, Ripper 29
Colman, Frank 30
Connors, Chuck 4, 108, 147
Cooper, Jackie 29
Cooper, Walker 114
Cox, Billy 41, 48
Craig, Roger 142, 145, 148
Cronin, Joe 21, 183
Crosby, Bing 3, 58, 63, 70, 71, 131, 139, 140
Crowley, Dan 15
Curtis, Jamie Lee 73, 74
Curtis, Tony 73
Cuyler, Kiki 183

Daley, Bud 126
Daniel, Dan 60, 61
Dark, Alvin 29, 121
Darling, Ron 163, 165, 167
Davis, Chili 182
Davis, Virgil 58
Dawson, Andre 181
Dean, Dizzy 9, 29, 77
Delahanty, Ed 177, 178
Delgado, Carlos 181
Del Grecco, Bobby 87, 94, 97, 99
Detroit Tigers 9, 20, 33, 90, 120
Dickey, Bill 15
Dickson, Murry 88, 96, 97, 109
Dietrich, Bill 22
DiMaggio, Dom 32, 45, 84
DiMaggio, Joe 8, 20, 21, 45, 81, 84, 180, 182
DiMaggio, Vince 44
Doby, Larry 120, 122

Doerr, Bobby 8, 81
Douglas, Paul 72, 73
Doyle, Charles J. 44, 45
Dreyfuss, Barney 38, 39, 57, 183
Droppo, Walt 95
Dunn, Adam 181
Durocher, Leo 121, 122
Dye, Jermaine 182
Dykstra, Lenny 163, 166

Easter, Luke 95, 96
Edmonds, Jim 182
Elliott, Bob 22, 131, 132
Elmira Pioneers 28
Elson, Bob 139
Ennis, Del 47, 90
Erautt, Ernie 132
Essick, Bill 15
Evans, Darrell 181
Evans, Dwight 182

Faye, Alice 71
Feller, Bob 32, 85, 121, 125
Fielder, Cecil 182
Finley, Steve 182
Fisk, Carlton 182
Fletcher, Elbie 41, 48, 49
Fondy, Dee 112
Forbes Field 1, 2, 45, 50, 62, 80, 82, 89, 102, 105, 110, 111, 148
Foster, George 182
Foster, Phil 148
Foxx, Jimmie 7, 181
Frick, Ford 136, 138, 140, 141
Friend, Bob 86, 110, 153
Frisch, Frankie 9, 22, 23, 29, 44, 52, 58, 183

Gables, Ken 41, 48
Gaetti, Gary 182
Galarraga, Andres 182
Galbreath, John 4, 58, 62, 63, 71, 87, 88, 92, 100, 101, 118, 119
Gant, Ron 182
Garagiola, Joe 90, 95, 97, 99, 104, 109, 114, 159
Garcia, Mike 121, 124, 125
Garms, Debs 1

Garner, James 71
Garrett, Wayne 157
Gavin, Pud 184
Gehrig, Lou 7, 15, 16, 20, 78, 181
Gehringer, Charlie 9, 33
Gentry, Gary 156, 157
Gerheauser, Al 49
Giambi, Jason 181
Gionfriddo, Al 41, 51
Glaus, Troy 182
Gomez, Ruben 121
Gonzalez, Juan 181
Gonzalez, Luis 182
Gooden, Dwight 162, 163, 165
Gordon, Joe 8, 81
Gornicki, Hank 41
Goslin, Goose 9
Gossage, Goose 184
Grant, James Mudcat 133
Grant, M. Donald 141, 157
Gray, Ted 83
Green, Shawn 182
Greenberg, Hank 4, 9, 16, 20, 26, 31, 32, 37, 59, 60, 61, 62, 63, 64, 65, 66, 68, 75, 90, 96, 99, 110, 118, 119, 123, 127, 128, 129, 131, 134, 137, 138, 139, 164, 165, 171, 182, 184
Griffey, Ken, Jr. 181
Grimes, Burleigh 30, 184
Grissom, Marv 121
Groat, Dick 87, 99, 109, 110
Gromek, Steve 125
Grove, Lefty 7, 85
Guerrero, Vladimir 181
Guintini, Ben 41

Haak, Howie 133
Hack, Stan 114
Hackett, Buddy 148
Hafey, Chick 178
Haines, Jesse 9, 29
Hall, Dick 87
Hallett, Jack 41
Hamey, H. Roy 58
Haney, Fred 108, 109

Index

Hanlon, Ned 184
Hano, Arnold 122
Harris, Bucky 159
Harris, Phil 4, 71, 144
Hartford Bees 28
Hegan, Jim 120
Heilmann, Harry 21
Heintzelman, Ken 41, 48
Helton, Todd 182
Henderson, Dave 167
Henderson, Ricky 178, 179
Hemus, Solly 141
Herman, Babe 86
Herman, Billy 63, 65, 159, 184
Hodges, Gil 91, 182
Hoeft, Billy 125
Hollywood Stars 8, 14, 17, 40, 85, 129
Hope, Bob 71, 72
Hopp, Johnny 81
Hopper, Jim 41
Hornsby, Rogers 7, 141, 182
Horton, Willie 182
Houtteman, Art 83, 121
Howard, Frank 182
Howard, Lee 41
Howard, Ryan 180, 182
Howerton, Bill 90
Hoyt, Waite 1, 184
Hughes, Tommy 52
Hunter, Torii 182
Hurst, Bruce 165, 166

Ibanez, Raul 182
Irvin, Monte 121

Jackson, Randy 114
Jackson, Reggie 181
Jagger, Dean 70
Janowicz, Vic 109
Jarvis, Roy 41
Johnson, Judy 159, 161
Johnson, Si 55
Johnson, Tom 58
Johnston, Harry 13, 14, 17
Johnston, Lefty 13, 17, 23
Jones, Andruw 181
Jones, Chipper 181
Jones, Cleon 153, 157
Justice, David 182

Kaline, Al 182
KDKA Radio 10
Keeler, Wee Willie 20
Kelley, Joe 177, 178, 184
Kennedy, Ray 58
Kennedy, Robert F. 29
Kent, Jeff 182
Killebrew, Harmon 181
Kiner, Barbara 161
Kiner, Beatrice Grayson 5, 6, 7, 11, 16, 17, 18
Kiner, DiAnn 169
Kiner, Kathryn Chaffee 12, 75, 114, 160
Kiner, Michael 75
Kiner, Ralph Macklin 5
Kiner, Ralph McPherran 1, 2, 3, 4, 5, 6, 7, 9, 10, 11, 12, 14,15, 16, 17, 21, 22, 23, 24, 25, 26, 28, 29, 30, 31, 33, 34, 35, 37, 40, 42, 43, 44, 45, 47, 50, 52, 53, 56, 59, 64, 65, 66, 67, 68, 69, 70, 71, 73, 74, 75, 76, 77, 79, 80, 82, 85, 88, 90, 91, 92, 95, 96, 98, 99, 100, 101, 102, 103, 104, 105, 106, 107, 108, 109, 110, 112, 113, 114, 115, 116, 117, 118, 119, 123, 124, 125, 127, 128, 129, 132, 134, 136, 137, 138, 139, 140, 144, 146, 148, 149, 150, 155, 157, 160, 161, 164, 165, 168, 169, 170, 171, 173, 174, 175, 176, 178, 179, 180, 182, 183
Kiner, Scott 75, 113
Kingman, Dave 162, 181
Klein, Chuck 180, 182, 184
Kluszewski, Ted 112
Knight, Ray 167
Koback, Nick 109
Konerko, Paul 181
Koosman, Jerry 154, 155, 158
Kranepool, Ed 142, 153
Krausse, Lew 28
Kuhn, Bowie 29, 161

Lanning, Johnny 41, 48
La Palma Park 44
Lary, Frank 125
Lavagetto, Cookie 33, 141
Law, Vernon 86, 110
Lazzeri, Tony 8
Leach, Tommy 2, 56
Lee, Carlos 182
Lee, Derek 182
Lee, Thornton 22
Leigh, Janet 72, 73, 74, 111
Lemon, Bob 41, 98, 121, 124, 125, 127, 136
Lemon, Jack 71
Lewis, John Norman 118
Lewis, Monica 69
Liddle, Don 122
Lindstrom, Freddie 1, 184
Lombardi, Ernie 8
Lopez, Al 4, 184
Lown, Turk 112
Luzinski, Greg 182
Lynn, Fred 182

Mack, Connie 184
Mackey, Biz 25
Maglie, Sal 28, 121
Mantle, Mickey 175, 181
Manusch, Heinie 1, 184
Maranville, Rabbit 184
Maris, Roger 104, 142
Martin, Pepper 9, 29
Martinez, Edgar 182
Martinez, Tino 182
Matthews, Eddie 112, 181
Mauney, Dick 52
May, Lee 182
Mays, Willie 121, 122, 181
Mazeroski, Bill 137, 183
McCarthy, Joe 76
McCarver, Tim 4, 69, 70, 164, 169, 170, 171, 176
McCovey, Willie 149, 181
McCullough, Clyde 81, 147
McGriff, Fred 181
McGwire, Mark 104, 181
McKechnie, Bill 109, 184
McKenzie, Ken 148
McKinney, Frank 58, 65
McNally, Dave 158
Medwick, Joe 9, 29

Index

Mesa, Pete 132
Metkivich, George 95, 97, 103, 131
Meyer, Billy 75, 78, 104, 105
Miller, Bob 125, 14.
Minosa, Minnie 133
Mitchell, Kevin 167
Mize, Johnny 55, 65, 76, 80, 81, 182
Montemayor, Felipe 87
Montreal Royals 46
Mulcahy, Hugh 31
Murphy, Bob 4, 143, 146, 168, 180
Murphy, Dale 182
Murray, Eddie 181
Musial, Stan 76, 82, 90, 98, 101, 181
Myers, Gary 149

Nagel, Bill 30
Nelson, Lindsey 4, 143, 146, 180
Nettles, Craig 182
New York Giants 21, 44, 51, 55, 90, 115, 121, 122, 131
Newhauser, Hal 121
Nipper, Al 166

O'Brien, Eddie 87
O'Brien, Johnny 87
O'Day, Hank 184
O'Doul, Lefty 131
Ojeda, Bob 163, 166
O'Malley, Walter 118, 135, 138
Orosco, Jesse 167
Ortiz, David 181
Ostermuller, Fritz 41, 48
Ott, Mel 181

Pacific Coast League 8, 13, 14, 15, 40, 85, 130, 136
Pagliaroni, Jim 150
Paige, Satchel 25
Palmeiro, Rafael 181
Palmer, Jim 158
Parker, Dave 182
Parnell, Mel 90

Parrish, Lance 182
Paul, Gabe 138
Payson, Joan 141, 144
Peck, Gregory 70
Peckinpah, Sam 39
Perez, Tony 182
Perris, Frederick T. 43
Perris Hill Park 43
Petit, Paul 85
Philadelphia Phillies 9, 31, 52, 151, 152
Piazza, Mike 181
Piersall, Jimmy 148
Pittsburgh Pirates 1, 2, 10, 14, 16, 17, 29, 38, 39, 40, 41, 48, 51, 52, 55, 56, 57, 58, 59, 61, 64, 66, 67, 72, 73, 78, 80, 85, 88, 95, 105, 111, 173, 179
Pollet, Howie 49, 55, 90, 109
Pope, Dave 132
Powell, Boog 182
Pujols, Albert 180, 181

Radatz, Dick 152
Ramirez, Aramis 182
Ramirez, Manny 181
Raschi, Vic 83
Reese, Pee Wee 97, 98
Regalado, Rudy 132
Reynolds, Allie 28, 117, 118, 119
Rice, Bob 58
Rice, Grantland 60
Rice, Jim 178, 182
Rickey, Branch 45, 46, 86, 87, 88, 94, 99, 100, 102, 104, 105, 107, 108, 128, 141, 184
Ripken, Cal, Jr. 181
Ripple, Jimmy 30
Rizzo, Johnny 44, 45
Robinson, Frank 158, 181
Robinson, Jackie 26, 27, 45, 46, 47, 66, 67, 68, 120, 133
Robinson, Jerry 26
Robinson, Mallie 26
Rodriguez, Alex 181
Rodriguez, Ivan 182
Rogan, Joe 25

Rolen, Scott 182
Rosen, Al 29, 120, 122, 123
Rowe, Schoolboy 9
Rowswell, Albert "Rosey" 58, 92, 93
Ruether, Dutch 16
Ruffing, Red 141, 147
Russell, Jim 52
Ruth, Babe 1, 7, 15, 16, 74, 78, 80, 82, 91, 98, 104, 173, 181
Ryan, Nolan 155, 163

St. Louis Cardinals 7, 22, 27, 29
San Diego Padres 8, 129, 130, 131, 155
San Francisco Seals 8
Sanders, Reggie 182
Santo, Ron 182
Sauer, Hank 30, 98, 112, 113, 115, 117
Schmidt, Mike 104, 149, 181
Schoendienst, Red 83
Schwall, Dick 150
Scott, Randolph 71
Scranton Red Sox 28
Scully, Vin 164, 180
Seaver, Charlie 132, 153
Seaver, Tom 132, 153, 154, 157, 158, 162
Selkirk, George 15
Sexson, Richie 182
Shea, William 140, 144, 151
Sheffield, Gary 181
Sierra, Ruben 182
Sievers, Roy 182
Simmons, Al 179, 182
Sinatra, Frank 4, 71
Slaughter, Enos 48, 76, 98
Smalley, Roy 112
Smith, Edgar 20
Smith, Reggie 182
Smith, Vinnie 41
Smith, Wendell 67
Snider, Duke 82, 97, 112, 147, 181
Soriano, Alfonso 181

Index

Sosa, Sammy 177, 181
Southworth, Billy 184
Spahn, Warren 28, 32, 152
Springfield Nationals 28
Stargell, Willie 149, 178, 179, 181, 183
Stengel, Casey 141, 142, 146, 148, 184
Stephenson, John 152
Stoneham, Horace 135
Strawberry, Darryl 162, 167, 182
Strincevich, Nick 49
Sukeforth, Clyde 105
Sunset League 43
Suttles, Mule 25

Tate, Al 41
Tatum, Goose 25
Taylor, Elizabeth 4, 70, 73, 161
Teixeira, Mark 180, 182
Tejada, Miguel 182
Terry, Bill 21
Thomas, Charley 45
Thomas, Frank 142, 181
Thome, Jim 181

Thurston, Hollis 17
Toporcer, Specs 27, 29
Traynor, Pie 1, 94, 183
Tucker, Forrest 71

Vance, Dazzy 1, 9, 184
Van Robays, Maurice 41
Vaughan, Arky 1, 183
Vaughn, Greg 182
Vaughn, Mo 182
Veeck, Bill 137

Waddell, Rube 1, 184
Wade, Gale 123
Wagner, Bill 140
Wagner, Honus 1, 2, 38, 105
Walker, Larry 182
Walsh, Junior 41
Waner, Lloyd 1, 183
Waner, Paul 1, 2, 77, 183
Waugh, Jim 94
Weiss, George 143, 144, 164
Weissmuller, Johnny 71
Welker, Herman 86
Welles, Willie 25
Wertz, Vic 120, 121, 122

West, Max 14
Westlake, Wally 78, 81, 90
White, Deacon 184
Wilhelm, Hoyt 121
Wilkes Barre Barons 28
Wilkie, Lefty 41
Wilks, Ted 90
Williams, Billy 178, 181
Williams, Esther 71
Williams, Ken 91, 92
Williams. Matt 182
Williams, Ted 8, 20, 21, 34, 60, 81, 83, 95, 130, 177, 178, 180, 181
Willis, Jim 112
Willis, Vic 184
Wilson, Mike 128
Winfield, Dave 181
Wright, Johnny 47
Wrigley Field 22, 110, 111, 115, 116
Wynn, Early 28, 124, 126, 127

Yastrzemski, Carl 178, 181

Zak, Frank 41

www.ingramcontent.com/pod-product-compliance
Ingram Content Group UK Ltd.
Pitfield, Milton Keynes, MK11 3LW, UK
UKHW042011140426
5217IPUK00015B/1099